C W Davies

CHRISTIAN THEO

SERIES E

Timothy Gorringe   Sere

CHRISTIAN THEOLOGY IN CONTEXT

Any inspection of recent theological monographs makes plain that it is still thought possible to understand a text independently of its context. Work in the sociology of knowledge and in cultural studies has, however, increasingly made obvious that such a divorce is impossible. On the one hand, as Marx put it, 'life determines consciousness'. All texts have to be understood in their life situation, related to questions of power, class, and modes of production. No texts exist in intellectual innocence. On the other hand, texts are also forms of cultural power, expressing and modifying the dominant ideologies through which we understand the world. This dialectical understanding of texts demands an interdisciplinary approach if they are to be properly understood: theology needs to be read alongside economics, politics, and social studies, as well as philosophy, with which it has traditionally been linked. The cultural situatedness of any text demands, both in its own time and in the time of its rereading, a radically interdisciplinary analysis.

The aim of this series is to provide such an analysis, culturally situating texts by Christian theologians and theological movements. Only by doing this, we believe, will people of the fourth, sixteenth, or nineteenth centuries be able to speak to those of the twenty-first. Only by doing this will we be able to understand how theologies are themselves cultural products—projects deeply resonant with their particular cultural contexts and yet nevertheless exceeding those contexts by being received into our own today. In doing this, the series should advance both our understanding of those theologies and our understanding of theology as a discipline. We also hope that it will contribute to the fast developing interdisciplinary debates of the present.

Athanasius of Alexandria

Bishop, Theologian, Ascetic, Father

David M. Gwynn

OXFORD

UNIVERSITY PRESS

OXFORD
UNIVERSITY PRESS

Great Clarendon Street, Oxford OX2 6DP
United Kingdom

Oxford University Press is a department of the University of Oxford.
It furthers the University's objective of excellence in research, scholarship,
and education by publishing worldwide. Oxford is a registered trade mark of
Oxford University Press in the UK and in certain other countries

First published 2012
Reprinted 2012

British Library Cataloguing in Publication Data
Data available

Library of Congress Cataloging in Publication Data
Data available

ISBN 978-0-19-921095-4

Printed in the United Kingdom by
the MPG Books Group Ltd

To My Parents
For Everything

Contents

Preface

Athanasius of Alexandria (*c.*295–373) has been a figure of inspiration and controversy from his own time to the present day. One of the greatest personalities of the fourth-century Church, Athanasius lived in a period of fundamental change for the Roman Empire and Christianity following the conversion of Constantine, the first Christian Roman emperor. Athanasius played a central part in shaping the identity of the Church during these formative years, and was remembered as a champion of orthodoxy and asceticism and a model for future bishops. He has never lacked for scholarly attention, and the present volume thus requires a short explanation.

Over the last few decades, modern scholarship has tended to focus around different aspects of Athanasius' life and thought. There have been numerous important studies of his theology (among the more recent are Pettersen, *Athanasius* (1995); Anatolios, *Athanasius: The Coherence of his Thought* (1998); and Weinandy, *Athanasius: A Theological Introduction* (2007)). Equally important work has developed our understanding of his ecclesiastical career (Barnes, *Athanasius and Constantius: Theology and Politics in the Constantinian Empire* (1993); Martin, *Athanase d'Alexandrie et L'Église d'Égypte au IVe siècle (328–373)* (1996)). Attention has also been increasingly paid to Athanasius' involvement in the rise of the ascetic movement in the fourth century (Brakke, *Athanasius and the Politics of Asceticism* (1995)) and to his dedication as a spiritual father and pastor (Ng, *The Spirituality of Athanasius: A Key for Proper Understanding of this Important Church Father* (2001)). Improved editions of Athanasius' writings have appeared, and a new survey of the latest Athanasian scholarship has now been published in the *Athanasius Handbuch* edited by Gemeinhardt (2011).

All these works have contributed significantly to our knowledge of Athanasius, his world, and his place in the wider history of Christianity. Yet there is no easily accessible modern book in English that draws together the different roles that he played and sets Athanasius within his broader context. The present volume aims to fill that void. It is intended in the first instance for students and teachers of courses in patristic theology and Late Roman history. There is extensive quotation from Athanasius' texts, for it is through his own words that we can best approach the man and his thought.

Footnotes have been kept relatively brief but provide guidance for further reading through the extended Bibliography. It is especially hoped that this book may encourage further dialogue between those who approach Athanasius from different traditions and perspectives, and particularly between theologians and historians who do not always communicate as frequently as they should.

The book opens with a short survey of Athanasius' life and the setting and purpose of his varied writings. The following four chapters are then organized around the Athanasian roles identified in the title. Each chapter provides an overview of Athanasius' activities and writings in the given sphere, with a focus upon the interrelationships between the different spheres and their importance in the wider context of the fourth century. The final chapter traces an outline of Athanasius' legacy for later Christian generations in the Greek east and the Latin west and in the Syriac, Armenian, and Coptic traditions.

Athanasius was a bishop, a theologian, an ascetic, and a pastoral father. These functions were not mutually exclusive. On the contrary, they were inseparable from each other, and all are essential to our understanding of Athanasius as an individual. This book provides an introduction to Athanasius' life and writings, and to the qualities that characterize his episcopal, theological, ascetic, and pastoral roles. But its central argument is that we must understand these different roles in relation to each other and within the context in which he lived. Only then can we do justice to Athanasius and his place in the history of Christianity and the Later Roman Empire.

I must, of course, offer my deepest thanks to all those whose generous assistance has made this volume possible. Lizzie Robottom of the OUP has offered patient support as deadlines have come and gone. David Brakke, Averil Cameron, Justin Champion, Mark Edwards, Peregrine Horden, and Bryan Ward-Perkins made time in their own busy schedules to read drafts of the text and offer numerous helpful criticisms and suggestions. I am also particularly indebted to Peter Gemeinhardt, both for his additional comments and for very kindly providing me with an advance copy of the proofs of his *Handbuch*. The responsibility for any remaining errors rests solely with me.

To friends and family who have heard far more about Athanasius than they ever expected, my thanks once more. Paul, Judith, Anthi, and Eleni have helped me to remember that there is life outside Athanasian studies. Teresa has been a source of inspiration and a sounding board, a voice on the phone that has kept me company throughout my labours. Jenny and Steve have always been there when I have needed them, be it in Spain or in London. This book is dedicated to my parents, Margaret and Robin, for debts that I cannot hope to repay.

David M. Gwynn

Royal Holloway
May 2011

Abbreviations

Byz.	*Byzantion*
CIG	*Corpus Inscriptionum Graecarum*
CSCO	Corpus Scriptorum Christianorum Orientalium
DOP	*Dumbarton Oaks Papers*
GRBS	*Greek, Roman, and Byzantine Studies*
HPA	*History of the Patriarchs of Alexandria*
HThR	*Harvard Theological Review*
IThQ	*Irish Theological Quarterly*
JAC	*Jahrbuch für Antike und Christentum*
JEA	*Journal of Egyptian Archaeology*
JECS	*Journal of Early Christian Studies*
JEH	*Journal of Ecclesiastical History*
JRS	*Journal of Roman Studies*
JThS, ns	*Journal of Theological Studies*, New Series
PO	Patrologia Orientalis
RSR	*Recherches de science religieuse*
StP	*Studia Patristica*
ThS	*Theological Studies*
VC	*Vigiliae Christianae*
ZAC	*Zeitschrift für Antikes Christentum*
ZKG	*Zeitschrift für Kirchengeschichte*
ZNW	*Zeitschrift für die neutestamentaliche Wissenschaft und die Künde der älteren Kirche*
ZPE	*Zeitschrift für Papyrologie und Epigraphik*

Chronology

1

Life and Writings

When Bishop Alexander was celebrating the day of Peter Martyr in Alexandria, he was waiting in a place near the sea after the ceremonies were over for his clergy to gather for a banquet. There he saw from a distance some boys on the seashore playing a game in which, as they often do, they were mimicking a bishop and the things customarily done in church. Now when he had gazed intently for a while at the boys, he saw that they were also performing some of the more secret and sacramental things. He was disturbed and immediately ordered the clergy to be called to him and showed them what he was watching from a distance. Then he commanded them to go and get all the boys and bring them to him. When they arrived, he asked them what game they were playing and what they had done and how. At first they were afraid, as is usual at that age, and refused, but then they disclosed in due order what they had done, admitting that some catechumens had been baptized by them at the hands of Athanasius, who had played the part of bishop in their childish game. (Rufinus, *Historia Ecclesiastica* X.15)

He [Athanasius] was the son of a principal woman, a worshipper of idols, who was very rich; and he was an orphan on the father's side. So when he grew up she wished to marry him to a wife, but he did not desire that. Then she intrigued against him, that he might fall with a woman who was a sinner, that she might involve him in the mire of matrimony; but he would not do it, for the Lord was keeping him for great things. And she used to take beautiful girls, and adorn them and perfume them, and make them enter to him into his chamber, and sleep near him and solicit him; but when he awoke he beat them, and drove them away . . . [finally, on the advice of an Alexandrian magician, his mother accepted that her son was a Christian] . . . She arose, and took him with her, and went with him to Alexander, and related to him the circumstances of Athanasius her son, and all his history. Then she was baptized, and her son also. (*History of the Patriarchs of Alexandria*, PO 1:407–8)

Athanasius of Alexandria was born in the last decade of the third century AD and died in May 373. His long life spanned a period of momentous change for the history of Europe and the Christian Church. The predominantly pagan Roman Empire within which Athanasius grew up was gradually transformed across the fourth century with the expansion of Christianity following the conversion of Constantine the Great in 312. Under the first Christian Roman emperor, the size, wealth, and power of the Church dramatically increased. The Christian religion itself entered into a formative age of redefinition. Church architecture and liturgy, clerical hierarchies, doctrinal creeds, and the canon of Scripture all took increasingly recognized forms. The new prominence of Christianity also gave a new significance to the divisions within the Church and the conflicts that flourished under Constantine and his successors.

It was into this complex environment that Athanasius was plunged when he became the bishop of Alexandria in 328. Across the next four and a half decades he would fight for his vision of Christianity, his conception of correct Christian belief and practice, and his leadership of the Egyptian Church. Athanasius' writings bring alive the doctrinal conflicts and ecclesiastical rivalries of his time, and reveal the rise of the ascetic movement and the tensions of living a Christian life in a rapidly changing world. A figure of controversy for many years, Athanasius by his death had become an elder statesman of the Church, remembered as a saint who devoted himself to the service of the faith.

We know all too little about Athanasius' early life. Unlike Augustine of Hippo a generation or more later, Athanasius did not compose an autobiographical work like the *Confessions*, and perhaps it was not in his character to do so. Even his date of birth is uncertain, with the traditional estimate of the last decade of the third century suggested by the debates upon his accession as bishop in 328 over whether he had reached 30, the canonical minimum age for entering the episcopate. As a child he lived through the Great Persecution that the pagan emperor Diocletian and his Tetrarchy unleashed upon Christianity in 303. The impact of that persecution on Egypt is graphically described by Eusebius of Caesarea, a man whom Athanasius would later come to know, although not as a friend, but there is no indication that Athanasius himself was directly touched by the violence of these years. He was still less than 20 when Constantine's conversion began Christianity's transformation into the imperial religion. Athanasius thus embarked upon his ecclesiastical career at a crucial moment in Christian history, and he would play an important role in shaping the development of the Church through this period of transition.

How did Athanasius come to the clerical life? There is no evidence from his writings to suggest that he was a convert, which may indicate that he was born to Christian parents, but we cannot trace with any certainty his early experiences or motives. The Latin ecclesiastical historian Rufinus early in the fifth century told the famous story quoted above, that Athanasius was seen by his predecessor Alexander of Alexandria performing the actions of a bishop in his childhood games. Athanasius played the role so well that Alexander had to confirm the baptisms that Athanasius had performed, and then took the young prodigy into his entourage. Rufinus' version was in turn adopted into the Greek ecclesiastical tradition, and remains the best-known account of Athanasius' induction into the clergy. Another explanation is provided by the Egyptian Coptic tradition in the *History of the Patriarchs of Alexandria*. According to this version, Athanasius was raised by a pagan mother whom he drove frantic by his insistence on a virtuous ascetic lifestyle. Finally, his mother brought him before Alexander, who baptized them both and oversaw Athanasius' education in the Scriptures.

The twin stories share a similar purpose, to identify Athanasius as a man marked out from his youth for greatness and to bind Athanasius closely with his predecessor Alexander. Neither story can be proven to be false, and at a stretch they might even be reconciled. Yet neither can be taken as proven historical fact. Here we must face one of the recurring problems of Athanasian scholarship. Athanasius' posthumous reputation as a hero of orthodoxy is testimony to his influence on later generations, but has also obscured the man behind the icon of the saint. Less than a decade after Athanasius' death, Gregory of Nazianzus celebrated the Alexandrian as a model bishop and orthodox champion in the *Funeral Oration* he delivered in Constantinople in May 380. The same heroic vision of Athanasius dominates the ecclesiastical historians who composed our earliest detailed narratives of the fourth-century Church. The Latin *Ecclesiastical History* of Rufinus that we have already encountered was followed in Greek by the Church histories of Socrates, Sozomen, and Theodoret, all of whom wrote in the first half of the fifth century. Their representations of Athanasius are largely uniform and unswervingly favourable, with the only contrary view preserved in the fragments of another early fifth-century ecclesiastical historian, the 'Neo-Arian' Philostorgius. Other eastern traditions hold Athanasius in equally high esteem, particularly the Coptic tradition in Egypt represented by the *History of the Patriarchs of Alexandria*. I will return to these varied works in my final chapter. Here it will suffice to emphasize that we should not discard the later traditions, which preserve how the bishop was remembered and draw upon sources often unavailable to us. For our understanding of the historical Athanasius, however, his own writings must take priority.

Rufinus and the *History of the Patriarchs* both assert that Alexander oversaw Athanasius' education. He received a thorough grounding in the Scriptures, and his writing style is powerful and evocative, although he does not appear to have shared the extensive training in classical literature and rhetoric of

some of his contemporaries.[1] Despite scholarly debate, all of Athanasius'
writings were composed in Greek. It has been suggested that Athanasius
also wrote in Coptic,[2] and it is entirely possible that he could speak the Coptic language. But all the extant Athanasian Coptic writings, like those preserved in Syriac and other eastern languages, appear to be translations from
Greek originals.[3] Athanasius' works form an impressive corpus. They range
from doctrinal treatises and ascetic exhortations to polemical apologia and
both public and private epistles. Each text had its own intended purpose and
audience against which it must be understood, while the corpus as a whole
reveals the evolution of his thought across half a century of almost cease-
less activity. In the next chapter I will trace Athanasius' ecclesiastical career
in detail. The following pages offer only a short chronological outline of the
major events of his life, placing his writings in their individual contexts.[4]

Whatever the truth of our stories of his childhood, Athanasius was
already a prominent figure in the Alexandrian church hierarchy when
he first emerges clearly in our historical record. The sources place great
emphasis on his relationship with Alexander (bishop 312–28), and it was
during the latter's episcopate that Athanasius attained the rank of deacon.
He was therefore a close observer to the disagreement between Alexander
and the Alexandrian presbyter Arius, which began the doctrinal debates
today known (rather inaccurately) as the 'Arian Controversy'. Alexander
and Arius came into conflict over how to define the divinity of the Son
and His relationship with the Father within the Trinity. The theological
implications of this conflict will again be discussed in a later chapter, but
in the aftermath of their dispute Alexander condemned Arius at a Council
of Alexandria in *c*.321.[5] Arius withdrew from Egypt but found support in

---

[1] For Athanasius' knowledge of Greek literary culture, see Stead (1976). According to
the panegyrical oration of Gregory of Nazianzus (*Oration* XXI.6), Athanasius studied non-
Christian literature only to avoid complete ignorance.

[2] Lefort (1933); Müller (1974).

[3] A number of Athanasian works survive only in Coptic, Syriac, and Armenian. This
includes the *Festal Letters* and a variety of ascetic writings (not all of which are authentic).
I will return to these eastern traditions in my final chapter.

[4] For a useful survey of older scholarship on many of the Athanasian works discussed in
the following pages, see Leemans (2000: 129–71), and also now the contributions in Gemeinhardt (2011: 166–282). On Athanasius' polemical writings, see also Gwynn (2007: 13–48). Editions and translations of the extant Athanasian writings are listed in the first section of the
Bibliography.

[5] Here and throughout, the chronology followed for the period between Arius' first clash
with Alexander and the Council of Nicaea is that proposed by R. D. Williams (1987: 48–61),
rather than the older model of Opitz (1934), who placed the outbreak of the controversy
in 318.

Palestine and Asia Minor, and the debates still simmered in September 324 when Constantine conquered the eastern half of the Roman Empire by defeating his rival Licinius and so united the Empire under his rule.

The arrival of Constantine in the east brought Athanasius and the rest of the Egyptian Church under the sway of a Christian emperor for the first time. In an effort to exploit this new situation, Alexander laid down his arguments against Arius in an *Encyclical Letter* circulated across the east in late 324 or early 325. It is not inconceivable that this document in fact represents Athanasius' earliest extant work, for in argument, style, and vocabulary there are notable similarities between the *Encyclical Letter* and Athanasius' later writings.[6] Athanasius is described in the *History of the Patriarchs* as Alexander's 'scribe', 'interpreter', and 'tongue', and as Alexander's deacon he may have had responsibility for drafting the text. Of course, the parallels between the *Letter* and Athanasius' later works may equally reflect the influence that his mentor inevitably exerted upon Athanasius' language and thought. Certainly Athanasius would seem to have established himself as Alexander's favoured aide and potential successor, and it was presumably in this capacity that he accompanied Alexander to one of the most remarkable events of Constantine's reign: the Council of Nicaea in June–July 325.

Later Christian tradition awarded Athanasius a leading role in what would become recognized as the first ecumenical ('universal') council of the Christian Church. This pious fiction is a further reflection of Athanasius' legacy, for by the time of his death fifty years later he had gained renown as the champion of the Nicene Creed, composed in 325, and as the leading foe of Arius, who was condemned at the council.[7] It is now well known that Athanasius' attitude towards the original Nicene Creed was rather more complex than his traditional image might suggest, a theme to which I will return in Chapter 3. In any case, in 325 Athanasius was only a young priest, albeit a member of the entourage of one of the leading bishops of the east. His writings make no claim to involvement in the crucial debates at Nicaea, even during the 350s when he came to emphasize the Nicene doctrines as the only true defence against the 'Arian heresy'. We can perhaps assume that he listened closely to the debates and discussed the issues with his bishop Alexander. We can also guess that Athanasius, like his contemporaries, was awestruck by the splendour and magnitude of

[6] This was argued in detail by Stead (1988).
[7] The claim first appears in Gregory of Nazianzus' *Oration* XXI in honour of Athanasius, composed less than a decade after Athanasius' death (XXI.14). This is another text to which I will return in my final chapter.

the largest gathering yet held in the history of the Church. However, as a deacon, he probably did not attend the gathering of bishops in the imperial palace to celebrate Constantine's *vicennalia*, which Eusebius of Caesarea memorably described as like 'an imaginary representation of the kingdom of Christ'.[8]

Athanasius returned home with Alexander to Alexandria, and we hear nothing more of him for the next few years, until April 328 when Alexander died. Alexander had nominated Athanasius his successor before his death, but the latter's election was far from smooth. The Egyptian Church was divided both over the theological questions raised by Arius and by the Melitian Schism, which had originated in the first decade of the fourth century over the treatment of those who had lapsed during the Great Persecution. Still young and relatively inexperienced, Athanasius had to work hard to secure his position. At the same time, the new bishop defined the theological principles that he would teach to his flock and from which he would never deviate. The foundations of Athanasius' subsequent career were laid down in his earliest episcopal writings, the great theological double treatise *Contra Gentes–De Incarnatione* and the first of over forty Easter *Festal Letters*.

There has been vast controversy over the date and context of the *Contra Gentes–De Incarnatione*.[9] The absence of any reference to 'Arianism' led older scholarship to propose a date of *c*.318, before Arius' conflict with Alexander. This requires Athanasius to have composed the work when he was little more than 20, and, while this is not inconceivable, most recent scholarship has preferred a date in the later 320s or early 330s. There is no reference to Arius or 'Arianism' in Athanasius' *Festal Letters* from those years, and his early episcopate provides a natural setting for a statement of his convictions. Whatever the precise date, the *Contra Gentes–De Incarnatione* represents the initial staging point for all analysis of Athanasius' theology. His later doctrinal works remained grounded in the principles he expressed in that first treatise. This must equally have been true of the many sermons Athanasius preached that are now lost to us, and the same values can be traced through the one major body of Athanasian pastoral writings that does survive: his *Festal Letters*.[10]

---

[8] Eusebius of Caesarea, *Life of Constantine* III.15.

[9] For a survey of twentieth-century debates, see Leemans (2000: 132–5), and also now Heil (2007).

[10] For the complex problems surrounding the extant *Festal Letters*, their transmission, and their numbering, see Lorenz (1986: 8–37), Camplani (1989: 17–196; 2003), and Barnes (1993: 183–91).

Like his predecessors in Alexandria, Athanasius wrote each year two letters concerning the Easter celebration for circulation to all the bishops subordinate to his see. The first short letter was despatched soon after Easter, and announced the date of Easter for the following year. The *Festal Letter* proper, a much longer work, was sent out in January or February of the year itself to confirm that date and to transmit Athanasius' Easter message to his churches. With the loss of Athanasius' sermons, the *Festal Letters* are priceless for our knowledge of his pastoral work, which is otherwise swallowed within his polemical and theological writings. They also provide a unique opportunity to trace how Athanasius' thought and self-presentation evolved across his long career.

There is a need for caution. Not all Athanasius' *Festal Letters* survive, and those that do are preserved almost exclusively in Syriac and Coptic rather than their original Greek. Most seriously, their chronological order remains a subject for debate. The traditional numeration of the *Festal Letters* derives from the Syriac *Festal Index* compiled after Athanasius' death.[11] The editors of the *Index* clearly had to assemble the letters into order themselves, and this depended almost entirely on analysis of their internal content. The *Festal Letters* contain almost no references to specific events and they do not record the year in which they were written. However, the day and month of the Easter in question are recorded, and these could be compared against existing tables of Easter dates for fourth-century Egypt.[12] A letter with a unique Easter date (that is, a date that occurred for Easter only once in Athanasius' episcopate) could thus be fixed with certainty. Unfortunately, many of the Easter dates recorded in Athanasius' *Festal Letters* were attributable to more than one year in his episcopate, and it is here that the problems lie.

In particular, the letters transmitted as I, IV, V, and XIV speak of only a six-day pre-Easter fast, whereas the other letters all refer to a forty-day Lenten fast. At some time between 334 and 338 the Egyptian practice shifted, and therefore *Festal Letters* II and III, which refer to the longer fast, must date to 352 and 342 respectively. The fragmentary *Letter* XXIV (assigned to 352) should be dated to 330, and *Letter* XIV (assigned to 342) to 331.

---

[11] The *Festal Index* comprises a short record of major events during Athanasius' episcopate. It was compiled to accompany a now lost collection of his *Festal Letters*, but at some point the *Index* became attached to the surviving Syriac corpus of the *Festal Letters* and so was preserved. For the complex transmission of the Syriac corpus, see further Camplani (1989: 115–29).

[12] For the calculation of Easter dates in the early Church, see Mosshammer (2008: esp. 162–89 on Athanasius' *Festal Letters* and the *Festal Index*, which Mosshammer prefers to call the Athanasian Index).

Letters I (329), IV (332), and V (333) retain their transmitted dates, but the attribution of *Letters* VI and VII to 334 and 335 remains uncertain.[13] I will return to the new Lenten fast in Chapter 5, for this is a development of some significance for understanding Athanasius' impact upon the Egyptian Church. But the chronological difficulties raised by the *Festal Letters* need to be remembered if we are to exploit the insights that they provide.

The tensions that Athanasius faced in the opening years of his episcopate were not slow to come to a head. In 332, Athanasius had to write his fourth *Festal Letter* from the court of Constantine, where he had been summoned to defend himself over charges of extortion and violence against the Melitians. Similar charges recurred again in 334, and culminated in his condemnation at the Council of Tyre in 335. Athanasius appealed to Constantine, but his plea was denied and he was exiled to the west, to the city of Trier. He returned to Egypt on Constantine's death in late 337, but fled again in 339 and came to Rome, while a rival named Gregory occupied his see. Athanasius was defended by a council called by Bishop Julius of Rome in 340, condemned by the Dedication Council of Antioch in 341, defended by the Western Council of Serdica in 343, condemned by the Eastern bishops of the same council,[14] and finally returned to Alexandria in 346.

Our major source for the dramatic events surrounding Athanasius' two periods of western exile is provided by the text known as the *Apologia contra Arianos*.[15] This work comprises an assemblage of documents covering the period 328–47, connected by an Athanasian narrative. The documents appear to have been assembled in a series of stages across the 330s and 340s, with the final touches to the narrative probably added in the late 350s. Nevertheless, the purpose of the collection remained consistent throughout: to defend Athanasius against the charges on which he was first condemned in 335. The documents preserved are selective, and their interpretation in the accompanying narrative is at times forced, but Athanasius' protestations of innocence and his self-presentation as the victim of an 'Arian' conspiracy proved highly compelling. His influence on contemporary opinion is already reflected within the *Apologia contra Arianos* itself,

---

[13] For a list of currently accepted dates, and those still under debate, see Barnes (1993: 188–9) and Camplani (2003: 613–20).

[14] The *Encyclical Letter* of the Eastern bishops in 343, preserved in Latin by Hilary of Poitiers (*Against Valens and Ursacius* I.II.1–29), is one of our very few pieces of evidence expressing the hostility felt towards Athanasius by a number of his eastern contemporaries.

[15] For the complex evolution of the text, see further Barnes (1993: 192–5) and Gwynn (2007: 16–19).

where his defence is taken up by the encyclical letter of the Council of Alexandria in 338 (quoted in *Apologia contra Arianos* 3–19), Julius of Rome's *Letter to the Eastern Bishops* in *c.*340/1 (20–35), and the letters circulated by the Western Council of Serdica in 343 (36–50). Later ecclesiastical traditions in east and west followed their lead, and Athanasius' suffering for the cause of orthodoxy became a symbol and a source of inspiration for subsequent generations.

During his second exile (339–46), as the *Apologia contra Arianos* gradually took shape, Athanasius also composed a number of other influential writings. His earliest complete polemical work was the *Epistula Encyclica* (also known as the *Epistula ad Episcopos*). This brief letter was written shortly after the arrival of his replacement Gregory as bishop of Alexandria in March 339 and Athanasius' flight from the city a few weeks later. Athanasius insisted to all who might read the letter in east or west that he was still the true and legitimate bishop against this 'Arian' imposter. Indeed, the *Epistula Encyclica* is the first work in which Athanasius explicitly depicts his opponents as an 'Arian party'. This party, which he named the 'Eusebians' (*hoi peri Eusebion*) after their alleged leader Eusebius of Nicomedia, features prominently throughout Athanasius' anti-'Arian' writings and plays a central role in his perception of himself as the innocent orthodox victim of a heretical conspiracy.

Athanasius' polarized division of the fourth-century Church into orthodox and heretical factions is highly subjective and serves an obvious purpose in defending his status as Alexandrian bishop in exile. It would be a serious error, however, to dismiss Athanasius' condemnation of his foes as 'Arian' as merely a device of polemical rhetoric. The theological issues at stake were real and fundamental, and Athanasius was not alone in the late 330s and early 340s in expressing renewed interest in Arius and the heretical teachings associated with him. Arius had died in Constantinople in 336, and it was most probably in the period 339–46 that Athanasius wrote one of his best-known letters, the *Letter to Serapion on the Death of Arius*, usually known as the *De Morte Arii*.[16] Concerned by debates in Egypt over whether Arius had died in communion, Athanasius prepared an account of Arius' death for his friend and colleague Serapion, the bishop of Thmuis in the Nile Delta.[17] Modern historians have questioned some elements of the

---

[16] For the chronology adopted here, rather than the older argument, which placed the *De Morte Arii* in 358, see Kannengiesser (1982: 992–4). Kannengiesser also proposed to date Athanasius' first *Letter to the Monks* or *Ad Monachos* to the same approximate time.

[17] For what is known of the life and writings of Serapion, who figures prominently in Athanasius' story, see Fitschen (1992).

story Athanasius tells, but his vision of Arius dying on a Constantinopolitan latrine is one of the most famous images in Christian heresiology.

Arius' death had not resolved the doctrinal debates that his teachings had in part caused. Athanasius' greatest composition during his second exile in the west underlined the scale and significance of those debates and provided a powerful statement of the threat that he believed the 'Arian heresy' posed to the Church. Taken together, the three *Orationes contra Arianos* form Athanasius' most extensive work of theology and polemic.[18] Their date and context are difficult to determine, not least because the *Orationes* as they stand may not have been composed as a uniform whole. But, whereas older scholarship favoured an approximate date of 356–60, modern analysis has placed the main stage of composition in the period 339–46.[19] In the *Orationes* Athanasius for the first time defined in detail the doctrines that he attributed to those he named as 'Arian'. At one level the *Orationes* are therefore the theological expression of the polemical argument presented in the *Epistula Encyclica* and the *Apologia contra Arianos*. Yet Athanasius goes far beyond the needs of that polemic, and his interpretation of the 'Arian Controversy' exerted a profound influence on later generations.

The *Orationes* are an invaluable but difficult source for the doctrinal questions troubling the Church in the decades following the Council of Nicaea. The first *Oratio* opens with Athanasius' denunciation of the errors of Arius, including a much debated précis of the latter's now fragmentary *Thalia*. Two other 'Arians' are also identified by name, the bishop Eusebius of Nicomedia and his friend Asterius 'the Sophist'. Athanasius insists that these three men share one and the same heresy, as do all those condemned as 'Arian'. The main body of the *Orationes* then focuses upon biblical exegesis. Scriptural passages that have been misused by the 'Arians' are interpreted correctly, from Athanasius' viewpoint, most notably the controversial verse Proverbs 8:22. Across all three *Orationes* Athanasius continually contrasts the heretical views of his opponents to the traditional orthodoxy of the Church that he represents, with a particular emphasis upon the full divinity of the Son as the essential guarantee for human salvation through Christ.

---

[18] The so-called fourth *Oratio contra Arianos*, which differs notably in argument and vocabulary from the other three, is not by Athanasius but may have been written by an unknown author at approximately the same time in *c*.340/1 (see Vinzent 1996). Kannengiesser (1982: 994–5; 1993a) also challenged the authenticity of the third *Oratio*, which he attributed to Apollinaris of Laodicea, but this argument has been widely rejected.

[19] For the evidence, see Kannengiesser (1982, 1983).

Throughout his years in exile Athanasius retained great support in Alexandria and Egypt, and his ecclesiastical and theological arguments won over many in both east and west. Gregory his rival died in 345, and Athanasius finally returned triumphantly to his city in 346, beginning a decade of relative peace. His *Festal Letters* from these years reflect his efforts to restore stability to the Egyptian Church under his leadership, efforts whose success was due in no small part to Athanasius' close relationship with the expanding monastic movement. He had always shown a keen interest in asceticism, and he had great respect for the ascetic lifestyle. The chronology and authenticity of the ascetic writings that have come down to us under Athanasius' name pose certain problems, but his genuine works include at least three works on virginity and a number of letters.[20] Athanasius particularly sought to promote ascetic values across the wider Church. An ideal means by which to achieve this end, and simultaneously to reinforce his position within Egypt, was the appointment of monks to vacant bishoprics. Monks were frequently reluctant to take clerical office, and in 354 Athanasius wrote his *Letter to Dracontius* to one such monk, in which he underlines his admiration for asceticism and the importance of ascetic values to his conception of the episcopate.

The 'Golden Decade' of 346–56 also witnessed a crucial shift in Athanasius' approach to the doctrinal controversies of the time. By the mid-fourth century Athanasius' fundamental theological principles were well established. So too was his construction of the 'Arian heresy' that he attributed to his foes. Yet something was missing. In the light of his later reputation as the great champion of Nicene orthodoxy, it may seem a surprise that the Council of Nicaea and its creed feature barely at all in Athanasius' extensive writings from the 330s and 340s. Only in the early 350s did this change, with the letter or treatise known as the *De Decretis Nicaenae Synodi*. The original date and context of the *De Decretis* remain controversial, and the addressee who had requested from Athanasius an account of Nicaea cannot be conclusively identified.[21] But the work was almost certainly composed in the period 350–5, and in these years Athanasius came to a new understanding of the significance of the great council he had attended as a

---

[20] Athanasius' first *Letter to Virgins*, which survived only in Coptic, was probably written 337–9 between his first and second exiles. His second *Letter to Virgins* survived in Syriac and was written after 346, while no firm date can be assigned to his work known as *On Virginity*, which was transmitted in both Syriac and Armenian versions. For a survey of these and other Athanasian and Pseudo-Athanasian ascetic writings, see Brakke (1994a).

[21] Athanasius, *De Decretis* 1. For the argument that the addressee in question was Liberius of Rome in 352, see Barnes (1993: 198–9).

young deacon in 325. For the first time in his extant writings, Athanasius in the *De Decretis* upholds the authority of the Council of Nicaea and represents the Nicene Creed as the sole bastion of orthodoxy against the 'Arian heresy'.

We should not exaggerate the impact of this shift upon Athanasius' own theology. His interpretation of the Nicene Creed in the *De Decretis* remained true to the principles he had laid down long before in the *Contra Gentes–De Incarnatione*. For the wider Church, however, Athanasius' exaltation of Nicaea had lasting implications. In the *De Decretis* Athanasius insisted that the Nicene Creed represented the traditional faith of Christianity. He further elaborated this argument in the *De Sententia Dionysii*, written shortly after the *De Decretis* and possibly to the same recipient, in which he defended the teachings of his predecessor Dionysius of Alexandria (bishop 247–64) as compatible with later orthodoxy.[22] Athanasius would not waver from these convictions, and by the end of the fourth century Nicaea was firmly established as the first ecumenical council and Athanasius as the champion of that council and its creed.

Athanasius' decade of peace after his return in 346 was not without ongoing tensions. Opposition in Egypt and the wider eastern Church still remained, and Athanasius' relationship with emperor Constantius II can only be described as strained. When Constantine died in 337, the Empire had been divided among his three sons: Constantine II (337–40), Constans (337–50), and Constantius II (337–61). Constantius took over the eastern provinces, while after the death of Constantine II in 340 Constans ruled in the west. Constans had supported Athanasius during the latter's western exile and helped influence his brother to allow Athanasius' return. But Constans was murdered in 350 after a coup by the usurper Magnentius, and by finally defeating the usurper in 353 Constantius consolidated the Empire under his rule. At this difficult time for the emperor, the controversial figure of Athanasius threatened the unity that Constantius wished to impose on Church and State. On the night of 8/9 February 356, a force of soldiers broke into the Church of Theonas in which the bishop was presiding over a vigil. Athanasius fled, and so began his third exile. Even after his replacement George entered Alexandria in February 357, however, Athanasius refused to depart from Egypt once more. Throughout the years 356–62 he survived in hiding in Alexandria and in the Egyptian

---

[22] Abramowski (1982), followed by Heil (1999: 22–71, 210–31), has argued inconclusively that the material attributed to Dionysius of Alexandria and his contemporary Dionysius of Rome in the *De Sententia Dionysii* derives from fourth-century forgeries.

desert, and during those years he wrote and circulated an impressive array of extremely influential writings.

The *Encyclical Letter to the Bishops of Egypt and Libya* was addressed to all the churches under Alexandrian leadership and written between Athanasius' expulsion in February 356 and George's arrival in February 357. The first major work of Athanasius' third exile, the letter defended his status as the true bishop of Alexandria and condemned the 'Arian' George. After summarizing his theological refutation of 'Arianism' from the *Orationes contra Arianos*, Athanasius then repeated in a slightly modified form his earlier account of the death of Arius. He thereby associated his contemporary opponents in the 350s with the earlier 'Arians' of the 330s and 340s. In 361 he further revised the *Encyclical Letter* to add a renewed denunciation of the Melitian schismatics for allying again with the heretics.

Three further Athanasian works all completed during 357 took up and expanded on the arguments of the *Encyclical Letter*. The first of these, the *Apologia ad Constantium*, was Athanasius' defence against charges of treason addressed to the emperor Constantius, and was begun before Athanasius' expulsion in February 356.[23] The bulk of the work was probably prepared in 353 or 354 when the pressure upon Athanasius was starting to build, and may indeed have been presented to the emperor in person. After his pleas for imperial favour had failed, Athanasius extended the *Apologia ad Constantium* in early 357 to protest his innocence and denounce the persecution of his followers that followed his flight and the subsequent arrival of George. These themes were further developed in the *Apologia de Fuga*, Athanasius' justification of why he had fled his see rather than face martyrdom, which was written in the second half of 357. The wide circulation of this work reflects Athanasius' concern to defend himself against accusations of cowardice and against those who believed that his flight had compromised his authority as bishop of Alexandria.[24]

The third and greatest of Athanasius' polemical writings of 357 is the *Historia Arianorum*, completed in the closing months of that year. The most violent polemical text that Athanasius ever wrote, the *Historia Arianorum* offers a highly selective account of the period from 335 to 357. Here as elsewhere in the works composed during his third exile, Athanasius presented the events of the 350s as a direct continuation of the conflicts of the

---

[23] For three different interpretations of the complex evolution of the text, see J.-M. Szymusiak (1987: 30, 55, 59–63), Barnes (1993: 196–7), and Brennecke (2006).

[24] Passages from the *Apologia de Fuga* were quoted by both Socrates (II.28, III.8) and Theodoret (II.15), and, according to the former (III.8), Athanasius read the work publicly at the Council of Alexandria over which he presided in 362.

330s and early 340s. He thus constructed the vision of a single overarching 'Arian Controversy', which would exert a huge influence upon later interpretations of the fourth-century Church. The *Historia Arianorum* is also well known for Athanasius' denunciation of Constantius, to whom he had appealed in the earlier *Apologia ad Constantium*. By the end of 357 any hope of an alliance with the emperor had faded, and Constantius was now an 'Arian' and the forerunner of Antichrist.

In the light of Athanasius' remarkable polemical output during 357, it is all too easy for the modern historian to focus exclusively on ecclesiastical politics and violence. Athanasius never lost sight of the deeper issues at stake. One of his most important compositions of this period, once again written in approximately 357–8, was the collection of *Letters to Serapion on the Holy Spirit*. Serapion of Thmuis had informed Athanasius that some Christian groups who accepted the full divinity of the Son denied that status to the Spirit. Athanasius' defence of the Holy Spirit marked a major step on the path from the Council of Nicaea, where the Spirit had been largely ignored, to the Council of Constantinople in 381, which upheld the divine equality of the Christian Trinity. The *Letters to Serapion* influenced Basil of Caesarea and Gregory of Nazianzus, the Cappadocian Fathers who played a central role in defining the doctrines adopted in 381, and demonstrated the evolution of Athanasius' theology as the questions under debate shifted in the middle years of the fourth century.

The other major theological work of Athanasius' third exile is the *De Synodis Arimini et Seleuciae*. If the *Historia Arianorum* represents Athanasius' definitive polemical interpretation of the fourth-century controversies, then the *De Synodis* represents the culmination of his doctrinal argument. In 359 Constantius summoned the dual councils of Ariminum (west) and Seleucia (east) to agree upon a single creed for the universal Church. Athanasius in response composed the *De Synodis*, written immediately after the eastern Council of Seleucia had broken up on 1 October 359, with further material added after Constantius' death in 361. He upheld again the Nicene Creed as the only symbol of orthodoxy, and contrasted that creed to the ever-changing arguments and councils of the 'Arians', which he quotes. The material that Athanasius preserves is an invaluable if selective source for his opponents' teachings, which are otherwise lost.[25] And by presenting the creeds proposed at Ariminum and Seleucia as the latest in a long succession of 'Arian' doctrines that began with Arius himself, he once more

---

[25] For a survey of what little is known of Athanasius' leading 'Arian' opponents and their writings, see Gwynn (2007: 116–24).

imposed his interpretation of the fourth-century debates as a single mono-lithic 'Arian Controversy'.

Yet the *De Synodis* is more than a recapitulation of Athanasius' earlier theological polemic. As in the *Letters to Serapion on the Holy Spirit*, Athanasius in the *De Synodis* showed that he was prepared to engage with the new doctrinal questions now troubling the Church. For the first time he qualified his polarized vision of the 'Arian Controversy' and acknowledged that not all those who questioned the authority of Nicaea must by defin-ition be 'Arian'. The majority of the eastern bishops at the Council of Seleucia in 359 distrusted the Nicene Creed, which described Father and Son as *homoousios* ('of one essence'). They preferred to describe the Son as *homoiousios* ('of like essence') or *homoios kat' ousian* ('like in essence') to the Father. Athanasius insisted upon the superiority of the Nicene Creed to these later formulations. But he was prepared to admit that those who expressed such language could be accepted as true Christians. It was an important step towards eventual resolution.

There is one final work that must be discussed in our catalogue of the great writings of Athanasius' third exile. The *Life of Antony* has been the sub-ject of vast debate concerning its authorship, its date, and its original lan-guage of composition.[26] Athanasius had known Antony, the great Egyptian hermit who was a crucial figure in the rise of the ascetic movement. Whether the traditional attribution of Antony's *Life* to Athanasius is correct cannot be definitively proven, but in style and content the work parallels closely his known writings and in the absence of conclusive evidence to the contrary his authorship should be accepted. Athanasius spent much of the period 356–62 in the company of the desert ascetics, and it was during those years that the *Life of Antony* was written. The experiences he shared with the ascetics further reinforced Athanasius' bond with this dynamic force within Egyptian Christianity, and none of his writings was to exert greater influence on later generations.

After Athanasius had been forced to flee in February 356, there was a year's delay until the Cappadocian George entered Alexandria to occupy the see in February 357. The new arrival was never secure and faced constant hostility from those who held Athanasius as their legitimate bishop. After almost being lynched in August 358, George increasingly withdrew from Alexandria, while the death of Constantius in 361 then deprived George

[26] The strongest challenge to Athanasius' authorship of the *Life* has come from Draguet (1980) and Barnes (1986), whose arguments are opposed by Brakke (1994c). For further bibli-ography on these debates, see Leemans (2000: 153–9).

of even imperial support. Following the accession of the pagan Julian 'the Apostate' (361–3), George finally met his fate at the hands of an Alexandrian mob. Freed from his rival, and under the protection of Julian's amnesty to all Christian exiles, Athanasius was restored to his city in February 362.

Athanasius' restoration was short lived, for in October 362 he received the rare accolade of being one of the few bishops to be forced into exile by the last pagan emperor. During his short return to Alexandria, Athanasius presided over a council, from which two documents survive: the fragmentary encyclical letter (the *Epistula Catholica*)[27] and a letter sent to Antioch in an effort to resolve the schism dividing the Christians of that city. Although this *Tomus ad Antiochenos* failed to achieve Antiochene unity, the theology of the letter marks a further evolution in Athanasius' approach to Trinitarian doctrines. His intervention in the affairs of Antioch, unsuccessful though it was, also bears witness to the international standing that Athanasius had attained in the Church by the later years of his episcopate.

The death of Julian in Persia in 363 permitted Athanasius to return from his short fourth exile. The reign of Jovian (363–4) briefly raised the possibility of an orthodox emperor, to whom Athanasius wrote (*Letter* LVI) to encourage imperial support for the followers of Nicaea. But Jovian died in 364, and under his eastern successor Valens (364–78) Athanasius faced his final period of imperial persecution in 365–6. By this stage, however, Athanasius' status both inside and outside Egypt was firmly established. The Cappadocian Basil of Caesarea admired him even when their purposes came into conflict, as Basil's letters regarding the schism in Antioch confirm. Athanasius' own letters travelled across the Mediterranean, from Asia Minor and Greece to Italy and North Africa. He had become an elder statesman, whose advice was sought and whose authority was respected throughout the Church.

In the closing years of his life Athanasius continued to enhance his reputation. He still wrote his *Festal Letters* to the churches of Egypt and Libya, and indeed perhaps the most famous of those letters dates to 367. *Festal Letter* XXXIX lays down the approved scriptural writings to be read by Athanasius' congregations, and so preserves the earliest extant list of biblical books to correspond with our New Testament. In the same year, Athanasius composed his last major polemical work, the *Epistula ad Afros*.[28] Sent,

---

[27] For the identification of this text, see Tetz (1988).

[28] The Athanasian authorship of the *Epistula ad Afros* has been questioned by Kannengiesser (1993b) and myself (Gwynn 2007: 15 n.12). Its authenticity has been defended by Stockhausen (2002) and is accepted here, as in most scholarship.

as the title suggests, to the churches of North Africa, Athanasius draws on the earlier *De Decretis* and *De Synodis* to restate his polemical construction of the 'Arian Controversy' to a new audience. To these letters we should perhaps also add the text now known as the *Historia acephala*.[29] This anonymous work survived in a Latin translation in Verona and has passed through a number of revisions, but the original was probably composed in Alexandria and possibly for the fortieth anniversary of Athanasius' election in 368. What is preserved provides an abbreviated survey of Athanasius' career from 346 until his death with a particular emphasis upon the persecutions he experienced. In addition to its value as a chronological source, the *Historia acephala* may in part reflect how Athanasius himself wished to be remembered.

By the fortieth anniversary of his accession to the Alexandrian see, Athanasius was in his 70s. But, even in his final years, his thought continued to evolve. Two of Athanasius' most influential private letters were composed at the very end of his life, the *Letter to Adelphius of Onuphis* in c.370 and the *Letter to Epictetus of Corinth* in c.372. Both letters were written in response to requests for advice on issues concerning the Incarnation. The *Letter to Epictetus* in particular addressed the relationship of the humanity and the divinity of Christ, a question that would underlie the great fifth-century controversies in which Athanasius would be recognized by all as a champion and symbol of the orthodox faith of the Church. His place in Christian tradition was already secure well before his death in May 373.

---

[29] Edited with a detailed introduction by Martin (1985).

2

Bishop

Like Athena springing fully grown from the head of Zeus, Athanasius of Alexandria emerges from the pages of history first and foremost as a bishop. We know almost nothing about him before his election in 328 to an office that he would occupy for over half his lifetime. In the course of his lengthy episcopate Athanasius redefined the bishop's role in Alexandria and Egypt, laying the foundations upon which his successors would build. He endured persecution and exile, some of which it might be argued he brought upon himself, and still preserved and indeed enhanced his authority and that of his see. Athanasius' long and complex ecclesiastical career provides the essential background against which we must set his theology and his ascetic and pastoral teachings.[1]

The late-antique bishop had many parts to play.[2] Within his church, he was a preacher and teacher, responsible for the doctrinal and pastoral guidance of his congregation. He led the celebration of the liturgy, and oversaw the distribution of bread to those in need. As a prominent social leader within his city, particularly following the conversion of Constantine, the bishop was also a central figure in civic administration and an important source of wealth and patronage. He represented the local community in Church gatherings, before imperial officials, and in the presence of the emperor. In this chapter the focus falls primarily upon Athanasius' involvement in the ecclesiastical politics of his age. It is a story of councils and episcopal rivalries, monastic alliances, and ever-shifting relations between the Alexandrian bishop and the imperial power. The story may be complicated, but it is important both for the history of the fourth-century Church and as the setting that shaped Athanasius' life and thought. In subsequent chapters

---

[1] More detailed outlines of Athanasius' career can be found in (among others) Tetz (1979a), Barnes (1993), Martin (1996), and the numerous contributions in Gemeinhardt (2011). On Egypt in Late Antiquity, see Bagnall (1993) and the articles collected in Krause (1998) and Bagnall (2007).

[2] For further general reading on the changing status and functions of the bishop in Late Antiquity, see Chadwick (1980), Liebeschuetz (1997), Drake (2000), Rapp (2005), and Lizzi Testa (2009).

we will explore how Athanasius fulfilled the wider roles expected of a
bishop, as guardian of orthodoxy, ascetic champion, and spiritual father.

Athanasius entered the episcopate at a seminal moment in the history
of the Christian Church and the Roman Empire. Sixteen years earlier the
emperor Constantine had embraced Christianity after the Battle of Milvian
Bridge outside Rome in October 312. The privileges and resources that he
then poured into the western Church were extended to the east after Constantine's defeat of Licinius in 324 united the Empire under his rule. When
Constantine summoned the great Council of Nicaea in 325, he affirmed the
new status of Christianity and of the bishops as the representatives of their
regions. As a newly appointed bishop in one of the Empire's leading cities,
Athanasius had a unique opportunity to influence the transformation that
Constantine's conversion had begun. But his election also came at a time of
great tensions within Egyptian Christianity and the wider Church. Before
we can focus upon Athanasius, we need to begin by sketching the context
in which the young bishop found himself when he took over the leadership
of the ancient and powerful see of Alexandria.

THE EPISCOPATE OF ALEXANDRIA BEFORE ATHANASIUS

Christianity reached Egypt very early, yet the origins and initial development
of the new religion in this corner of the Mediterranean world remain
largely unknown. There was unquestionably considerable diversity in the
forms that early Egyptian Christianity took. Much of our evidence for what
is known as Christian 'Gnosticism' derives from Egypt, most notably the
collection of manuscripts discovered at Nag Hammadi in 1945. The older
argument that Gnosticism was the dominant force within early Christianity in Egypt has been widely rejected, however, in favour of a more fluid
model in which a variety of forms of Christianity coexisted for at least the
first two centuries AD.[3]

The status of the Alexandrian Church and its leadership within
Egyptian Christianity during these early centuries was equally fluid.
Later tradition would trace an unbroken line of patriarchs back to Mark
the Evangelist, the founder of the Church of Alexandria who was subsequently martyred by the pagans of the city. The historical accuracy of

---

[3] On early Egyptian Christianity, see Roberts (1979), Griggs (1990), and the articles in Pearson
and Goehring (1986). On the early bishops of Alexandria and their authority in the Egyptian
Church, see Martin (1996: 17–214), Jakab (2001), Davis (2004), and Wipszycka (2007).

that tradition is very difficult to determine.[4] We cannot assume that the earliest Christian community in Alexandria followed a single recognized bishop, for the monarchical episcopate became established as the most common form of Christian leadership only during the second and third centuries. The first men in the Alexandrian line of succession are nothing more than names to us. This starts to change only with Demetrius, whose episcopate is conventionally dated to 189–231. It may have been under Demetrius' guidance that the succession list of bishops from Mark was originally composed. Certainly it was in these years on either side of AD 200 that Alexandrian claims to authority within Egyptian Christianity began to become a reality.

Demetrius held the see of Alexandria at a crucial time. In addition to the Gnostics who continued to flourish in this period, his contemporaries included the two great intellectuals of early Egyptian Christianity: Clement (*c*.160–215) and Origen (*c*.185–253). To maintain control over the definition of doctrinal orthodoxy and the instruction of new candidates for baptism, the bishop had to establish himself as the undisputed head of the Alexandrian Church. Demetrius' conflict with Origen, which eventually led to the latter's departure to Palestine, reflects these tensions but also their resolution. The catechetical school of Alexandria that Origen had made famous now came under clear episcopal direction. Demetrius' third-century successors Heraclas (231–47), Dionysius (247–64), Maximus (264–82), and Theonas (282–300) all served as heads of the school before they entered the episcopate.[5]

From Demetrius onwards the bishops of Alexandria thus imposed themselves as the highest theological voice within their Church. Theirs was not the only voice, as the clash between Alexander and his presbyter Arius would demonstrate, but after Origen's passing there were no serious internal conflicts for the rest of the third century. This unity was vital as imperial persecution fell upon Christianity under the emperors Decius in 250 and then Valerian in 257. The leadership provided by Dionysius, whose episcopate spanned both outbreaks of persecution, was essential in holding the Alexandrian Church together through these trials. Dionysius did have to explain his failure to accept martyrdom, a criticism that Athanasius would later face in his turn. Through his endurance he further strengthened the

---

[4] The evidence is discussed in Davis (2004: 1–14).

[5] The status of the catechetical school during the fourth century is uncertain. It was once believed that Athanasius appointed the renowned biblical scholar Didymus the Blind to head the school during his episcopate, but the evidence for this (Rufinus, XI.7) is dubious: see Layton (2004: 15–18).

growing authority of his see, and set a precedent for future bishops of Alexandria, including Athanasius, to follow.

It is during the third century that we also find the Alexandrian episcopate exerting increasing influence over the wider body of Egyptian Christianity. This was aided by the geography and history of Egypt itself, which favoured centralization to a greater extent than in other regions of the eastern Mediterranean. Ever since her foundation by Alexander the Great, Alexandria had been the centre of Egyptian government under both Ptolemaic and Roman rule. Within her sphere of influence the metropolis on the Nile Delta was by far the largest urban centre, unlike her occasional rival Antioch in Syria, whose bishops never achieved the same local power over the surrounding cities. Perhaps in part for these reasons, we find little opposition in our sources to Alexandrian claims to leadership. The *Festal Letters* announcing the date of Easter for the Egyptian Church, the circulation of which by the bishop of Alexandria was symbolic of that leadership, are first attested with certainty once again under Dionysius.[6] The same bishop was engaged in extensive correspondence with Fabius of Antioch and Dionysius of Rome, taking his place alongside those men among the chief representatives of the universal Christian faith.

By the dawn of the fourth century the Alexandrian see's claims to authority were firmly established. The title *papas* (pope), used for a bishop of Alexandria some fifty years before its first attestation in Rome,[7] accurately reflects the prestige the office held. We see this confirmed in 325 by the sixth canon of the Council of Nicaea: 'Let the ancient customs hold good which are in Egypt and Libya and Pentapolis, according to which the Bishop of Alexandria has authority over all these places.'[8]

Such was the legacy that Athanasius inherited in 328. Yet it is not so easy to determine how far Alexandrian leadership over Egyptian Christianity actually extended in reality before Athanasius' election. Much of our evidence derives from later texts such as the *History of the Patriarchs*, which assume that the earlier bishops of Alexandria already held the powers they would possess in the time of Athanasius' great successors Theophilus and

---

[6] Eusebius of Caesarea, *Historia Ecclesiastica* VII.20; see Camplani (2003: 25–7).

[7] Dionysius refers to his predecessor Heraclas as 'our blessed pope' in a letter quoted by Eusebius of Caesarea, *Historia Ecclesiastica* VII.7.4. The earliest known Roman use of the term is in a catacomb inscription of *c*.300.

[8] On the context to this canon, see still Chadwick (1960).

Cyril.[9] Alexandrian authority did grow markedly in the third century, but that authority was still contested when Athanasius took office. The challenges that he faced are encapsulated by two men who had come to prominence under his predecessors and whose conflict with the Alexandrian see would cast a long shadow over Athanasius' episcopate: Melitius of Lycopolis and Arius.

The Melitian Schism that divided the fourth-century Egyptian Church originated during the Great Persecution and parallels in many respects the better-known Donatist Schism in North Africa.[10] Melitius of Lycopolis was a bishop and confessor from Upper Egypt who was imprisoned in 305/6 together with Peter of Alexandria (bishop 300–11).[11] The relatively mild terms that Peter set for the readmission of Christians who lapsed under the persecution were rejected by Melitius, who began to ordain others who shared his more rigorous attitude. After his return from the mines in 311 and Peter's death later the same year, Melitius organized his followers into a parallel 'Church of the Martyrs'.

So significant was the following that Melitius attracted that his schism received close attention at Nicaea in 325. The council ruled that Melitius and his clergy should retain their positions, although inferior in status to the equivalent clergy of the majority Egyptian Church, which now followed Athanasius' mentor Alexander. Properly elected Melitian bishops could even succeed catholic bishops when the contested sees became vacant. This attempted reconciliation failed after Alexander's death, and Athanasius clashed repeatedly with the Melitians right down to the 360s. The *Breviarium Melitii*, the list of Melitian clergy that Melitius submitted to Alexander, records a Melitian presence all along the Nile Valley.[12] Melitius' rigorist teachings particularly appealed to those who held ascetic values, and much of our knowledge of the movement derives from papyri preserved from Melitian monastic communities. The speed and scale with which Melitius' message spread highlighted two of the major difficulties that Athanasius would face: the need to unite Alexandria more closely with the rest of Egypt and the potential dangers related to the rise of asceticism.

[9] This is also the difficulty raised by the *History of the Episcopate of Alexandria* recently identified by Camplani from a new Ethiopian manuscript. Camplani (2006) has proposed that this text may have been compiled in the late fourth century, shortly after the death of Athanasius, and may therefore reflect his construction of Alexandrian authority.
[10] On the origins and nature of the Melitian Schism, see Bell (1924: 38–99), Barnard (1973), Martin (1974; 1996: 219–389), and Hauben (1998).
[11] For the life and legend of Peter, see Vivian (1988).
[12] Preserved in Athanasius, *Apologia contra Arianos* 71.

Entire volumes have been written on the career and teachings of Meli-tius' contemporary Arius.[13] Doomed to be remembered as the greatest heresiarch of the fourth century, Arius was a pious and ascetically minded cleric who first emerges clearly in our sources in the later 310s as the pres-byter of the Alexandrian parish church of 'Baucalis'.[14] The location of Bau-calis cannot be identified with certainty, but as the presbyter of his own church Arius possessed considerable status and developed a strong follow-ing. His controversial doctrines will be discussed in the next chapter, but in some respects Arius was another representative of the intellectual tradition of Alexandrian theology that went back to Clement and Origen. Inten-tionally or not, Arius challenged episcopal authority over doctrine, and his local power base gave him an initial platform and made him difficult for his bishop Alexander to control.

Alexander's response to the threat posed by Arius sheds valuable light on the resources available to an early fourth-century Alexandrian bishop. After his initial rebuke of Arius failed to quell the presbyter, Alexander summoned a Council of Alexandria in *c*.321. The assembled clergy sup-ported their leader, and Arius withdrew into exile. Sadly for Alexander, Arius received support in Palestine and Asia Minor. Alexander reacted by rallying his own allies outside Egypt. In *c*.322 he wrote to his namesake Alexander of Byzantium/Thessalonica denouncing Arius' heresy.[15] Dur-ing the same period Arius gained the notable patronage of Eusebius of Nicomedia, bishop of the eastern imperial capital, and tensions continued to mount. After Constantine's defeat of Licinius in September 324 had brought the whole Roman Empire under a Christian emperor, Alexander (possibly aided by his scribe Athanasius) spelt out his arguments in detail in an *Encyclical Letter* intended for the entire eastern Church. Many of the polemical themes of this letter would recur in Athanasius' later writings, including the construction of the 'Arian heresy' and the attack on Eusebius of Nicomedia as the heresy's leader. Alexander thus prepared the ground for the condemnation of Arius at Nicaea.

When Athanasius inherited the Alexandrian see from Alexander in 328, he immediately became a figure of the highest importance in the

---

[13] The standard work is R. D. Williams (1987). Later tradition tried to link Arius and Melitius together, although the evidence is very dubious: see R. D. Williams (1986).

[14] Epiphanius, *Panarion* 69.1.2. See further Haas (1997: 269–71).

[15] This letter is quoted in Theodoret, I.4, who identifies the recipient as Alexander of Byzantium (I.3). It is more likely that the letter went to yet another Alexander, the bishop of Thessalonica, who would subsequently write in support of Athanasius before the latter's first exile (his letter is quoted in Athanasius, *Apologia contra Arianos* 66).

eyes of the Church. Ecclesiastically and theologically, Alexandria already stood in the forefront of Christianity, and Athanasius accepted the burden of continuing that tradition. But Athanasius also inherited the ongoing problems that neither Alexander nor Nicaea had been able to resolve. The rival Melitian hierarchy threatened his authority particularly outside Alexandria. Arius still had supporters, both within Egypt and beyond. Two Libyans at Nicaea had chosen to share Arius' exile rather than sign his condemnation, and Eusebius of Nicomedia and other easterners sympathetic to Arius were prepared to exert pressure on his behalf. These and other challenges awaited the new bishop as Athanasius embarked on the long career that would shape the fortunes of Alexandria and Christianity for centuries to come.

THE EARLY YEARS: FROM ELECTION TO EXILE (328–35)

According to the introduction to the *Festal Index*, Alexander died on 17 April 328. On 8 June Athanasius was elected in his place. The two-month interregnum hints that all was not well. There seems no reason to doubt that Athanasius was Alexander's preferred heir, and yet his succession was far from smooth. Unfortunately, the exact circumstances are lost behind the veil of later apologetic and polemic.[16] In the *Encyclical Letter* of the Council of Alexandria that Athanasius summoned in 338, any suggestion that his election had been disputed is brushed aside as the slander of his accusers:

They say that 'after the death of Bishop Alexander, a certain few having mentioned the name of Athanasius, six or seven bishops elected him clandestinely in a secret place'. This is what they wrote to the Emperors, having no scruple about asserting the greatest falsehoods. We are witnesses and so is the whole city and the province too that the whole multitude and all the people of the catholic Church assembled together as with one mind and body, and cried, shouted, that Athanasius should be bishop of their Church, made this the subject of their public prayers to Christ, and conjured us to grant it for many days and nights, neither departing themselves from the church nor suffering us to do so. (Quoted in Athanasius, *Apologia contra Arianos* 6)

This account was written a decade after the event, following Athanasius' return from his first exile. Defending his legitimacy as bishop of Alexandria

---

[16] For contrasting interpretations of the difficult evidence for Athanasius' election, see Barnard (1975: 329–36), Girardet (1975: 52–7), and Arnold (1991: 25–48). On episcopal elections more broadly in Late Antiquity, see Norton (2007).

had become paramount, and was the primary mission of the council that composed the *Encyclical Letter*. We are, therefore, justified in hesitating before we accept the claim that Athanasius was welcomed with universal approval. Some contemporaries at least believed his election had been engineered by a secret minority, and this was well known to the fifth-century ecclesiastical historians.[17] Other traditions reported that the Melitians and the 'Arians' both sought to impose their own candidates on the Alexandrian see.[18] Ultimately, the exact circumstances in which Athanasius was elected bishop perhaps do not greatly matter. But the fact that his election was contentious does. From the moment of his accession Athanasius faced an urgent challenge to reunite his divided episcopate and establish himself as the true leader of the Egyptian Church.

The earliest extant works composed by Athanasius as bishop make no reference to the controversy surrounding his election. This is not a surprise. The subject was not one he would wish to raise, and in any case was hardly appropriate to the *Festal Letters*, which comprise his first episcopal writings. Those letters, combining exegesis and exhortations for the faithful, set the tone for Athanasius' approach to his pastoral obligations, which will be discussed further in Chapter 5. They also represented a statement of his authority, declaring his right to determine the date of Easter for the Egyptian Church. Athanasius reinforced his new status by travelling widely, touring the Thebaid in 329–30 (*Festal Index* 2) and Pentapolis and Ammoniaca in 331–2 (*Festal Index* 4). The devoted following that he built up during these early years was to prove crucial, for the tensions were beginning to rise that would lead inexorably to Athanasius' initial condemnation and exile in 335.

For our knowledge of the events leading up to and surrounding the Council of Tyre in 335 at which he was condemned we depend almost entirely on Athanasius' polemic and the documents preserved within his works.[19] The evidence may be tendentious, but a basic outline is not too difficult to reconstruct, however controversial its interpretation. Immediately upon his accession Athanasius came into conflict with the Melitians, who challenged his authority as bishop and brought accusations against him. A first vague accusation in 330/1 regarding the misuse of linen vest-

---

[17] Socrates, I.23; Sozomen, II.17; Philostorgius, II.11.
[18] Epiphanius, *Panarion* 68.7.2–4 (Melitians), 69.11.4–6 ('Arians').
[19] For a more detailed analysis of these events and the problems raised by our evidence, see Barnes (1993) and Gwynn (2007).

ments was quickly dropped. But more serious charges were raised in 332, which caused Constantine to summon Athanasius for a hearing. Athanasius was accused of causing his presbyter Macarius to break a sacred chalice in a Melitian church and of bribing an official named Philumenus. Those charges in turn were dismissed, as Athanasius reports in *Festal Letter* IV, which he sent from Constantine's court in Nicomedia. New charges were then raised, alleging that Athanasius was responsible for the murder of the Melitian bishop Arsenius. In 333/4 Constantine ordered an episcopal council to gather at Caesarea in Palestine to investigate, but Athanasius informed the emperor that Arsenius had been found alive and the council was abandoned. Yet even this could not quiet Athanasius' accusers. Finally, Athanasius was found guilty at the Council of Tyre in 335, and after a last desperate appeal to the emperor was banished to Gaul.

In the polemical writings that Athanasius composed in the years following his first exile, his explanation for his fate is clear and consistent. He was the victim of an 'Arian conspiracy'. Although his primary accusers were the Egyptian Melitians, they had formed an alliance as far back as 330 with their 'secret friend' (*krupha philos*) Eusebius of Nicomedia. Eusebius, who had been attacked in Alexander's *Encyclical Letter* for his support for Arius before Nicaea, wished to see Arius restored to the Church. Athanasius stood in his way and threatened to expose his 'Arian' beliefs. Therefore Eusebius and his associates, whom Athanasius names *hoi peri Eusebion* ('the ones around Eusebius' or 'the Eusebians'), worked through the Melitians to have Athanasius condemned: 'All the proceedings against me, and the fabricated stories about the breaking of the chalice and the murder of Arsenius, were for the sole purpose of introducing impiety into the Church and of preventing their being condemned as heretics' (Athanasius, *Apologia contra Arianos* 85).

It is necessary to draw out the implications of this Athanasian polemic. First, he is entirely innocent of the various charges that have been alleged against him. Secondly, although those charges were concerned with his behaviour not with theology, the true motive behind the attacks is that he has defended orthodoxy against heresy. Thirdly, his chief accusers are not Egyptian schismatics but 'Arians', heretics who threaten the entire Church. The Council of Tyre was a direct continuation of the earlier conspiracy against him and was controlled by the 'Eusebians'. They organized the commission of enquiry that was sent from Tyre to Egypt to investigate the charges against Athanasius and fabricated its findings. When Athanasius appealed to the emperor, the 'Eusebians' then came to court to secure his downfall. His condemnation and exile were the work of a small heretical faction, not the legal judgment of the eastern Church or of the emperor Constantine.

Should we accept Athanasius' protestations of innocence and his presentation of his accusers as 'Arians'? This question has increasingly troubled modern scholars, although Christian tradition from the late fourth century onwards strongly embraced the Athanasian line. There are certain factors that might encourage doubts. Athanasius describes his foes as an 'Arian party', the 'Eusebians', throughout the narrative of the *Apologia contra Arianos*, which he wrote after his first exile. In the documents that he quotes within that work from before 335, and in his own *Festal Letters* from those years, the sole accusers identified are the Melitians. The first attacks upon a 'Eusebian conspiracy' occur in the letters written by Athanasius and his followers at the Council of Tyre itself. This may indicate that at Tyre Athanasius finally recognized the true source of his sufferings. Or it may indicate that Athanasius began to represent his opponents as 'Arians' only when he realized his condemnation was imminent, and then reinterpreted his earlier career accordingly.

Uncertainty also surrounds the exact charges on which Athanasius was condemned and whether he was in fact guilty of any of the crimes attributed to him.[20] In his writings Athanasius focuses upon two charges: that he murdered Arsenius (which it seems he disproved, as he produced Arsenius alive)[21] and that he was responsible for Macarius breaking a Melitian chalice (a charge unclear even in the *Apologia contra Arianos*, where Athanasius argues that nothing happened but that, if it did happen, it did not matter). These were charges that Athanasius believed he could refute. There were other charges that he does not mention, including the dispute over the legality of his election and accusations of violence against the Melitians.

One rare contemporary Melitian letter written shortly before the Council of Tyre suggests that the last charge in particular may have had a basis in truth:

I have written to you in order that you might know in what affliction we are; for he [Athanasius] carried off a bishop of the Lower Country and shut him in the Meat Market, and a priest of the same region he shut in the lock-up, and a deacon in the

---

[20] The difficulties posed by any reconstruction are visible in the markedly disparate interpretations of Tyre that have been proposed by Girardet (1975: 66–75), Drake (1986: 193–204), Arnold (1991: 143–63), and Barnes (1993: 22–5).

[21] The story that Athanasius actually identified Arsenius as among those present at Tyre does not appear in any Athanasian work, only in Sozomen, II.25.10.

principal prison, and till the 28th of Pachon [23 May] Heraiscus too had been confined in the camp—I thank God our Master that the scourgings which he endured
have ceased—and on the 27th he caused seven bishops to leave the country. (*Papyrus
London* 1914)[22]

Papyrus London 1914 is no less potentially tendentious than Athanasius'
writings. All conclusions are therefore subjective, and a modern reader
must make up his or her own mind which evidence to accept. Athanasius believed himself to be the victim of a 'Eusebian' conspiracy, and this
was the argument he and his Egyptian followers presented to the assembled bishops at Tyre. Despite its influence on later Christian tradition, as
a defence at his trial the polemic failed. Rightly or wrongly, the council
(which represented a considerable bloc of the eastern Church) found
Athanasius guilty.[23] Athanasius did not wait for the verdict. Leaving Tyre,
according to *Festal Index* 8 in an open boat, he set out for the imperial court.
The emperor Constantine takes up the story:

As I was entering on a late occasion our eponymous and all-fortunate *patria* of
Constantinople (I chanced at the time to be on horseback), on a sudden the bishop
Athanasius with certain others whom he had with him approached me in the middle of the road, so unexpectedly as to occasion me much amazement. God, who
knows all things, is my witness that I should have been unable at first sight even
to recognize him, had not some of my attendants, on my naturally inquiring of
them, informed me both who it was and under what injustice he was suffering.
(Constantine, *Letter to the Bishops assembled at Tyre*, quoted in Athanasius, *Apologia
contra Arianos* 86)[24]

Constantine was concerned that the council might not have given Athanasius a fair hearing, and in his letter he summoned the bishops to court to
explain their judgment. In fact a delegation from Tyre was already on the
way, and arrived scarcely a week after Athanasius.[25] A final hearing then took

---

[22] This famous text was first published by Bell (1924: 53–71). The attempt of Arnold (1989,
developed in more detail in 1991: 62–89) to argue that the subject here is not Athanasius is
unconvincing: see DiMaio (1996) and Hauben (2001: 612–14).

[23] Socrates (I.28) estimated there were sixty bishops at Tyre, to which must be added the
forty-eight Egyptian bishops who accompanied Athanasius. The council was certainly more
representative of the eastern Church than Athanasius' presentation of Tyre as the vehicle of
his 'Eusebian' opponents might suggest.

[24] A longer version of this Constantinian letter is preserved in Gelasius of Cyzicus, *Historia
Ecclesiastica* III.18. As Gelasius' version includes a further section in praise of Athanasius' piety,
which it is difficult to believe that Athanasius would have removed, it is likely that Athanasius'
text is the original and that of Gelasius reflects later additions, probably made by Gelasius
himself (Ehrhardt 1980: 55–6).

[25] For the chronology, see *Festal Index* 8 and Peeters (1945).

place before the emperor. Athanasius claims, although without evidence, that the 'Eusebians' now raised a further charge to arouse Constantine's anger. They alleged that Athanasius had threatened to withhold the corn shipments that sailed from Egypt to Constantinople. Whether this is true or not, Constantine concluded that Athanasius was to be punished. On 7 November 335 the bishop departed into exile in Gaul.

BETWEEN EAST AND WEST: THE FIRST AND SECOND EXILES (335–46)

We hear very little about Athanasius' first experience of exile. In title he remained the bishop of Alexandria, for Constantine refused to allow the election of a replacement.[26] He suffered no physical mistreatment, and on his arrival in Gaul he resided in Trier, the imperial residence of Constantine's oldest son Constantine II, whom he befriended. There he waited for the opportunity to return home. That opportunity came with the death of the elder Constantine on 22 May 337, and the division of the Empire between his sons.[27] Constantine II, now the senior emperor in the west, provided Athanasius with a letter of recommendation, and the bishop set out for the east.

Athanasius did not travel directly to Alexandria. His return was the subject of controversy. In the eyes of many eastern bishops Athanasius had been condemned by a legitimate council of the Church, and required the approval of a council before he could be restored. Although he had been exiled by Constantine the Great, his critics could argue, the emperor's death did not affect his status. Athanasius' route home suggests that he knew his position remained insecure. The support of Constantine II was valuable, but more important was the blessing or at least the permission of the latter's brother Constantius, who now ruled the east. Travelling through the Balkans, Athanasius met his new emperor at Viminacium in Moesia.[28] No report of their meeting survives, but Constantius evidently raised no

---

[26] In *Epistula Encyclica* 6, Athanasius refers to a certain Pistus appointed by the 'Eusebians' over the 'Arians' in Alexandria before Gregory. For what little is known of Pistus and his career, see Schneemelcher (1974a: 313–15) and Klein (1977: 68–71).

[27] Theodoret, I.30, uniquely claims that Constantine ordered Athanasius' recall just before his death.

[28] Athanasius refers to the meeting in *Apologia ad Constantium* 5. No context is given in that text, but Barnes (1993: 33–4) must be correct to place it here.

immediate objections, and Athanasius was permitted to travel onwards. His journey took him to Constantinople and through Syria–Palestine, and according to his opponents he used this opportunity to restore other condemned bishops and impose by violence his nominees on a number of sees.[29] He had already begun to prepare for a struggle before he arrived in Alexandria on 23 November 337.

The faithful followers who had mourned his exile doubtless welcomed Athanasius back. But this was not a triumphal homecoming. Constantius was swiftly under pressure from eastern bishops who demanded that Athanasius be returned into exile. The tension is clearly visible from *Festal Letter* X, which Athanasius wrote for the Easter of 338.[30] The letter opens with Athanasius' declaration that he has fulfilled the traditional duty of the bishop of Alexandria by informing his flock of the date of Easter even from 'the ends of the earth' (Trier):

Although I have travelled all this distance from you, my brethren, I have not forgotten the custom which obtains among you, which has been delivered to us by the Fathers, so as to be silent without notifying to you the time of the annual holy feast, and the day for its celebration. For although I have been hindered by those afflictions of which you have doubtless heard, and severe trials have been laid upon me, and a great distance has separated us; while the enemies of the truth have followed our tracks, laying snares to discover a letter from us, so that by their accusations, they might add to the pain of our wounds; yet, the Lord strengthening and comforting us in our afflictions, we have not feared, even when held fast in the midst of such machinations and conspiracies, to indicate and make known to you our saving Easter-feast, even from the ends of the earth. (X.1)

In the main body of the letter, Athanasius contrasts those who persecute with the endurance and mercy of the faithful (X.4–5) and presents the only detailed theological attack on 'Arianism' to be found anywhere in his *Festal Letters* (X.8–9). The overall tone is one of resistance against an imminent threat. Throughout 338 Athanasius sought to rally support in Egypt and from the wider Church. It was at this time that the monk Antony made a famous visit to Alexandria and spoke against the 'Arians' (*Festal Index* 10; *Life of Antony* 69). A council of Egyptian bishops was summoned to Alexandria, and circulated an *Encyclical Letter* (quoted in *Apologia contra*

---

[29] This charge is raised in the *Encyclical Letter* of the eastern bishops who attended the abortive Council of Serdica in 343, on which see further below. Cf. Sozomen, III.21.

[30] *Festal Letter* X is the longest of the extant *Festal Letters*, and the only letter to have received a detailed edition and monograph: Lorenz (1986). For the importance of the letter to Athanasius' pastoral mission, see Ch. 5.

Arianos 3–19) in defence of Athanasius' position. The charges on which
he had been condemned in 335 and the Council of Tyre itself were dismissed as the product of a Melitian–'Eusebian' conspiracy. Their accusations were nothing more than 'an impiety on behalf of the Ariomaniacs,
which rages against piety so that, when the orthodox are out of the way,
the advocates of impiety may preach whatever they wish without fear' (5).
Therefore it is necessary for true bishops everywhere to come to the aid of
the cause of orthodoxy, 'to welcome this, our declaration, to share in the
suffering of our fellow bishop Athanasius, and to show your indignation
against the Eusebians' (19).

The efforts of Athanasius and his followers were in vain. In late 338 he
was condemned once more by a Council of Antioch, which met in the
presence of Constantius. Unlike in 335, this time a replacement, Gregory
of Cappadocia, was appointed to take control of the Alexandrian see. He
entered the city on 22 March 339, and on 16 April (Easter Monday) Athanasius fled. His *Epistula Encyclica*, the first work of his second exile composed
in mid-339, appealed to all Christians to denounce his rival as an 'Arian'
who had brought persecution to Alexandria.[31] Supported by the Prefect
Philagrius, Gregory is alleged to have rallied gangs of Jews and pagans,
who burnt one church, assaulted Athanasius' followers, and then attacked
the church in which Athanasius himself resided (*Epistula Encyclica* 3–5). The
true scale of the violence is difficult to assess from Athanasius' rhetoric.[32]
The church that was burnt was probably the Church of Dionysius, whose
location in Alexandria is unknown, while the cathedral church in 339 from
which Athanasius was expelled was the Church of Theonas (*Festal Index* 11)
at the north-western end of the city.[33] The new bishop, Gregory, unsurpris-
ingly sought to establish his authority by occupying the main Alexandrian
churches during the great Easter celebrations. He also took over the chief

[31] For a fuller survey of Athanasius' arguments in this letter, see Schneemelcher (1974*a*:
esp. 325–37), and Gwynn (2007: 51–7).

[32] Athanasius described the events of 339 again later in his *Historia Arianorum*. In addition
to the crimes recounted in the *Epistula Encyclica*, the 'Arians' are reported to have 'so persecuted the bishop's aunt, that even when she died he [Gregory] would not suffer her to be
buried' (13). Strangely, Athanasius never even mentioned this personal outrage in his original
version of those events.

[33] For the architecture and topography of late-antique Christian Alexandria, see Haas
(1997) and Martin (1998) and the wider Egyptian studies of Grossman (2002) and McKenzie
(2007). On the importance of Christian topography to the fourth-century ecclesiastical conflicts, see Gwynn (2010).

civic functions of the episcopate, particularly the distribution of bread, the pastoral significance of which will be discussed further in Chapter 5.

Gregory's appointment placed still greater pressure on Athanasius to defend his innocence and his status as legitimate bishop of Alexandria. After his flight from the city, he travelled back to the west to seek support from those who had aided him during his earlier exile. Between 339 and 346 Athanasius resided in Italy and Gaul, but he continued to look towards Egypt. Through considerable effort he succeeded in circulating *Festal Letters* in some of these years, although on occasion he was able to send only the brief notification that recorded the date of Easter. *Festal Letter* XIII, written for the Easter of 341, emphasizes that distance could not separate him from his congregations: 'Although the opponents of Christ have oppressed you together with us with afflictions and sorrows; yet, God having comforted us by our mutual faith, behold, I write to you even from Rome. Keeping the feast here with the brethren, still I keep it with you also in will and spirit' (XIII.1).

Athanasius devoted the majority of the letter to a meditation on the appropriate theme of the persecution of the faithful and the need for endurance. Nor were *Festal Letters* the only correspondence that Athanasius exchanged from exile with his Egyptian followers. It was in these years that Athanasius most probably wrote two of his best-known epistles. One, discussed further in the chapter on asceticism, was Athanasius' first *Letter to the Monks*. The second was the *Letter to Serapion on the Death of Arius* or *De Morte Arii*. Writing in response to debates within Egypt over whether Arius had died in communion with the Church, Athanasius asked Serapion to pass on his judgement to those in dispute. Because of the machinations of the 'Eusebians', Athanasius declared, Arius had been given permission to attend worship in Constantinople. But, on his route to the church, he felt the need to enter a privy, and there ' "falling headlong he burst asunder" [Acts 1:18]...[and] he was deprived of both communion and his life' (3). The divine judgement that Arius suffered, modelled on the scriptural fate of Judas, condemned both the man and his heresy.

All these letters reinforced Athanasius' claim to authority over the Egyptian Church. They also demonstrated Athanasius' awareness that there were larger issues facing contemporary Christianity than just his personal concerns. The rise of asceticism was one such development that Athanasius was pleased to support, and later sources credited him with the promotion of ascetic practices in the west during this time. Far more worrying in Athanasius' eyes, however, were the theological developments then taking place in eastern Christianity. In 341 a major council met in Antioch to celebrate the dedication of the city's new great church. The doctrinal significance of this Dedication Council will again receive more attention in a later chapter. But the creed that the council composed revealed directions in eastern theology that Athanasius at least regarded as heretical. It was in this context that Athanasius began his longest theological and polemical work, the three *Orationes contra Arianos*. The condemnation of his opponents as 'Arian' vindicated Athanasius' claims to innocence and legitimacy. Nevertheless, there is no questioning the sincerity of his conviction that fundamental principles of Christian doctrine were at stake, a conviction that the western bishops who rallied to his defence came to share.

On his arrival in the west, Athanasius had been welcomed by Julius, the bishop of Rome. At Julius' summons, a council of Italian bishops met in the Roman city in late 340 or 341 and re-examined Athanasius' case. The council declared Athanasius innocent, and Julius wrote to the eastern bishops then gathered in Antioch to announce this verdict.[34] His letter is quoted by Athanasius in *Apologia contra Arianos* 20–35.[35] The accusations against Athanasius are declared to be false and Gregory's appointment is uncanonical and a cause of persecution. Julius has derived his interpretation of events from Athanasius (although he does not explicitly repeat Athanasius' condemnation of his opponents as 'Arian'), and his arguments do not have independent historical value. Nor did Julius' letter have any apparent impact on eastern opinion. Yet the letter is an important document. Julius' public statement of support for Athanasius enhanced the latter's standing in the west, and established a relationship between Athanasius and the Roman see that endured throughout his life and would benefit a number of his Alexandrian successors. Julius' exchange with the bishops in Antioch also hardened a growing rift between Christians in east and west, in which the fate of Athanasius was one of the major causes of dispute.

These tensions between east and west finally came to a head at the abortive Council of Serdica in 343. Athanasius was not the only exiled eastern bishop in the west whose status was controversial. He had been joined in Rome by Marcellus of Ancyra, who had been condemned on theological

---

[34] The eastern gathering was most probably the Dedication Council, but the relative chronology of both that council and Julius' letter is difficult to determine. On this debate, see Eltester (1937: 254–6), Schneemelcher (1977), and Barnes (1993: 57–9).

[35] Julius' letter has primarily been studied as a source for the position of the see of Rome in the fourth-century Church. The letter concludes with Julius' claim that, with regards to the Church of Alexandria, 'the custom has been for word to be written first to us, and then for just decisions to be defined from here' (35). This has aroused considerable controversy: see Twomey (1982: 382–6), Hess (2002: 184–90), and Chadwick (2003: 15–16).

grounds in 336, and by Asclepas of Gaza. The need to resolve both the fates of the exiles and the ongoing doctrinal debates led Constans, Constantine's youngest son and the sole western emperor after the death of Constantine II in 340, to agree with his brother Constantius to summon a joint gathering of eastern and western bishops.[36] The council was set to meet in the Balkan city of Serdica. Unfortunately, the full gathering never took place. The easterners refused to allow the presence of the exiles, whose episcopal authority they denied, and the westerners refused to meet in their absence. The two contingents therefore held their own gatherings. Each council composed *Encyclical Letters*, defending their position and condemning the other.[37]

Far from resolving the tensions, the twin councils of 343 widened the east–west divide. For our knowledge of Athanasius, however, their respective *Encyclical Letters* offer a unique opportunity to compare the arguments of his supporters with those of his foes. The Western *Encyclical Letter* (*Apologia contra Arianos* 42–50) defended the innocence of all the eastern exiles but particularly Athanasius. Like Julius of Rome, the western bishops at Serdica dismissed the charges against Athanasius as entirely false and denounced Gregory as an imposter. Unlike Julius, they also repeated Athanasius' condemnation of his eastern foes as 'Arian'. To quote from the conclusion to their letter:

It was necessary for us not to remain silent, nor to pass over unnoticed their calumnies, imprisonments, murders, woundings, conspiracies by means of false letters, outrages, stripping of virgins, banishments, destruction of churches, burnings, translations from small cities to larger dioceses, and above all, the insurrection of the ill-named Arian heresy by their means against the orthodox faith. We have therefore pronounced our dearly beloved brethren and fellow-ministers Athanasius, Marcellus and Asclepas, and those who minister to the Lord with them, to be innocent and clear of offence, and have written to the diocese of each, that the people of each Church may know the innocence of their bishop and may esteem him as their bishop and expect his coming.[38] And as for those who like wolves have invaded their churches, Gregory at Alexandria, Basil at Ancyra and Quintianus at Gaza, let them

---

[36] In our orthodox sources Constans is presented as the chief protagonist for the council, and Athanasius later had to defend himself against charges of turning Constans against his brother: *Apologia ad Constantium* 2–4.

[37] For a discussion of the course of the two councils and their texts, see De Clercq (1954: 334–62), Girardet (1975: 106–54), Barnard (1983: 63–118), and Hess (2002: 93–11)1.

[38] Athanasius quotes their letters to the Church of Alexandria and to the bishops of Egypt and Libya in *Apologia contra Arianos* 37–41.

neither give them the title of bishop, nor hold any communion at all with them, nor receive letters from them, nor write to them. (Quoted in *Apologia contra Arianos* 47)

The Eastern *Encyclical Letter*, preserved in Latin by Hilary of Poitiers (*Against Valens and Ursacius* I.II.1–29), understandably offers a very different interpretation.[39] Theologically, the easterners were far more concerned with Marcellus of Ancyra than with Athanasius, for reasons we will explore in the next chapter. It was Marcellus' heresy that they accused the western bishops of adopting. Athanasius, of course, maintained that the underlying cause of the accusations he faced was his defence of orthodoxy against 'Arianism'. For the eastern bishops, his name was synonymous rather with violence and illegality. Their letter provides a rare glimpse of how Athanasius was seen from the other side:

In the case of Athanasius, formerly bishop of Alexandria, you are to understand what was enacted. He was charged with the grave offence of sacrilege and profanation of the holy Church's sacraments. With his own hands he broke a chalice consecrated to God and Christ, tore down the august altar itself, overturned the bishop's throne and razed the basilica itself, God's house, Christ's house, to the ground. The presbyter himself, an earnest and upright man called Scyras, he delivered to military custody. In addition to this, Athanasius was charged with unlawful acts, with the use of force, with murder and the killing of bishops. Raging like a tyrant even during the most holy days of Easter, he was accompanied by the military and officials of the imperial government who, on his authority, confined some to custody, beat and whipped some and forced the rest into sacrilegious communion with him by various acts of torture (innocent men would never have behaved so). Athanasius hoped that in this way his own people and his own faction would get the upper hand; and so he forced unwilling people into communion by means of military officials, judges, prisons, whippings and various acts of torture, compelled recusants and browbeat those who fought back and withstood him. (Quoted in Hilary of Poitiers, *Against Valens and Ursacius* I.II.6)

What weight to place on these two highly polemical documents, modern readers may decide for themselves. The *Encyclical Letters* each use very similar language and accuse their respective opponents of much the same crimes. The verdict of the Western Council of Serdica confirmed Athanasius' standing in the west, where Athanasius would later find a powerful

---

[39] One of the addressees of this letter was Donatus, the schismatic bishop of Carthage. When the Donatists cited the Eastern encyclical in order to claim support from churches outside Africa, Augustine's friend Alypius pointed out that the letter had to be heretical as it attacked Athanasius and Julius of Rome (Augustine, *Letter* 44.5.6).

source of support during his conflict with Constantius in the 350s. Athanasius also retained the patronage of Constans, with whom he is known to have attended worship in Aquileia in 345.[40] But the majority of the eastern Church remained hostile towards Athanasius, and Gregory was still recognized as the bishop of Alexandria. It was only after Gregory's death in 345 that Athanasius, having received imperial permission, was finally allowed to return home.

THE GLORIOUS RETURN AND THE GOLDEN DECADE (346–56)

He was welcomed with branches of trees, and garments with many flowers and of varied hue were torn off and strewn before him and under his feet. There alone was all that was glorious and costly and peerless treated with dishonour. Like, once more, to the entry of Christ were those that went before with shouts and followed with dances; only the crowd which sung his praises was not of children only, but every tongue was harmonious, as men contended only to outdo one another. I pass by the universal cheers, and the pouring forth of unguents, and the nightlong festivities, and the whole city gleaming with light, and the feasting in public and at home, and all the means of testifying to a city's joy, which were then in lavish and incredible profusion bestowed upon him. Thus did this marvellous man, with such a concourse, regain his own city. (Gregory of Nazianzus, *Oration* XXI.29)

Athanasius' triumphal entrance into Alexandria on 21 October 346, which Gregory of Nazianzus compared to Christ's entry into Jerusalem, is one of the iconic episodes of his episcopate. The death of Gregory of Alexandria the previous year had left the see vacant, and so the returning bishop faced no immediate competition. But this cannot explain the depth of joy expressed for his restoration. Athanasius reaped the benefit from the loyal following that he had built up in his first decade and nurtured through his *Festal Letters* and other writings from exile. Gregory had failed either to win over or to break that Athanasian support, and, although he held the Alexandrian see for some seven years, he left no discernible legacy. Athanasius had seen off his first serious rival.

---

[40] In *Apologia ad Constantium* 15, Athanasius states that he had seen Constans worshipping at Aquileia in a church still under construction. *Festal Index* 17 confirms the year as 345, for in that year Athanasius sent his *Festal Letter* from the same city.

Nevertheless, we should not be carried away by the dramatic rhetoric. His long absence in the west had left Athanasius with considerable work to do if he was to re-establish his authority not only in Alexandria but across Egypt and Libya.[41] Clergy appointed by Gregory might occupy some local churches, and more seriously the Melitian movement with its rival hierarchy continued to exist. We gain a measure of the challenge Athanasius faced and of his response from *Festal Letter* XIX, written upon his return for Easter 347. The letter begins with an invocation of Paul to celebrate Athanasius' restoration: ' "Blessed is God, the Father of our Lord Jesus Christ" [Ephesians 1:3], for such an introduction is fitting for an epistle, and more especially now, when it brings thanksgiving to the Lord, in the Apostle's words, because He has brought us from a distance and granted us again to send openly to you, as customary, the Festal Letters' (XIX.1).

The main body of the letter then proclaims at length that only the true Christian can celebrate the Easter festival and understand the Law and the nature of sacrifice. 'The feast of the Passover is ours, not that of a stranger' (XIX.1). Those who feign to act lawfully and piously will be rejected by the Lord, a rebuke that is addressed against the Jews but also against the heretics who misinterpret the Scriptures. Athanasius' language can be interpreted as a warning to those who have fallen away during the years of his exile, but the polemic of *Festal Letter* XIX is less violent than the anti-'Arian' rhetoric of the letters he composed after his earlier return in 338. In 347 Athanasius could feel more secure, and he urges all to give thanks to God as he himself gives thanks that the Lord 'did not deliver us over to death, but brought us from a distance, even as from the ends of the earth, and has united us again with you' (XIX.8).

Athanasius follows his exhortation by reaffirming the date of Easter and of the forty-day Lenten fast. The letter also contains a highly significant postscript: 'I have also thought it necessary to inform you of the appointment of bishops, which has taken place in the stead of our blessed fellow-ministers, that you may know to whom to write, and from whom you should receive letters' (XIX.10). The list that follows names the bishops appointed to sixteen sees from Syene to Clysma. The previous occupants of the sees died in Athanasius' years in exile (with the exception of Artemidorus of Panopolis, who has requested a coadjutor, because of his age and infirmity), and their successors are now confirmed in office. By asserting his right to confirm these appointments through his *Festal Letter*, Athana-

---

[41] For further discussion see Barnes (1993: 94–7).

sius made a powerful statement of his authority over the Egyptian Church. He also ensured the support of the men who now occupied these sees, further strengthening his position in Egypt beyond Alexandria.[42]

Athanasius' list of appointments includes three men who are said to have 'reconciled to the Church'—Arsenius of Hypsele, Isidorus of Xois, and Paulus of Clysma—as well as Amatus and Isaac of Nilopolis, who have reconciled with each other. Arsenius, who is recognized in the letter as the sole bishop of Hypsele, is the same Melitian cleric who had been involved in the charges against Athanasius at the Council of Tyre. Isidorus and Paulus are named as colleagues of the bishops in their respective sees, just as Isaac has reconciled with Amatus in Nilopolis. It is entirely possible that Isidorus, Paulus, and Isaac are all also Melitians who have acknowledged Athanasius' authority. These defections suggest that the schism was losing momentum by the 340s, although Athanasius would come into conflict with the Melitians again in the 360s.

Festal Letter XIX is our clearest evidence for Athanasius' efforts to reaffirm his authority outside Alexandria after his return from his second exile. In this context, we might also consider the letter that he wrote to the ascetic Dracontius a few years later in *c*.354. Athanasius' purpose was to persuade Dracontius to accept episcopal office. A fuller discussion of this letter and of Athanasius' relationship with the Egyptian monks belongs in a later chapter, but that relationship provided an important additional source of support for Athanasius' ecclesiastical position. Dracontius did indeed serve as the bishop of Hermopolis Parva, and in his appeal Athanasius names a number of other monk-bishops, including Serapion of Thmuis. Like the men named in *Festal Letter* XIX, these monk-bishops could be relied upon to remain loyal to Athanasius and in turn to aid him to retain the loyalty of the wider ascetic community. That alliance was to prove its value once more when Athanasius' third exile began in 356.

In the light of the reception that Athanasius received upon his return in October 346, his position within his city already possessed firm foundations on which to build. The charitable distribution of bread and oil was back under his control, a means to rally support and a proof of his legitimate

---

[42] Athanasius had already sent a similar list of approved bishops from the west in either *c*.337 or *c*.339/40. It appears at the end of the document preserved in the *Festal Index* as *Festal Letter* XII, which is actually a personal letter that Athanasius wrote from exile to his friend Serapion of Thmuis. Athanasius asked Serapion to circulate the Easter message he enclosed, including the list of appointments, to the Egyptian churches. On the known bishops of Egyptian sees in the fourth century, see Worp (1994).

authority. He likewise led by personal example, through preaching and
spiritual direction, although this pastoral role as always is hardest to trace
because of the nature of our evidence. Athanasius benefited here from an
important development in the Christian topography of Alexandria.[43] The
Caesareum, the imperial cult temple on the harbour in the centre of the
city, was now converted into the new great church of Alexandria. Work
had not quite reached completion when Athanasius used the church to
celebrate Easter in *c*.351. He had to explain his action to Constantius, as the
emperor had financed the construction of the church, which had not been
dedicated.[44] According to Athanasius, the enormous multitude gathered
for the feast had forced his hand, but, while this may attest to his popularity
in his city, the premature use of the church was one of the complaints that
led to his third exile.

The conversion of the Caesareum of Alexandria from pagan temple to
Christian church serves as a reminder that Athanasius lived in an age of
great religious change. His entire episcopal career was a reflection of the
new prominence that the Church enjoyed from the reign of Constantine
onwards. Yet the rapid expansion of Christianity in the fourth-century
Roman Empire is scarcely visible from Athanasius' writings. In one of his
earliest works he does celebrate the spread of the Church. 'Every day in
every place He [the Saviour] invisibly persuades such a great multitude of
Greeks and barbarians to turn to faith in Him and all to obey His teaching'
(*De Incarnatione* 30). As we will see in the next chapter, however, even in
the *Contra Gentes–De Incarnatione* Athanasius' attacks on paganism are subordinated to his theological concerns. Elsewhere in his works there is little
reference to pagans, except when they are alleged to have allied with his
heretical foes,[45] or to pagan practices.[46] The primary threats to Athanasius' authority came from within Christianity, from 'Arians' and Melitians,
not from pagans. But, through his efforts to secure Church unity and to
strengthen the position of the bishop of Alexandria, Athanasius played his
part in establishing Christianity as the dominant religion of late-antique
Egypt.

It was probably during the years in the middle of the fourth century
that Athanasius also made one of his most lasting contributions to the

---

[43] For bibliography, see n. 33 above.

[44] Athanasius, *Apologia ad Constantium* 14–18; see Barnes (1993: 113–14) and Heinen
(2002).

[45] On this rhetorical theme, see D. H. Williams (1997).

[46] One exception is Athanasius' condemnation of pagan oracles (*Life of Antony* 31–5, *Festal
Letter* XLII (AD 370)). See further Frankfurter (1998: esp. 187–9).

authority of the Alexandrian Church beyond the traditional limits of his see. His role in the story, it must be said, was relatively minor. A young Syrian named Frumentius was brought as a captive to the king of Aksum (ancient Ethiopia). Having risen to a position of trust and encouraged the spread of Christianity in the kingdom, Frumentius was allowed to return to the Mediterranean. Rather than go home, he came to Alexandria to inform Athanasius that a bishop needed to be sent to oversee the Aksumite Church. Athanasius wisely rewarded the messenger and sent Frumentius back as the first bishop of Aksum. Ethiopian Christianity would look to Egypt for leadership from that time onwards, extending still further the reach of Athanasius' see.[47]

By the early 350s Athanasius' situation seemed secure. More than any previous bishop of Alexandria, he had succeeded in unifying the Egyptian Church behind his banner and had rallied the desert ascetics to his cause. Internal opposition remained, both on theological grounds and among the surviving Melitian communities, but their voices were muted. This achievement is a tribute to Athanasius' ecclesiastical and pastoral leadership. The troubles that were soon to befall him originated not within Egypt but in the broader political and doctrinal developments taking place elsewhere in the Roman Empire.

When Athanasius had returned to Alexandria in 346, rule of the Empire was still divided between the brothers Constans in the west and Constantius in the east. The murder of Constans in 350 after the coup of Magnentius deprived Athanasius of his imperial champion. In the eastern Church those hostile to Athanasius had not ceased to campaign against him. There was a brief respite after his restoration, with two of his enemies Ursacius and Valens even submitting a 'Recantation' of the charges Athanasius had faced early in 347 (quoted in *Apologia contra Arianos* 58). This 'Recantation' was withdrawn in *c*.350/1, after Athanasius had been condemned once more by a council of eastern bishops at Antioch in 349. The bishops appealed to Constantius for support. Faced with a usurper in the west while struggling to contain the Persian Empire to the east, the emperor fully shared the bishops' desire for unity. As he expanded his power westward in 350–3, Constantius came to the increasing conviction that the main threat to that

---

[47] Our main source for this episode is Rufinus, X.9–10, copied by Socrates, I.19, and in turn Sozomen, II.24. Rufinus misdates the conversion of Aksum to the time of Constantine in order to avoid placing this event in the reign of the 'heretical' Constantius. See Munro-Hay (1997).

unity, at least within the Church, lay with the divisive figure of Athanasius in Alexandria.

In 351, as Constantius advanced through the Balkans against Magnentius, an episcopal council met in his presence in the city of Sirmium in Pannonia. The council condemned bishop Photinus of Sirmium, a follower of Marcellus of Ancyra, and may likewise have condemned Athanasius. At the same time, the council issued a creed that included anathemas against any who misused the *ousia* language accepted at Nicaea. Discussion of the theological content of the ongoing debates will be left until the next chapter, but Sirmium in 351 marks the beginning of a concerted campaign to impose doctrinal and ecclesiastical harmony on the Church. After the defeat of Magnentius in 353 had given Constantius sole rule over the Empire, this campaign gathered momentum, with Athanasius now clearly the primary target. A new council of bishops was summoned to Arles that year and ordered to denounce Athanasius. A further council in Milan in 355 faced the same demand.[48]

Athanasius did not lack for supporters who resisted on his behalf. The alliances formed during his years in the west held strong. Paulinus of Trier, to whose city Athanasius had come as an exile back in 335, opposed the decisions made at Arles. So too did Liberius of Rome, who had succeeded Julius in 352 and who maintained his predecessor's defence of Athanasius' innocence. At Milan the Italian bishop Eusebius of Vercellae insisted that the council subscribe to the Nicene Creed before reaching any further decisions. All three resisting bishops were sent into exile, together with Dionysius of Milan and Lucifer of Cagliari. It was in these tense years that defence of Athanasius and defence of Nicaea became inextricably intertwined in the west, and Athanasius would not forget the sufferings of the westerners on his behalf.

Amid the gathering clouds, Athanasius refused to sit passively and wait for his enemies to strike. An embassy headed by Serapion of Thmuis was sent to Constantius in Milan in 353 (*Festal Index* 25). The first version of Athanasius' *Apologia ad Constantium* was probably prepared around the same time to refute charges of disloyalty towards the emperor, and may have been delivered to Constantius by Serapion's embassy. These appeals do not seem to have had any effect, but Athanasius' other great literary pro-

---

[48] For more detailed narratives of the complex events of these years, see Barnes (1993), D. H. Williams (1995b), and Beckwith (2008).

duction of these years was to prove far more influential. For Athanasius as for his contemporaries, questions of ecclesiastical politics were inseparable from matters of doctrine. The *De Decretis Nicaenae Synodi*, the first work in which Athanasius explicitly made the Nicene Creed the cornerstone of orthodoxy, was composed in the early 350s and may indeed have encouraged the western emphasis on Nicaea at Milan. Longer term, the *De Decretis* was to prove a pivotal contribution to the evolving theological debates of the fourth century. In the short term, nothing could avert the storm that was about to break over Athanasius' head.

FLIGHT TO THE DESERT: THE THIRD EXILE (356–62)

It was night, and some of the people were keeping a vigil preparatory to a communion on the morrow, when the *dux* Syrianus suddenly came upon us with more than 5,000 soldiers, having arms and drawn swords, bows, spears, and clubs. With these he surrounded the church, stationing his soldiers near at hand in order that no one might be able to leave the church and pass by them. Now I considered that it would be unreasonable to desert the people during such a disturbance, and not rather to endanger myself on their behalf. Therefore I sat down upon my throne and desired the deacon to read a psalm, and the people to answer 'For His mercy endureth for ever' [Psalm 136:1], and then all to withdraw and depart home. But the *dux* having now made a forcible entry and the soldiers having surrounded the sanctuary for the purpose of apprehending us, the clergy and those of the laity who were still there cried out, and demanded that we too should withdraw. But I refused, declaring that I would not do so until they had retired one and all. Accordingly I stood up, and having bidden prayer, I then made my request of them, that all should depart before me, saying that it was better that my safety should be endangered than that any of them should receive hurt. So when the greater part had gone forth and the rest were following, the monks who were there with us and certain of the clergy came up and dragged us away. (Athanasius, *Apologia de Fuga* 24)

On the night of 8/9 February 356 Athanasius was presiding over a vigil when the *dux* Syrianus and his soldiers stormed the Church of Theonas. This assault, which marked the beginning of Athanasius' third period of exile, is one of the best-documented episodes of his entire career. Exceptionally, we possess three descriptions of the event written by those who were present, two composed by Athanasius (*Apologia ad Constantium* 25; *Apologia de Fuga* 24–5) and a third by his followers, who sent a letter of protest to Constantius immediately after the attack (quoted in *Historia Arianorum*

81). Although these were written by eyewitnesses favourable to each other, there are some interesting differences between these reports. According to Athanasius, the attack was coordinated by the 'Arians', and he did every-thing in his power to ensure the safety of his congregation before being forcibly removed by his companions. The letter of his followers makes no reference to 'Arian' involvement and presents the bishop in a slightly less heroic light. After he had been seized, he 'fell into a state of insensibility and appearing as if dead, he disappeared'. Whatever the truth, Athanasius was forced to abandon the Church of Theonas, the old Alexandrian episco-pal church, and flee. A few months later a further assault fell upon the new great church of the Caesareum (*Historia Arianorum* 54–7).[49] The ground had been prepared for the arrival of Athanasius' new replacement as bishop of Alexandria, George of Cappadocia.

The third exile of Athanasius has inspired many stories. Unlike in 339 when he fled to the west, in 356 Athanasius refused to abandon his home-land. That he was able to remain active in Egypt throughout the six years of his exile is an immense tribute to his pastoral labours of the preceding decade and to the loyalty he inspired. Athanasius' exact movements are as impossible for us to trace as they were for the imperial authorities, who never ceased to hunt him. Some of his time was spent within Alexandria, according to one tradition concealed by a devoted virgin.[50] He also trav-elled widely among the desert ascetics. Never was the close relationship Athanasius had established with the monks more important than in these dangerous years. Their shared experiences further consolidated this bond, as did the composition of the *Life of Antony*.

There is a romantic flavour to the accounts of narrow escapes and heroic resistance that surround Athanasius as he evaded capture. Yet these were years of hardship and suffering. George of Cappadocia presented a greater threat to Athanasius' followers than had his predecessor and fellow coun-tryman Gregory in 339–45. Gregory's authority had largely been confined to Alexandria, and there is limited evidence for his efforts to impose his power over the wider Egyptian Church. George was never secure even within Alexandria, where he arrived in February 357 but left in October 358 after almost being lynched and did not return until 361. But he benefited from stronger state support than had Gregory, and the ongoing presence of Athanasius intensified the efforts of George's supporters. The numerous

---

[49] On these conflicts, see further Haas (1997), 281–6.

[50] Palladius, *Lausiac History* 63. *Festal Index* 32 for 359/60 reports that during the search for Athanasius the virgin Eudaemonis was tortured.

works that Athanasius composed throughout his exile offer a grim narrative of escalating violence whose rhetorical exaggeration cannot conceal the very real anguish of persecution.[51]

The years 356–62 saw the greatest concentration of Athanasius' polemical, theological, and ascetic writings. Against the challenge of George, like that of Gregory two decades before, Athanasius had to maintain his legitimacy as the bishop of Alexandria. He continued to compose and circulate *Festal Letters* when the opportunity arose, notably *Festal Letter* XXIX for Easter 357, the surviving fragments of which celebrate the Old Testament patriarchs who stood strong against affliction. But more remained at stake than his personal prestige. New ecclesiastical and doctrinal currents were sweeping through mid-fourth-century Christianity. The works of Athanasius' third exile lay down his interpretation of those currents and of the course the true Church had to follow to secure its future.

The essential themes of Athanasius' literary campaign are immediately plain from the earliest work of his third exile: the *Encyclical Letter to the Bishops of Egypt and Libya*. Writing such an encyclical in the aftermath of his expulsion in February 356 was itself a statement of intent that he would defend his claim to the Alexandrian episcopate. The bulk of the letter represents a theological refutation of 'Arianism', largely summarized from the *Orationes contra Arianos*. Here, as throughout his writings of 356–9, Athanasius insisted that his contemporary opponents were the direct successors of his earlier 'Eusebian' foes. They therefore shared the same 'Arian heresy' that he attributed to the 'Eusebians' and led the same conspiracy against orthodox bishops like himself. The importance of this argument is that Athanasius interpreted the conflicts of the later 350s as a continuation of those of the 330s and early 340s. Thus he constructed his hugely influential vision of a single monolithic 'Arian Controversy'. He steadily expanded upon this vision first in the *Apologia ad Constantium* and the *Apologia de Fuga*, and then in increasing detail in the *Historia Arianorum* and the *De Synodis*.

One of Athanasius' aims was, of course, to maintain his innocence against the charges on which he found himself once more in exile. He continued to denounce his condemnation at Tyre as the work of a heretical conspiracy, and extended this to include the more recent accusations.

---

[51] Examples include the forty laypeople beaten with the thorny branches of palm trees (*Apologia de Fuga* 6–7), a presbyter who was kicked to death by the 'Arian' Secundus of Ptolemais (*Historia Arianorum* 65), and numerous bishops banished to the deserts and mines (*Historia Arianorum* 72). On religious violence in this period, see more generally Hahn (2004), Gaddis (2005), and Sizgorich (2009).

The new charges included treason (confronted in the *Apologia ad Constantium*) and cowardice (the *Apologia de Fuga*), but the primary motive of his accusers was still to spread their impiety (*Apologia ad Constantium* 26; *Apologia de Fuga* 2).[52] In these later works, Athanasius does not stand so alone. He is one of a number of orthodox bishops who are all victims of the same 'Arian' persecution, including Eustathius of Antioch (exiled in 327), Marcellus of Ancyra, and less well-known figures such as Euphration of Balanae and Cyrus of Beroea (*Apologia de Fuga* 3; *Historia Arianorum* 4–7). Whatever the varied charges upon which these men were individually condemned, in Athanasius' eyes their only real 'crime' was their hatred of the 'Arian heresy'.

The historical evidence for this so-called purge of the orthodox is rather weaker than Athanasius suggests.[53] None of the alleged victims can be proven to have been persecuted by 'Arians', nor were their fates determined by a single conspiracy. Nevertheless, Athanasius' polemic is an important indicator of how he viewed the wider Church from his concealment in Egypt in the late 350s. The contemporary attack on the western bishops who defended him and Nicaea is presented as a continuation of the conspiracies against him and his fellow exiles in the 330s and 340s (*Apologia de Fuga* 3–5; *Historia Arianorum* 33–45). Such an interpretation vindicated his innocence and so his legitimacy as the true bishop of Alexandria. But, more fundamentally, Athanasius' argument was a rallying call to Christians everywhere to resist the heresy that he believed was taking over the Church.

For no other reason than for the sake of their own impious heresy they have plotted against us and against all the orthodox bishops from the beginning. For behold, that which was intended long ago by the Eusebians has now come to pass, and they have caused the churches to be snatched away from us, they have banished the bishops and presbyters not in communion with themselves, as they wished, and the people who withdrew from them they have shut out of the churches, which they have handed over to the Arians who were condemned so long ago. (*Encyclical Letter to the Bishops of Egypt and Libya* 22)[54]

---

[52] For a discussion of the charges that Athanasius attempts to refute in these two works, and their respective contexts, see Barnes (1993: 113–26).

[53] Elliott (1992) and Gwynn (2007: 136–47).

[54] The quoted passage comes from the material inserted into this *Encyclical Letter* (originally written in 356) in 361.

Not all the accusations that threatened Athanasius' episcopal standing could be resolved through the denunciation of his 'Arian' foes. The charge of cowardice, to which he responded in the *Apologia de Fuga*, was a serious matter in a Christian culture that placed great weight on the heroism of martyrdom.[55] This was a particular concern within Egypt, where the Melitians who threatened Athanasius' authority styled themselves the 'Church of the Martyrs'. Athanasius had a very real need to justify his flight into hiding after the attack on the Church of Theonas in February 356. In the *Apologia de Fuga*, he maintained that he had thought of his congregation before himself and that the teaching of Scripture vindicated his decision. Moreover, his miraculous escape from the church was itself proof of divine favour: 'When Providence had thus delivered us in such an extraordinary manner, who can justly lay any blame [upon us], that we did not give ourselves up to those who pursued us, nor turned back and presented ourselves [to them]? This would have been plainly to show ingratitude to the Lord' (25).

There were precedents from Egyptian Christian tradition to which Athanasius could appeal for support. Dionysius of Alexandria, the great third-century bishop, had survived the persecutions of both Decius and Valerian. The hermit Antony, according to Athanasius' *Life*, had come forward at the time of the Great Persecution but had been preserved by God for the benefit of others (*Life of Antony* 46). Still, Athanasius' flight remained a source of some embarrassment for his supporters. In the later Coptic tradition, the *History of the Patriarchs* imagined that he had in fact surrendered himself to Constantius, only to be rescued from death by divine grace.[56]

Constantius personified Athanasius' other episcopal dilemma, which concerned not only his personal standing but his vision of the place of the Church in an increasingly Christian Empire. What loyalty did a bishop owe to an emperor whom he believed was acting in support of heresy?[57] The relationship of Christianity to the Roman State had been transformed by the conversion of Constantine, which had been welcomed by a Church reeling from the Great Persecution. Like the vast majority of his contemporaries, Athanasius expressed nothing but respect for the first Christian

[55] On the context and theological justification of Athanasius' defence of his flight, see Pettersen (1984) and Leemans (2003).

[56] This episode and the presentation of Athanasius in the *History of the Patriarchs* are discussed further towards the end of Ch. 6.

[57] Among the many modern studies of Athanasius' view of the relationship between Church and State, note the works of Nordberg (1964), Barnard (1974), and Barnes (1993: esp. 165–75). On the reign of Constantius, see also Klein (1977).

emperor. Even his first exile in 335 was attributed solely to the machinations of the 'Eusebians', who misled the pious ruler. The same respect is
extended to Constantius throughout Athanasius' writings down to his third
exile and the *Apologia ad Constantium*. Both in the original text written in
c.353–6 and in the passages added in mid-357 Constantius is addressed as
'the most pious and religious Augustus'. The change in tone in the *Historia
Arianorum*, written later in 357, is startling. Constantius is not merely under
the influence of the 'Arians'. He is the leader of the heretics, the forerunner
of the Antichrist.

Whether this remarkable shift in language represents an equally dramatic
change in Athanasius' feelings regarding the emperor is impossible to determine. He must have been at least wary of the emperor who had supported
the imposition of first Gregory and then George in his place. In the *Historia
Arianorum* Athanasius reinterpreted the events of the previous two decades
to hold Constantius responsible for every action of the 'Arians' against the
orthodox. 'Those who hold the doctrines of Arius have indeed no king but
Caesar; for through him the fighters against Christ accomplish everything
they wish' (33). In response to the threat of a heretical emperor, Athanasius proclaimed the Church's freedom from secular interference. This doctrine of the separation of Church and State is summed up in Athanasius'
quotation of a letter written to Constantius by the Spanish bishop Ossius
of Cordova. The aged Ossius, who had once been Constantine's episcopal
aide at Nicaea, warned Constantius to reconsider his actions:

Cease these proceedings, I beseech you, and remember that you are a mortal man.
Be afraid of the day of judgement and keep yourself pure thereunto. Do not intrude
yourself into ecclesiastical affairs, and do not give commands to us concerning
them, but learn them from us. God has put into your hands the kingdom; to us He
has entrusted the affairs of His Church; and as he who would steal the Empire from
you would resist the ordinance of God, so likewise fear on your part lest by taking
upon yourself the government of the Church you become guilty of a great offence.
It is written, 'Render unto Caesar the things that are Caesar's, and unto God the
things that are God's' [Matthew 22:21]. Neither therefore is it permitted to us to
exercise an earthly rule, nor have you, Sire, any authority to burn incense. (Quoted
in *Historia Arianorum* 44)

Yet Athanasius did not actually oppose the involvement of the emperor
in Church affairs. Even in the *Historia Arianorum* he refused to criticize
Constantine, whose support for orthodoxy is contrasted to Constantius'
'Arianism'. Throughout his career he repeatedly appealed to and welcomed imperial assistance on his own behalf. In addition to his flight to

Constantine after the Council of Tyre, Athanasius' restoration in 337 was supported by Constantine II, and after the deaths of Constantius and Julian he would write to Jovian upon that emperor's accession in 363. Athanasius' hostility to Constantius is directed not against the principle of imperial involvement in the Church, but against imperial support for the 'wrong' Christians. It was a dilemma that every subsequent Christian generation would face, reflecting the change wrought for better and for worse by state support for the Church from Constantine onwards.

The *Historia Arianorum* marked the culmination of the apologetic writings of Athanasius' third exile. At the same time, he defined his construction of the ongoing theological debates in the *De Synodis Arimini et Seleuciae* begun in 359. Athanasius' representation of contemporary events as the continuation of a single 'Arian Controversy' would become the standard interpretation of the fourth-century ecclesiastical conflicts. This triumph, however, lay in the future. In the late 350s, the old expression 'Athanasius *contra mundum* [against the world]' was not so far from the truth. His support remained strong in Egypt, and he still had allies elsewhere in the east as well as in the west. But the joint councils of Ariminum and Seleucia in 359, which provoked the *De Synodis*, were a further statement of Constantius' desire to establish unity in the Church, and the creed that those councils were pressured to endorse was regarded at least by Athanasius as 'Arian'. It seemed that Athanasius was fighting a losing struggle. Then in November 361 his fortunes changed once more. Constantius died, at the comparatively young age of 44. The new emperor was Julian 'the Apostate' (361–3), the last pagan to rule the Roman Empire.

THE FINAL YEARS (362–73)

The accession of Julian had one immediate consequence for Athanasius' benefit. George had never endeared himself to the population of Alexandria and had spent much of his episcopate away from the city. He returned only on 26 November 361, just before news arrived of Constantius' death. The bishop was seized and imprisoned, and a month later he was lynched (*Historia acephala* 8), whether by pagans or Athanasius' supporters is unknown. Julian had already declared an amnesty to all bishops exiled under his Christian predecessor, and Athanasius reclaimed his city in February 362. Just as he had on his return from his first exile, Athanasius immediately presided over a Council of Alexandria. Part of his aim was to reaffirm his authority over the Egyptian Church, which he appears to have achieved with very little difficulty. The other aim of the council was to seek a resolution to the situation in Antioch, where the Nicene Christian population was split between two factions. These twin purposes are reflected in the two documents preserved from the council: the *Epistula Catholica* and the *Tomus ad Antiochenos*.

What is now known as the *Epistula Catholica* contains part of the council's encyclical letter and concerns the acceptance into communion of bishops who had subscribed to the councils of 359–60. This will have applied to any Egyptian clergy appointed by George, as well as many bishops across east and west. In a conciliatory gesture, the conditions set were not overly restrictive, but required subscription to Nicaea and recognition of the full divinity of the Holy Spirit. The *Tomus ad Antiochenos* had a more specific audience in mind. It was addressed to the divided Nicene Christians of Antioch, urging unity. This document is of considerable importance for Athanasius' theological development, to which we will return in the next chapter. It is also a statement of his ecclesiastical vision for the Nicene Church.[58]

In certain respects the Antiochene Church was a microcosm of the fourth-century Church as a whole.[59] In 362 the Christian congregations in the city were divided between no fewer than three factions. Euzoius, who followed the doctrinal programme that had been promoted by Constantius, was ignored by the *Tomus* as an 'Arian'. But two groups within Antiochene Christianity each claimed to represent Nicene orthodoxy. Paulinus led those who had remained loyal to Eustathius, the bishop exiled in 327. His rival Meletius was more suspect in Athanasius' eyes as he had been ordained by the 'Arian' Eudoxius of Constantinople, although he too had come to endorse the authority of Nicaea and his congregation was larger than that of Paulinus. The *Tomus* has a bias in favour of Paulinus, who is identified by name, whereas Meletius' following is referred to as 'those who assemble in the Old [Church]'. But the chief concern is to unite both blocs behind the condemnation of 'Arianism' and support for the Nicene Creed.

Since we rejoice with all those who desire reunion, but especially with those that assemble in the Old [Church], and as we glorify the Lord exceedingly, as for all things so especially for the good purpose of these men, we exhort you that concord

---

[58] A far more cynical view of the *Tomus* and its purpose is offered by Elliott (2007).

[59] For a short overview on the Antiochene schism, see Spoerl (1993), and, on the period of the *Tomus*, see Karmann (2009). On the late-antique city of Antioch and its Christian history more broadly, see Liebeschuetz (1972) and Wallace-Hadrill (1982).

be established with them on these terms, and, as we said above, without further conditions, without namely any further demand upon yourselves on the part of those who assemble in the Old [Church], or Paulinus and his fellows propounding anything else, or aught beyond the Nicene definition. (*Tomus ad Antiochenos* 4)

The mission to reunite the Antiochene Nicenes was doomed to fail. Paulinus, who had previously been only a presbyter, was ordained bishop over his congregation before the *Tomus* arrived. He remained apart from Meletius, who was recognized as legitimate bishop of Antioch by much of the eastern Church. Yet, even in failure, the *Tomus* is at least indicative of Athanasius' vision and the status he had gained through his long struggle for orthodoxy. The ease with which he reasserted his authority in Egypt and his immediate involvement in wider affairs are a testament to his achievement in the years of desert exile. Through his example and writings, Athanasius had retained his following in Egypt and the west, and, as the Nicene Creed gained increasing support in the east, so too did Athanasius' reputation rise. His prominence was reflected when Julian, who preferred to avoid direct persecution of Christians, made him an exception and in October 362 ordered that he go into exile. As he fled, Athanasius is said to have prophetically told his companions, 'let us retire for a little while, friends; it is but a small cloud which will soon pass away' (first quoted in Rufinus, X.35).

Athanasius' prophecy was swiftly fulfilled. The death of Julian in Persia in June 363 permitted Athanasius to return from his short fourth exile. The new emperor was the Christian soldier Jovian (363–4).[60] Athanasius came to meet the emperor on the latter's arrival in Antioch, as too did the 'Arian' Lucius, who had been appointed as successor to George. Jovian is reported to have dismissed the protests of Lucius and requested from Athanasius a statement of the orthodox faith. In response, Athanasius wrote a letter laying down the Nicene Creed and urging the emperor to reject the followers of Arius. The *Letter to Jovian* (*Letter* LVI) is a further reminder that Athanasius did not oppose imperial intervention in the Church, as long as that intervention was in the service of the correct faith. His hopes were quickly dashed. Jovian did apparently endorse Nicaea. But this time, Athanasius' prediction that as a religious emperor 'you will truly have your heart also in the hand of God and you will peacefully enjoy a long reign' (*Letter* LVI.1) proved wide of the mark. Jovian died after a reign of just eight

---

[60] On Jovian and Athanasius, see Barnard (1989) and Stockhausen (2006).

months. His successor in the east was Valens (364–78), who returned to the
theological programme of Constantius. His initial policy towards Athanasius was one of persecution, and in late 365 the bishop withdrew into hiding to avoid arrest (*Historia acephala* 16). This fifth and last period in exile
was very brief. In February 366 Valens allowed him to return unmolested,
and so he remained until his death.

As he entered the closing years of his life Athanasius had become an
'elder statesman', venerated in Egypt and respected throughout the Nicene
Church.[61] Even now challenges remained. Within Egypt, the Melitian
Schism still endured. After their prominent role in Athanasius' first exile,
the Melitians disappear from his writings until the later 350s. In the *Life of
Antony* the hermit is reported to have avoided all contact with the schismatics (68, 89). In the *Historia Arianorum* (78–9) and the material added to
the *Encyclical Letter to the Bishops of Egypt and Libya* in 361 (22) the Melitians
are alleged to have supported George of Alexandria. This is then followed
by a series of anti-Melitian passages in Athanasius' *Festal Letters* of the late
360s, which may indicate a Melitian resurgence in Upper Egypt around this
time.[62] One of those passages occurs in *Festal Letter* XXXIX for Easter 367,
the famous letter that defined the canon of Scripture. Athanasius condemns
the Melitians for their use of apocryphal books, stamping his authority
once again over the beliefs and practices of the Egyptian Church.

Outside Egypt, the ecclesiastical and theological controversies continued
unabated. In the west, the name of Athanasius carried a powerful weight.
His final major polemical work was written in 367 to the bishops of Roman
Africa: the *Epistula ad Afros*.[63] There is little new in this work's theological
argument, which is lifted from the earlier *De Decretis* and *De Synodis*. What
is more striking is that, by writing the *Epistula ad Afros*, Athanasius has
claimed the responsibility for urging the African bishops to greater efforts
in support of orthodoxy. He upholds the supremacy of Nicaea against
those who defend the Council of Ariminum, and expresses surprise that
one such man, Auxentius of Milan, has been allowed to remain in his episcopate (10). Auxentius had been ordained by Athanasius' old rival Gregory
of Alexandria, which may have increased his concern. A similar condemnation of Auxentius appears in one of Athanasius' very last works, the *Letter*

---

[61] 'Elder statesman' is the title for the relevant chapter in Barnes (1993:152–64).

[62] *Festal Letters* XXXVII (364), XXXIX (367), XLI (369). See further Camplani (1989: 262–82).

[63] Athanasius states that he wrote on behalf of all the bishops of Egypt and Libya, 'for
we all are of one mind in this, and we always sign for one another if any chance not to be
present' (*Epistula ad Afros* 10).

to Epictetus of Corinth in *c*.372, which he wrote in response to a request for advice on the correct doctrine of Christ.

In the eastern Nicene churches Athanasius was no less admired, although increasingly the baton for the defence of orthodoxy had passed from him to the Cappadocian Fathers led by Basil of Caesarea.[64] A number of letters from Basil to Athanasius survive from these years. Their tone was unvaryingly respectful, for, 'the worse the diseases of the churches grow, the more do we all turn to your Excellency, in the belief that your championship is the one consolation left to us in our troubles' (Basil, *Letter* 80). Yet there is also a note of frustration. Like the majority of the eastern Nicene bishops, Basil recognized Meletius as the true bishop of Antioch. Athanasius and the western churches, however, still recognized Paulinus, and, despite Basil's pleas (*Letters* 66, 67, 69), Athanasius would never agree to accept communion with Meletius.[65] Basil similarly urged Athanasius to convince the west to condemn Marcellus of Ancyra (*Letter* 69.2), who had been defended back at Western Serdica but whose heresy was a major focus of opposition in the east. Here too Basil was unsuccessful. In this correspondence the younger man is looking to the future of the Church, while Athanasius' loyalty to former friends is rooted in the past.[66] Nevertheless, Basil has no doubt of the debt that his generation owed to Athanasius, 'who from his boyhood fought a good fight on behalf of true religion' (*Letter* 82).

DEATH AND AFTERMATH

'On the seventh of Pachon [2 May 373], he departed this life in a wonderful manner' (*Festal Index* 45). The last few years of Athanasius' episcopate were, at least by the standards of his previous career, relatively uneventful. His position was not under serious threat, his authority respected throughout the Nicene Church. When he died in May 373, the episcopate passed as he desired to the presbyter Peter, who took office as Peter II (373–80). Yet the challenges that Athanasius had faced for so long did not dissipate upon his

[64] On the career and writings of Basil, see Rousseau (1994: esp. 294–9 on his exchanges with Athanasius). There is a new assessment of his relationship with Athanasius in Heil (2006).
[65] After Athanasius' death, Basil would claim that Athanasius had desired communion with Meletius but was prevented by 'the malice of counsellors' (*Letter* 258, to Epiphanius, *c*.377).
[66] 'I myself once asked the blessed Pope Athanasius what his attitude towards Marcellus was. He neither defended him nor showed dislike for him, but only suggested with a smile that he had come close to depravity, but that he considered that he had cleared himself' (Epiphanius, *Panarion* 72.4.4). See Lienhard (1993, 2006) and Spoerl (2006).

death. Immediately upon his election, Peter was arrested on Valens' orders and fled into exile to Rome, while the 'Arian' Lucius occupied his see. Peter remained in exile until 378, when he returned shortly before the Goths killed Valens at the Battle of Adrianople, and on his own death was succeeded by his brother Timothy (bishop 380–5).

At first glance it might be tempting to view the exile of Peter as a sign that nothing had really changed. The bishop of Alexandria was still vulnerable to imperial persecution, and Peter shared the fate that had so often afflicted his mentor Athanasius. In truth, of course, the office that Peter inherited in 373 was very different from that to which Athanasius had been elected amid controversy back in 328. Athanasius' long episcopate had transformed the status of the Alexandrian see within both Egypt and the wider Church. He had united the Egyptian clergy behind him, a unity reinforced by his alliance with the powerful ascetic movement, which included a number of prominent monk-bishops. Through his long struggle for orthodoxy against 'Arianism', Athanasius had raised Alexandrian doctrinal authority to an unprecedented height. His periods of western exile and the links he had maintained with colleagues in west and east had placed Alexandria at the heart of a network that spanned the Mediterranean world.

When we examine Peter's career more closely, it provides a testimony to the achievements that his predecessor had wrought. Even Peter's exile bears witness to the pressures that Athanasius had kept in check during his final decade, and Peter benefited greatly from the prestige that he inherited. His reception in the west owed much to Athanasius' close ties with Rome, and, when Peter returned to Alexandria, he carried with him a statement of support from the Roman bishop Damasus. As the head of the Alexandrian Church, Peter was also regarded as a natural authority on matters of doctrine. A year before the Council of Constantinople in 381, Valens' eastern successor Theodosius I passed a law in which he defined as orthodox all those who shared 'the religion that is followed by the Pontiff Damasus and by Peter, Bishop of Alexandria' (*Theodosian Code* XVI.1.2, February 380).

Later generations would hold up Athanasius as a model for future bishops to emulate. His triumph owed much to his endurance in adversity and to his dedication to his see. But to understand Athanasius' life and legacy we have to look beyond the narrative of ecclesiastical politics. Athanasius' episcopal career is inseparable from his commitment to theology and asceticism and to the pastoral duties of a spiritual father. The Egyptian Coptic Church would have good reason to look back on Athanasius as their second founder, and it was on his achievements that his two greatest Alexandrian successors, Theophilus (385–412) and Cyril (412–44), would build.

3

Theologian

No history of Christian doctrine may omit the name of Athanasius of Alexandria. In theology, as in all other aspects of Christianity, the fourth century was a time of definition and transformation. Athanasius was one of the central figures of this formative age. Despite the controversy that surrounded so much of his episcopate, his doctrinal influence grew stronger as the century progressed and laid the foundations for later generations of theologians. He was remembered for his understanding of the Trinity and the relationship between God and His creation, rooted in a profound belief in human salvation through the Incarnation of God's Son and Word. His condemnation of his opponents, although much removed from their actual teachings, established 'Arianism' as the archetypal heresy that denied the divinity of Christ. In his later years Athanasius embraced the original Nicene Creed as the strongest bastion for orthodoxy against this 'Arian heresy', and extended his defence of the full godhood of the Son to the Holy Spirit. He also placed an increasing emphasis on the union of humanity and divinity in the Incarnate Word, and so moved towards the Christological questions debated in the following century.[1]

The best known of Athanasius' theological writings are the great treatises. The earliest, the *Contra Gentes–De Incarnatione* (*c*.328–35), already reveals the doctrinal principles that Athanasius would uphold throughout his life. He expressed these principles in a more polemical form in the three *Orationes contra Arianos* (*c*.339–46), which constructed his interpretation of the fourth-century debates as an 'Arian Controversy' polarized between the orthodoxy that he represented and the heresy of his foes. The same polemical construction is visible in the *De Decretis Nicaenae Synodi* (*c*.350–5), Athanasius' first explicit endorsement of the Nicene Creed of 325, and the *De Synodis Arimini et Seleuciae* (359–61). In this

---

[1] Modern scholarship on Athanasius' theology is vast. For older works see the bibliography of Butterweck (1995). Among recent studies note particularly Widdicombe (1994: 145–249), Pettersen (1995), Anatolios (1998), Behr (2004: 168–259), Morales (2006), and Weinandy (2007).

last work Athanasius acknowledged that not everyone whose teachings differed from his own was by necessity an 'Arian'. The desire for compromise is similarly attested in the *Tomus ad Antiochenos* despatched from Alexandria in 362 as Athanasius sought to heal some of the rifts that had opened in the previous decades. To these treatises we must add a number of shorter but no less important works. They include Athanasius' *Letters to Serapion on the Holy Spirit* (*c.*357–8) and other personal letters like those to Adelphius (*c.*370) and Epictetus (*c.*372), the latter of which was widely read in the fifth century for its meditation on the natures of Christ.

In this chapter we will trace the background against which Athanasius' theology emerged and the evolution of his beliefs across the long course of his life. It is all too easy through modern eyes to regard matters of doctrine as the concern of bishops and intellectuals separated from the travails of everyday life. For Athanasius and his contemporaries, this was far from the truth. The issues at stake lay at the very heart of the Christian faith: the relationship between God and humanity and the promise of salvation through the Incarnation. Athanasius' involvement in the controversies was thus inseparable from his obligations as a bishop and a pastoral and ascetic leader. It is perhaps the greatest strength of Athanasius as a theologian that he could express concepts of such importance in language that everyone could understand and never lost sight of why the questions mattered for the wider Christian world.

ARIUS, ALEXANDER, AND NICAEA: THE ORIGINS OF THE FOURTH-CENTURY THEOLOGICAL CONTROVERSIES

The evolution of Christian theology is a long and complex story.[2] In the decades following the death of Christ in *c.*33 AD, the religion that we know as Christianity took shape only gradually. The first communities of believers did not have a fixed organizational structure or an agreed canon of Christian Scripture. Each individual community preserved its own interpretation of Christ's message, and creeds were not yet written that

---

[2] Accessible introductions can be found in Kelly (1972, 1977), McGrath (1994), Behr (2001), and Pelikan (2003), and the edited collections of Di Berardino and Studer (1996) and Evans (2004).

sought to capture the faith of the wider Church. A number of the definitive elements of our modern understanding of the Christian religion took their full form in the fourth century. This process of definition had begun before the conversion of Constantine but accelerated rapidly with the appearance of a Christian emperor. The contribution that Athanasius would make to the definition of Christianity extended beyond theology and the role of episcopal authority to the rise of the ascetic movement and the scriptural canon.

Amid the diversity of the early Christian movement, however, there was also a remarkable sense of unity. The early Christians themselves held strongly that all their communities everywhere belonged to a single Church. They also held in common the fundamental theological values that underlay the Christian faith. They were monotheists who worshipped one God, but a God who was expressed through a Trinity of Father, Son, and Holy Spirit. The second member of that Trinity, the Son, had become Incarnate in the man Jesus Christ. Through His birth to Mary, His life and teachings, and His death on the cross, the Incarnate Son made possible the salvation of humanity in the world to come.

Far more controversial was how these doctrines should be understood and their implications. How should the Christian faith comprehend the Trinity and the relationship between God and humanity? Against the polytheistic cults that dominated the Roman Empire in which Christianity developed, the new religion emphasized monotheism. In comparison to monotheistic Judaism, from which the first Christians had emerged, the crucial differences lay in the Trinity and the Incarnation of the Son. But how could monotheism and the Trinity be reconciled? Did a hierarchy exist within the persons of the Trinity? In very simple terms, how could God be both One and Three? The Incarnation raised further concerns. Christian salvation was achieved through the divine Son of God, who lived and died as a human man and rose again from death. Did the divine Son experience the changes and sufferings of the body? Did the Incarnation compromise His divinity and render Him lesser than God the Father? How could Christians conceive of Jesus Christ who was simultaneously both divine and human and yet a single being? Such questions in turn led to debates over the nature of God and how the Incarnation could bridge the gulf that separated the divine from the rest of creation.

The early Christians recognized that a true understanding of God was beyond the scope of human comprehension. Human thought and language cannot embrace the divine, and belief ultimately rests upon faith not reason.[3] Yet the issues at stake were too crucial to the Christian religion to be left unexamined. A number of alternative interpretations were debated and condemned in the second and third centuries AD. There were those who placed such emphasis upon the monotheistic unity of the Godhead that they appeared to reduce the Trinity to three faces or modes and reject the distinct identities of Father, Son, and Spirit. This became known as 'Modalism' or 'Sabellianism', and not only neglected the Trinity but undermined the individual presence of the Son in the Incarnation. At the opposite extreme lay those who so separated the members of the Trinity that they taught three independent Gods ('Tritheism'). Still others sought to avoid the implications of involving the divine in human suffering by arguing that, in Christ, the Son took on a phantasmal or impassible body and so only seemed to share such experiences. This was 'Docetism' (from the Greek *dokeō*, 'to seem') and was believed to deny the truth of the Incarnation on which salvation rested. Few Christians followed these respective teachings in the fourth century, but they cast a shadow that influenced Athanasius and many of his contemporaries. Unfortunately, it was far easier to renounce those in error than to find agreement on the positive expression of Christian orthodoxy.

We gain some insight into the difficult questions under debate from the extensive writings of the Alexandrian theologian Origen (c.185–253).[4] One of the most controversial of early Christian thinkers, Origen was a wide-ranging teacher whose legacy can be traced in the arguments of men on all sides of the fourth-century controversies. He emphasized the superiority of the Father over the Son, and it has been argued that he followed a 'subordinationist' theology of three unequal members within the Trinity. No less important to Origen, however, was the unique status of the Son as the Word, Wisdom, and Power of God. The very name Father requires the existence of the Son, and God cannot be without His Word and Wisdom. Therefore Origen proposed the eternal generation of the Son, who was always with the Father. This raised once more the problem of how to speak of Father and Son as united yet distinct. Origen on at least one occasion spoke of Father, Son, and Spirit as three *hypostases* (using

---

[3] 'The things that have been handed down by faith ought not to be measured by human wisdom, but by the hearing of faith' (Athanasius, *Letter to Serapion on the Holy Spirit* I.17).

[4] On Origen and the much-debated question of his impact upon the fourth-century doctrinal debates, see Patterson (1982), Hanson (1987), Ayres (2004b: 20–30), and the articles collected in Bienert and Kühneweg (1999). For the influence of Origen's teachings on Athanasius, see Lyman (1993) and Widdicombe (1994).

the word *hypostasis* to mean individual existence).[5] But he denied that the Son derived from the Father's *ousia* (essence), a term that he regarded as imposing materialist ideas upon the immaterial God. He preferred to speak of the Son as a product of the Father's will.

All the key points raised by Origen's teachings—the status of Father, Son, and Spirit within the Trinity; the eternity of the Son and the signifi-cance of His titles Word, Wisdom, and Power; the generation of the Son; and the meaning of the terms *hypostasis* and *ousia*—would come to a head in the fourth-century theological controversies. For our understanding of the background to the controversies, what needs to be emphasized is that, when Athanasius was born in *c*.295, there was no agreed orthodox interpretation on any of the questions under dispute. Nor was there a uni-versally agreed mechanism by which orthodoxy could be determined and imposed. The development of Christian theology in the fourth century has aptly been described as a 'search for orthodoxy, a search conducted by the method of trial and error'.[6]

In later Christian tradition, the fourth-century debates were remem-bered as the 'Arian Controversy'.[7] The heresy of the Alexandrian presbyter Arius, although condemned at the first ecumenical Council of Nicaea in 325 for denying the divinity of the Son of God, rallied supporters and threatened to dominate the Church. Almost single-handedly, Athanasius, the champion of orthodoxy, defeated the 'Arian' threat and secured the triumph of the Nicene Creed. Modern scholars are all too aware of the dangers inherent in this oversimplified narrative. The traditional interpret-ation of the 'Arian Controversy' owes much to Athanasius' own polemical construction of 'Arianism', to which we will return later in this chapter. 'Orthodoxy' and 'heresy' were neither as self-evident nor as polarized as the polemic would suggest, and the fourth century witnessed a wide spectrum of different viewpoints that cannot be categorized as 'Nicene' or 'Arian'.[8] The resolution of the debates was long in doubt, and the eventual triumph of what became Nicene orthodoxy does indeed owe much to Athanasius' dedication and theological genius. But, before we turn to the theology of Athanasius in detail, it is true that any account of the controversies must

---

[5] Origen, *Commentary on John* 2.75. See further Logan (1987).

[6] Hanson (1988: p. xx).

[7] In addition to Hanson (1988), see now in general Ayres (2004b) and Behr (2004).

[8] For an introduction to the problems raised by the categories 'orthodoxy' and 'heresy' in early Christianity, see Bauer (1971), Le Boulluec (1985), R. D. Williams (2001b), and the articles collected in Elm, Rebillard, and Romano (2000).

begin with the conflict between Arius and his bishop Alexander of Alexandria and with the Council of Nicaea.

The difficulties involved in studying the theology of Arius (*c*.250–336) are many and well known.[9] His posthumous reputation as the greatest heresiarch of the fourth century colours all later judgements, and his surviving writings are limited. We possess three short texts: the *Creed and Letter* that Arius sent to Alexander of Alexandria in 320/1 (in Athanasius, *De Synodis* 16); Arius' short *Letter to Eusebius of Nicomedia* in *c*.321/2 (Theodoret, I.5); and a *Creed* that Arius and his friend Euzoius submitted to Constantine in an attempt to secure recognition of their orthodoxy, probably in 333 (Socrates, I.26). Athanasius also provides two extensive summaries of Arius' most notorious work, the *Thalia*. The first, in *Oratio contra Arianos* I.5–6, is an Athanasian paraphrase rather than a verbatim quotation and will be discussed further under Athanasius' construction of 'Arianism'. More authentic is the material preserved in *De Synodis* 15, which corresponds closely to Arius' other letters and creeds.[10] These works cannot give us a complete sense of Arius' teachings but do enable us to identify his characteristic arguments and why they aroused such great contention.

We acknowledge One God, alone unbegotten, alone eternal, alone without beginning, alone true... who begot an only-begotten Son before eternal times, through whom He has made both the ages and the universe; and begot Him, not in semblance, but in truth; and that He made Him subsist at His own will, unalterable and unchangeable; the perfect creature [*teleion ktisma*] of God, but not as one of the creatures; offspring [*gennēma*], but not as one of things begotten;[11] not as Valentinus pronounced that the offspring of the Father was an emanation; nor as Manichaeus taught that the offspring was a portion *homoousios* to the Father; or as Sabellius, dividing the Monad, speaks of a Son-Father. (Arius, *Letter to Alexander*, *De Synodis* 16)

Throughout his extant writings, Arius repeatedly emphasizes the unique divinity of God the Father. Contrary to some accusations, he did not deny the divinity of the Son, but Arius certainly subordinated the Son to the Father. The Son is God but not true God. He cannot be eternal because He is begotten and therefore has a beginning, and for the same reason He

---

[9] In addition to the standard work of R. D. Williams (1987, 2001a), see also Böhm (1991) and now Löhr (2005, 2006).

[10] For various assessments of these *Thalia* passages, see Stead (1978), Kannengiesser (1981, 1985a), and R. D. Williams (1985).

[11] Arius describes the Son as a *ktisma* (creature) and a *gennēma* (offspring) but never as a *poiēma* (a thing made). The importance of this distinction for our understanding of Athanasius' polemic will be discussed later in this chapter.

cannot share in the *ousia* of the unbegotten Father. The Son 'has nothing proper [*idios*] to God according to personal subsistence [*hypostasis*], for He is neither equal nor *homoousios* with Him... The Father is alien according to essence [*ousia*] to the Son, because He exists without beginning' (*Thalia, De Synodis* 15). Moreover, the Son cannot fully know the One God, who is transcendent and unknowable. 'It is clear that for one who has a beginning to encompass by thought or apprehension the one who is without beginning is impossible' (*Thalia, De Synodis* 15). The Son is Word, Wisdom, and Power, but He received these qualities from the Father, who possesses them inherently and eternally.

The generation of the Son occurred before time and the ages. But 'He was not before He was begotten' (*Letter to Alexander, De Synodis* 16), for He had a beginning and cannot possess the eternity of the Father. Nor does the Son share the *ousia* of the Father, and so Arius taught that the Son was created by the Father's will. He was a creature (*ktisma*), although not like any other created being. In one text Arius even referred to the Son as coming into existence 'out of nothing [*ex ouk ontōn*]' (*Letter to Eusebius of Nicomedia*, Theodoret, I.5).[12] However, for Arius the Son is a unique and perfect creature, who unlike other creatures is unalterable and unchangeable. Later claims that Arius taught that the Son changed and suffered derive from Athanasius' polemic and find no support in Arius' original writings.[13]

In the light of his heretical reputation, it is important to underline the sincerity of belief that inspired Arius' controversial teachings. Arius sought to maintain the status of the Father against those whom he believed over-exalted the Son and blurred their distinct identities within the Trinity. He initially came into conflict with his bishop Alexander over the latter's teaching of 'God always, the Son always'. For Arius, if the Son was eternal, then He must also be unbegotten, and this compromised the uniqueness of both the Father and His only-begotten Son. It was the Son who became Incarnate as man, and, while Arius does not attribute human suffering or weakness to the Son, he saw the Incarnation as further evidence that the Son was different by nature from the Father. The begotten Son similarly could not be one in essence (*homoousios*) with the unbegotten Father, and such a teaching led to the errors of Manichaeism or to the Sabellian Modalism that Arius particularly feared.

[12] For the significance of this doctrine, see May (1994).
[13] These later polemical claims have exerted a powerful influence on modern scholarship. This is particularly true of the arguments of Gregg and Groh (1981), who hold that Arius' Son advanced in virtue as a model for Christian salvation, and Hanson (1985), who believed that Arius emphasized the Son as a God who suffered in the Incarnation.

Arius thus shared the theological concerns of other third- and early fourth-century Christians over how to conceive of the Trinity and the Incarnation. His language is highly philosophical, but the points he raised were genuine and not easy to refute. Nevertheless, among some contemporaries Arius' doctrines aroused immediate hostility. Many eastern bishops feared Sabellianism no less than Arius did, but, in his desire to maintain the separation of Father and Son, Arius had gone too far. To teach that the Son came into existence out of nothing and could not even know His Father threatened to undermine the Son's divinity entirely. If the Son was so inferior to the Father, could He truly fulfil the Christian promise of human salvation? This was the reaction of the earliest opponents of Arius, led by Alexander of Alexandria.

The evidence for Alexander's doctrinal teachings is no more extensive than for those of Arius. Two letters survive, one addressed to his namesake Alexander of Byzantium/Thessalonica in *c.*322 (Theodoret, I.4) and the *Encyclical Letter* that he circulated across the eastern Church in late 324 or early 325 (Socrates, I.6). Both letters are primarily concerned to denounce Arius rather than to present Alexander's own definition of orthodoxy. The *Encyclical Letter* in particular provides the earliest systematic polemical description of the 'Arian heresy':

What they have invented and assert, contrary to the Scriptures, are as follows: God was not always a father, but there was when God was not a father; the Word of God was not always, but came to be out of nothing [*ex ouk ontōn*]; for the ever-existing God has made Him who did not previously exist, out of the non-existent. Therefore indeed there was once when He was not. For the Son is a creature [*ktisma*] and a thing made [*poiēma*]. He is neither like the Father according to essence [*kat' ousian*], nor true Word by nature of the Father, nor true Wisdom. He is one of the things made and one of the generated beings, being inaccurately called Word and Wisdom, since He came to be Himself through the proper Word of God and the Wisdom in God, in which indeed God made everything and also Him. Therefore indeed He is changeable and mutable by nature, as are all rational beings, [and] the Word is foreign and alien and separate from the essence of the Father. And the Father is unintelligible to the Son, for the Word neither perfectly and exactly knows the Father, nor is He able to see Him perfectly. (Alexander, *Encyclical Letter*, Socrates, I.6)

Alexander's construction of 'Arianism' directly foreshadows the polemic of Athanasius in both content and rhetorical style.[14] Like Athanasius, Alexander combines elements of Arius' original teachings with implications

---

[14] For the argument that this letter was in fact drafted by Athanasius, see Stead (1988).

that he has drawn from Arius' words, and so attributes to Arius conclusions that the latter would never have accepted. We will explore this rhetorical approach in more detail when we turn to 'Athanasian Arianism' below. But the polemic reveals clearly the dangers that Alexander saw in Arius' theology. If the Son has a beginning, and is foreign to the *ousia* of the Father whom He does not know perfectly, then how can He be the Father's eternal Word and Wisdom? If He is a creature, then how can He be the one through whom creation came into being? Alexander disregards Arius' distinction that the Son is a creature but not like other creatures. If the Son is a creature, then He has been reduced to the level of all creatures, created from nothing and changeable by nature, and is no longer our God and Saviour.

In contrast to the errors of Arius, Alexander offered his understanding of the traditional faith of the Church. The eternal and only-begotten Son of the Father is not one of the creatures but the Word through whom the Father brought forth creation. 'How is He unlike the Father's *ousia*, who is "His perfect image" [Colossians 1:15] and "the brightness of His glory" [Hebrews 1:3]?' (Alexander, *Encyclical Letter*, Socrates, I.6). The Son is always immutable and was not changed by the Incarnation, and His knowledge of the Father is perfect. Alexander's teachings again foreshadow those of his successor and pupil Athanasius, although Athanasius would surpass his master and develop these doctrines in far greater depth.

After Arius had been expelled from Egypt by Alexander in *c.*321, he gained support elsewhere in the east, notably from the church historian Eusebius of Caesarea in Palestine and from Eusebius of Nicomedia, the bishop of the eastern imperial capital. It was this wider escalation of the controversy that led Alexander to circulate his *Encyclical Letter*. When Constantine conquered the eastern regions of the Empire in 324, the divisions were of a magnitude that required imperial involvement. The Council of Nicaea in June–July 325 would come to be remembered as the first ecumenical ('universal') council of the Church.[15] The traditional number of 318 bishops in attendance is legendary (it is the number of Abraham's servants in Genesis 14:14), but there were some 220 bishops present from across the east and a few from further afield.[16] No *Acta* (minutes) from the council survive, and reconstruction of the debates that took place is largely impossible. The theological decisions of the council, however, are at first sight fairly straightforward. Arius was

---

[15] There is a convenient survey of what is known of the council in Luibheid (1982).
[16] On the tradition of the '318 fathers', see Aubineau (1966). There is a tentative reconstruction of the original signature lists of Nicaea in Honigmann (1939: 44–8).

condemned, a sentence confirmed by Constantine, who sent him into exile. And a creed was composed, which for the first time sought to represent the agreed orthodox faith of the wider Church.[17]

We believe in one God, Father Almighty, Maker of all things, seen and unseen; and in one Lord Jesus Christ the Son of God, begotten as only begotten of the Father, that is of the essence [*ousia*] of the Father, God of God, Light of Light, true God of true God, begotten not made, of one essence [*homoousios*] with the Father, through whom all things came into existence, both things in heaven and things on earth; who for us men and for our salvation came down and was incarnate and became man, suffered and rose again the third day, ascended into the heavens, and is coming to judge the living and the dead; and in the Holy Spirit. But those who say 'there was a time when He did not exist', and 'before being begotten He did not exist', and that 'He came into being from non-existence', or who allege that the Son of God is from another *hypostasis* or *ousia*, or is alterable or changeable, [or created[18]], these the catholic and apostolic Church condemns. (Nicene Creed of 325)

At one level, the original Nicene Creed was clear and unequivocal. The most extreme formulations associated with Arius were rejected, particularly the Son's creation from nothing and any suggestion that He came into existence in time or was subject to change. The Son is not only God but is true God and is begotten of the *ousia* of the Father, although it is not explicitly stated that He is eternal. The creed thus firmly safeguarded the essential Christian understanding of the divinity of the Son who became Incarnate for our salvation.

Yet Nicaea failed to remove the tensions troubling eastern Christianity. The creed itself raised almost as many questions as it resolved. Some of those questions only gradually emerged in the course of the fourth-century controversies. The status of the Holy Spirit within the Trinity, included almost as an afterthought at Nicaea, became a subject of debate from the 350s onwards. The terms *ousia* and *hypostasis*, used effectively as synonyms in the Nicene anathemas, would later be redefined and play a crucial role in expressing orthodox Trinitarian faith. We will return to Athanasius' involvement in these developments in the second half of this chapter. But, even for many of those present at Nicaea, elements of the creed were a cause for concern, above all the description of the Son as *homoousios* ('of one essence') with the Father. *Homoousios* was not a scriptural term, and its meaning was highly ambiguous. It could be interpreted as implying materialist ideas of God,

---

[17] On the development of creeds within the Church, see Kelly (1972) and Young (1991).

[18] This anathema, which appears only in Athanasian versions of the creed, will be discussed later in this chapter.

a concern already held by Origen, or as uniting Father and Son so closely together as to lead to the Sabellian Modalism that many easterners feared. Those doubts were expressed by Eusebius of Caesarea, who wrote home to his see in 325 to explain his acceptance of the creed (quoted in Socrates, I.8). Eusebius accepted *homoousios* and 'from the *ousia* of the Father' only in the broadest sense of teaching the unity of Father and Son, and spoke for much of the eastern Church in his distrust of the language of Nicaea.

The Council of Nicaea was one of the greatest events of Constantine's reign, and as long as he lived there was no open challenge to the Nicene Creed. After his death in 337, the theological debates reignited with increased force. Distrust at the implications of Nicaea and the word *homoousios* had increased in the 330s because of the teachings of Marcellus, bishop of Ancyra. Like Arius he was eventually condemned as a heretic and accused of doctrines he may not have held, but Marcellus certainly emphasized the unity of Father and Son to an extent that others regarded as Sabellian.[19] In the 340s and 350s a number of councils composed creeds condemning such views and expressing different interpretations of the Son's divinity and status relative to the Father. It was also in the early 350s that the Nicene Creed attracted renewed attention, when Athanasius first upheld Nicaea as the strongest defence against teachings he regarded as 'Arian'. The controversies continued past Athanasius' death in 373 and even beyond 381, when the second ecumenical Council of Constantinople revised the Nicene Creed into the form used in most church services down to the present day. The final stages of the fourth-century debates were dominated by the three Cappadocian Fathers—Basil of Caesarea, Gregory of Nazianzus, and Gregory of Nyssa—who in orthodox tradition completed the work that Athanasius had begun.

THE EARLY THEOLOGY OF ATHANASIUS: *CONTRA GENTES–DE INCARNATIONE* AND THE *ORATIONES CONTRA ARIANOS*

Athanasius was elected bishop of Alexandria three years after the Council of Nicaea. The issues raised in the conflict between Arius and Alexander were still being debated, and the controversy over his election made it

---

[19] On Marcellus' teachings and his role in the controversies, see Seibt (1994), Lienhard (1999), and Parvis (2006).

important for Athanasius to establish his doctrinal as well as ecclesiastical position. It is in this context that we should most probably set his earliest theological work: the double treatise *Contra Gentes–De Incarnatione*.[20] Like Athanasius' later writings, the double treatise had a practical purpose. In contrast to his fellow Alexandrian Origen a century before, Athanasius was not a theoretical or intellectual theologian. The questions that inspired his teachings were those that concerned his congregations and the wider Christian people. Already in this early text we find Athanasius engaging with the fundamental doctrines of Christianity: the revelation of God and salvation for man made possible through the Incarnation of the Son.

The stated purpose of the *Contra Gentes*, repeated in the opening chapter of the *De Incarnatione*, was to demonstrate that the Christian faith was not irrational. Pagans might mock the crucifixion and resurrection:

If they had really applied their minds to His divinity they would not have mocked at so great a thing, but would rather have recognized that He was the Saviour of the universe and that the cross was not the ruin but the salvation of creation. For if, now that the cross has been set up, all idolatry has been overthrown, and by this sign all demonic activity is put to flight, and only Christ is worshipped, and through Him the Father is known, and opponents are put to shame while He every day invisibly converts their souls—how then, one might reasonably ask them, is this still to be considered in human terms, and should one not rather confess that He who ascended the cross is the Word of God and the Saviour of the universe? (*Contra Gentes* 1).

The triumph of Christianity over paganism was a theme of immediate relevance for Athanasius' audience in the reign of Constantine. Athanasius presents an extended attack upon pagan idolatry and the falsity of the pagan gods (*Contra Gentes* 8–29). But this is not the primary purpose of his double treatise. The attack on paganism is incorporated within a broader theological argument that encapsulates Athanasius' understanding of God and creation and of the purpose of the Incarnation. Christ's sacrifice on the cross heralded the decline of paganism, which Athanasius and his readers were now witnessing in the increasingly Christian Constantinian Empire. For Athanasius, however, the full significance of the Incarnation lay in bridging the gulf that separated God and creation and enabling humanity to 'become divine'.

Fundamental to Athanasius' entire theology is his conception of a complete ontological division between God and the world He created

---

[20] Edition and English translation in Thomson (1971).

from nothing.[21] The Godhead, eternal and immutable, is utterly separate by *ousia* (essence) and *physis* (nature)[22] from the created order, brought into existence in time and mutable. Yet God is not distant from His creation. Those who are created cannot bridge the gulf between themselves and the divine. Revelation and salvation for humanity must come from God through His love, expressed above all through the Incarnation of His Son.

Immediately after the opening of the *Contra Gentes*, Athanasius declares that all creation owes its existence to the transcendent Christian God. But God did not allow His transcendence to divide Him completely from His creatures, for in His love He made humanity in His likeness.

For God, the creator of the universe and king of all, who is beyond all being and human thought, since He is good and bountiful, has made humanity in His own image through His own Word, our Saviour Jesus Christ; and He also made humanity perceptive and understanding of reality through its similarity to Him, giving it also a conception and knowledge of its own eternity, so that as long as it kept this likeness, it might never abandon its concept of God or leave the company of the saints, but retaining the grace of Him who bestowed this on it, and also the special power given it by the Father's Word, it might rejoice and converse with God, living an idyllic and truly blessed and immortal life. (2)

God is by nature good, and so too His creation was good. In His goodness, however, He created humanity with free will, and through that free will humanity turned away into error and evil (3–7). Athanasius' attack on idolatry in the *Contra Gentes* represents paganism as a product of that turn towards evil (8–29). The pagan gods are not true gods but are part of creation (the sun and moon), lifeless works of art (statues) or human beings falsely honoured as gods (Zeus, Apollo). 'Their worship and deification is the beginning not of piety, but of godlessness and all impiety, and proof of great deviation from the knowledge of the one and only true God, I mean the Father of Christ' (29). Even so, God did not abandon humanity, and through His love humanity could still seek to know God. The likeness of God remained visible within human souls (30–4), and He was revealed through creation itself (35–9).

God, who is good and loves humanity and who cares for the souls He has made, since He is by nature invisible and incomprehensible, being above all created being, and therefore the human race would fail to attain knowledge of Him in that they

---

[21] This doctrine is the foundation for the study of Anatolios (1998).

[22] For Athanasius' use of the terms *ousia*, *physis*, and also *hypostasis*, see Torrance (1995: 206–12). In Athanasius' writings all three terms are virtually synonyms, although there are nuances between them.

were made from nothing while He was uncreated—for this reason God so ordered creation through His Word that although He is invisible by nature, yet He might be known to humanity from His works. (35)

The closing passages of the *Contra Gentes* affirm that creation must not be attributed to any other power, but solely to the Christian God acting through His Word. It is the Word who binds all creation together, as it is written in the Scriptures (40–6). Yet men in their folly set aside the true God and honour false deities and created things (47). There the *Contra Gentes* ends and the *De Incarnatione* begins. In the opening words of the *De Incarnatione* Athanasius condemns again the pagan error of worshipping idols and their ignorance of God's providence and His Word. He then sets the Incarnation firmly within this context, for it was in order to rescue humanity from its errors that the Word Himself took on a created form. And 'although He is incorporeal by nature and Word, yet through the mercy and goodness of His Father He appeared to us in a human body for our salvation' (1).

In the *De Incarnatione*, as in the *Contra Gentes*, Athanasius first emphasizes that creation itself was good. Humanity turned away from God through free will and so fell into evil (3–5). Nor was humanity able to reverse its decline. But the loving God would not abandon those He had created, and so the Word became Incarnate:

For since the Word realized that human corruption would not be abolished in any other way except by everyone dying—but the Word was not able to die, being immortal and the Son of the Father—therefore He took to Himself a body which could die, in order that, since this participated in the Word who is above all, it might suffice for death on behalf of all, and because of the Word who was dwelling in it, it might remain incorruptible, and so corruption might cease from all humanity by the grace of the resurrection. (9)

The corruption from which humanity was liberated by the Word originated in the error of turning away from God. Through the Incarnation, therefore, the Word not only renewed humanity but restored its ability to know God. Those who had fallen into error worshipped idols and resorted to magic and astrology, and paid no heed to the lessons given through the Laws and the Prophets (11–12). But, as humanity had originally been made in the likeness of God, so 'the Word of God came in His own person, in order that, as He is the Image of His Father, He might be able to restore humanity who is in the image' (13). And through His works, culminating in Christ's death and resurrection, the Word provided revelation of God's love and providence.

In two ways our Saviour had compassion through the Incarnation: He both rid us of death and renewed us; and also, although He is invisible and indiscernible, yet by His works He revealed and made Himself known to be the Son of God and the Word of the Father, leader and king of the universe. (16)

Only through the Incarnation of the divine Son and Word, Athanasius maintains, could salvation and revelation be received by humanity. Only through His life and death as a created man could the Word enable humanity to cross the otherwise unbridgeable gulf between the mortal and divine. The remaining two-thirds of the *De Incarnatione* further reinforce this presentation of the Incarnation against possible opposition. Athanasius particularly seeks to explain the necessity and importance of Christ's death and resurrection (20–32), the most difficult Christian teachings for non-Christians to accept. This is followed by a refutation of those who refuse to acknowledge the Incarnation, both Jews (33–40) and pagans (41–55). At the end of his refutation of paganism, Athanasius concludes with a summary of his understanding of salvation. It contains perhaps the most famous lines Athanasius ever wrote:

Just as if someone wishes to see God, who is invisible by nature and in no way visible, he understands and knows Him from His works, so he who does not see Christ with his mind, let him learn of Him from the works of His body, and let him test whether they be human or of God. And if they be human, let him mock; but if they are recognized to be not human but of God, let him not laugh at what are not to be mocked, but rather wonder that through such simple means these divine things have been revealed to us, and that through death immortality has come to all, and through the Incarnation of the Word the universal providence and its leader and creator the Word of God Himself have been made known. For He became human that we might become divine; and He revealed Himself through a body that we might receive an idea of the invisible Father; and He endured insults from human beings that we might inherit incorruption. (54)

'He became human that we might become divine (*theopoiēthōmen*)'. These words encapsulate Athanasius' vision of salvation as a process of 'deification' or 'divinization'.[23] By this he did not mean that humans could become gods in the same manner as God Himself. Only God is divine by nature. But through participation with the divine Word, made possible by the Incarnation, humanity could be made perfect and free from sin and

---

[23] On the doctrine of deification and its development across the history of Christianity, see Nispel (1999), Russell (2004), and the articles collected in Finlan and Kharlamov (2006) and Christensen and Wittung (2007).

preserve the knowledge and unity with God that was lost when men and
women turned away into error. Athanasius was by no means the first theologian to understand salvation in these terms. It was the clarity of his vision
and the power of his language that made his presentation hugely influential on subsequent Christian generations.

There is a further element to Athanasius' vision of salvation which,
though controversial at the time when he wrote, was to prove equally influential for the development of orthodox Christianity. For Athanasius, it was
not sufficient merely to say that salvation was achieved through the Incarnation. The one who became Incarnate for our sakes had to be the eternal
and true Son and Word of the Father. None could bridge the ontological
divide of God and humanity except a mediator who was Himself divine by
nature. As we shall see shortly, this is a central theme throughout Athanasius' anti-'Arian' writings. The great danger that Athanasius saw in 'Arianism' was precisely the separation of the Son from the Father to an extent
that he believed made the Son's saving work impossible. The Son as the
true Word and Wisdom of the Father is a recurring theme in the *De Incarnatione*, and is already made explicit near the end of the *Contra Gentes*:

> His holy disciples teach that everything was created through Him and for Him, and
> that being good offspring of a good Father and true Son, He is the Power of the
> Father and His Wisdom and Word; not so by participation, nor do these properties
> come to Him from outside in the way of those who participate in Him and are
> given wisdom by Him, having their power and reason in Him; but He is Wisdom
> itself, Word itself, and Himself the Father's own Power, Light itself, Truth itself,
> Justice itself, Virtue itself, and indeed Stamp, Effulgence and Image. In short, He is
> the supremely perfect issue of the Father, and is alone Son, the express Image of
> the Father. (46)

According to the standards of later orthodoxy, there are two potential
weaknesses revealed by this summary of the theological arguments of the
Contra Gentes–De Incarnatione. The importance that Athanasius placed on
the full divinity of the Son left unresolved the question of how to speak
of Father and Son as one God and yet distinct identities within the Trinity.[24] This was a difficulty faced by all early fourth-century theologians who

---

[24] On Athanasius and the unity of God, see Robertson (2007: esp. 139–51 on the *Contra
Gentes–De Incarnatione*). Athanasius continued to struggle with how to express the distinction
between Father and Son in the later *Orationes contra Arianos*: 'they are two, because the Father
is Father and is not the Son, and the Son is Son and not the Father. But the nature is one, for
the offspring is not unlike the parent, for it is his image, and all that is the Father's is the Son's'
(*Oratio* III.4).

emphasized the unity of Father and Son, and could lead to suspicion of Sabellianism in some parts of the eastern Church. Athanasius is far more careful in his language than his contemporary Marcellus of Ancyra, who was eventually condemned for this error. The problem lay less in Athanasius' conception of the Trinity than in the limitations of the available terminology, an issue that was addressed by the Cappadocian Fathers.

The second difficulty concerns Athanasius' Christology, how he understood the humanity and divinity of the Incarnate Christ. This has proved more of an issue for modern scholars. It has been suggested that Athanasius reduced the human body of Christ to merely the tool of the Word, who 'fashioned for Himself in the virgin a body as a temple, and appropriated it for His own as an instrument in which to be known and dwell' (*De Incarnatione* 8).[25] Others have argued that Athanasius taught a 'spacesuit' Christology, in which the divine Word puts on His body like a suit and does not share in the body's human experiences.[26] Such criticisms are in part projecting back upon Athanasius the controversies of the fifth century, when the relationship of the two natures of Christ became the major focus for debate. The *Contra Gentes–De Incarnatione* is in any case not primarily concerned with analytical Christology, and naturally emphasizes the role of the divine Word. Nevertheless, Athanasius did not entirely separate the Word from the experiences of Christ's body, even though the divinity could not itself suffer.[27]

When the theologians who speak of Him say that He ate and drank and was born, understand that the body was born as a body and was nourished on suitable food. But God the Word, who was with the body yet orders the universe, also made known through His actions in the body that He Himself was not a man but God the Word. But these things are said of Him, because the body which ate and was born and suffered was no one else's but the Lord's; and since He became human, it was right for these things to be said of Him as a man, that He might be shown to have a true, not a phantasmal, body. (*De Incarnatione* 18)

Athanasius here is beginning to move towards the concept known as the communication of idioms. This approach to expressing the mystery of the Incarnation, more closely associated with his greatest successor Cyril of Alexandria (bishop 412–44), allows the attribution of the properties of

[25] This is a central theme of the interpretation of Athanasius in Grillmeier (1975). See the comments of Anatolios (1998: 70–3).
[26] The 'spacesuit' analogy comes from Hanson (1988: 448).
[27] On the question of divine suffering in early Christian debate, see Gavrilyuk (2004).

each of Christ's two natures to the other. Athanasius' insistence that 'the body which ate and was born and suffered was no one else's but the Lord's' associates the divine Word with the properties of His human body. He would further develop such arguments later in his life, notably in his *Letter to Epictetus* in *c*.372, which was much quoted in the fifth century. Although his teachings were again limited by his terminology, the humanity of the Incarnate Christ no less than His divinity was essential to Athanasius' deification model of salvation.

When the *Contra Gentes–De Incarnatione* was written (*c*.328–35), Athanasius was still a relatively young man. Across some forty years of controversy and teaching, he would never deviate from the fundamental principles laid down in that first double treatise. His conception of the Incarnation and the divine grace that was given to humanity through the Word underlay his promotion of the ascetic movement in Egypt and the pastoral wisdom that he preached to his congregations. Seen against this theological background, Athanasius' involvement in the ongoing fourth-century debates was inevitable. It is true, as we saw in the preceding chapter, that his attacks on 'Arianism' from the late 330s onwards served his ecclesiastical interests. The assertion that his condemnation at Tyre was the work of a 'heretical conspiracy' vindicated his innocence and his legitimacy as orthodox bishop of Alexandria. The sincerity of his convictions regarding the theological issues at stake, however, cannot possibly be questioned. The 'Arian heresy' that Athanasius believed his opponents propagated struck at the very heart of his own theology and threatened to undermine the faith in salvation that he taught.

In the following section we will look at Athanasius' polemical construction of 'Arianism' in detail, beginning with the three *Orationes contra Arianos* that he composed in *c*.339–46.[28] Before we do so, it is worthwhile to consider briefly what further light the *Orationes* may shed on the teachings that Athanasius presented in the *Contra Gentes–De Incarnatione*. Against the challenge of 'Arianism', Athanasius emphasized even more strongly the full divinity of the Son. As he wrote in the opening argument of the first *Oratio contra Arianos*:

For behold, we speak openly from the divine Scriptures concerning the pious faith, and we hold [it] as a lamp on a lampstand, saying that He is true by nature

---

[28] For a far more detailed analysis of the *Orationes contra Arianos* than can be attempted here, see Meijering (1996–8).

and legitimate Son of the Father, that He is proper to his essence, only-begotten Wisdom, and true and only Word of the Father. He is not a creature, nor a thing made, but proper offspring of the essence of the Father. Therefore He is true God, existing *homoousios* with the true Father; while other beings, to whom He said, 'I said you are gods' [Psalm 82:6], had this grace from the Father only by participation of the Word through the Spirit. For He is the expression of the Father's Person, and Light from Light, and Power, and very Image of the Father's *ousia*. For this again the Lord said, 'he who has seen Me, has seen the Father' [John 14:9]. Always He was and is, and never He was not. For since the Father is eternal, eternal also must be His Word and Wisdom. (I.9)

This passage is exceptional, for it contains the only description of the Son as *homoousios* to the Father found anywhere in Athanasius' writings prior to the early 350s. But Athanasius maintains the Son's full divinity throughout the three *Orationes* and His role in bridging the ontological gulf between the divine and the created world for revelation and salvation.

All things partake of the Son Himself according to the grace of the Spirit coming from Him. This shows that the Son Himself partakes of nothing. Rather, what is partaken from the Father is the Son. For, as partaking of the Son Himself, we are said to partake of God, and this is what Peter said, 'that you may be partakers in the divine nature' [2 Peter 1:4]; as the Apostle says also, 'Do you not know that you are a temple of God?' [1 Corinthians 3:16] and 'We are the temple of the living God' [2 Corinthians 6:16]. And seeing the Son, we see the Father; for the thought and comprehension of the Son is knowledge about the Father, because He is His proper offspring from his *ousia*. (I.16)

Across the *Orationes contra Arianos* Athanasius likewise reaffirms the doctrine of Christian salvation through deification. Only through the intercession of the true Son who took on created human nature could humanity have been saved.

For humanity would not have been deified if joined to a creature, or unless the Son were true God. Nor would humanity have been drawn into the Father's presence, unless the one who had put on the body was the true Word by nature. And as we would not have been delivered from sin and the curse, unless it had been by nature human flesh which the Word put on (for we would have had nothing in common with what was foreign), so also humanity would not have been deified, unless the Word who became flesh had been by nature from the Father and true and proper to Him. (II.70)

Athanasius also clarifies the significance of deification and the gift that we receive from salvation. The adoption of humanity by grace through the Incarnation cannot exalt humanity to share the uncreated nature of God:

Because of the grace of the Spirit which has been given to us, we come to be in Him, and He in us. And through His becoming in us, and we having the Spirit, it is reasonable that, since it is the Spirit of God, we are considered to be in God and God in us. Not then as the Son is in the Father, do we also become in the Father; for the Son does not merely participate in the Spirit in order to be in the Father. Nor does He receive the Spirit, but rather supplies it Himself to all. And the Spirit does not unite the Word to the Father, but rather the Spirit receives from the Word. And the Son is in the Father, as His proper Word and Radiance; but we, apart from the Spirit, are foreign and distant from God, and by participation of the Spirit we are knit into the Godhead. (III.24)

Yet through our deification in Christ, humanity has been freed from sin and death. For, although the divine Word could not suffer in His divinity, He took upon Himself the suffering of the body for our salvation. 'It was fitting that the Lord, in putting on human flesh, put it on entirely with the passibilities proper to it; so that, as we say that the body was proper to Him, so also we may say that the passibilities of the body were proper to Him alone, though they did not touch Him according to the Godhead' (III.32). Only by this means could salvation be achieved. 'If the works of the Word's Godhead had not taken place through the body, humanity would not have been deified. And again, if the properties of the flesh had not been attributed to the Word, humanity would not have been thoroughly delivered from them' (III.33). But the divine Word did take on the properties of the flesh and overcame them. And so:

We no longer die according to our former origin. But from now on, since our origin and all the weakness of flesh has been transferred to the Word, we rise from the earth, the curse from sin having been removed, because of Him who is in us, and who has become a curse for us. And reasonably so; for as we are all from earth and die in Adam, so being regenerated from above of water and Spirit, in Christ we are all enlivened; the flesh being no longer earthly, but being henceforth made word, by reason of God's Word who for our sake became flesh. (III.33)

The passages quoted here are necessarily selective, but they demonstrate the continuity of Athanasius' theology from the *Contra Gentes–De Incarnatione* to the *Orationes contra Arianos*. The language of the three *Orationes* is far more explicitly polemical, and Athanasius reacted to the threat he perceived in 'Arianism' by placing even greater stress on the Son's full divinity. He also refined his presentation of the doctrine of deification and the relationship between the divine Word and the human body in the Incarnation. These were differences of emphasis not of interpretation. The fundamental principles of Athanasius' theology remained unchanged, as they would throughout his involvement in the fourth-century controversies.

For our understanding of Athanasius' theology, the *Orationes contra Arianos* have one final important contribution to make. A central element in Athanasius' approach to Christian doctrine has not yet been discussed: his exegesis of Scripture.[29] Like every Christian, Athanasius looked to the Holy Scriptures for guidance and inspiration. The canon of Scripture was not universally defined in the early fourth century, an ongoing debate in which Athanasius' part is discussed in Chapter 5. The majority of the books contained in the modern Bible were already recognized as authoritative, however, and in a very real sense the controversies of the fourth century were controversies over how the Scriptures should be read.[30] The issues at stake could not be settled merely by the citation of scriptural texts. The interpretation of the language of Scripture was crucial, and this is an essential theme of Athanasius' three *Orationes*.

After an initial condemnation of 'Arianism' (I.1–10), all three *Orationes* are structured around the exegesis of a series of scriptural texts. According to Athanasius, these texts were brought forward by the 'Arians' to support their belief in the reduced divinity of the Son. We must always treat Athanasius' presentation of his 'Arian' opponents with caution, but it is probable that the interpretation of the passages he cites was a subject of debate. They included Philippians 2:9–10 ('Therefore God also has highly exalted Him, and given Him the name which is above every name; that in the name of Jesus every knee should bend, of things in heaven and things in earth and things under the earth' (*Oratio* I.37–45)); Psalm 45:7–8 ('You have loved righteousness and hated iniquity, therefore God, your God, has anointed you with the oil of gladness above your fellows' (*Oratio* I.46–52)) and a lengthy discussion of Proverbs 8:22 ('The Lord created me a beginning of His ways for His works' (*Oratio* II.19–72)). The third *Oratio* focuses upon passages from the Gospels. The 'Arians' are reported to have emphasized texts that attributed weakness or ignorance to Christ, such as Matthew 26:39 ('Father, if it be possible, let this cup pass from Me') and Mark 13:32 ('Of that day and that hour knows no man, nor the angels in heaven, nor the Son, but only the Father'). Athanasius himself drew particularly on John's Gospel for several of his favourite passages: 'I and the Father are One' (John 10:30), 'Whoever has seen Me has seen the Father' (John 14:9), and 'I am in the Father and the Father is in Me' (John 14:10).

---

[29] On Athanasius and the Bible, see in general Ernest (2004), and also Metzler (1997).

[30] There is a helpful introduction to the place of Scripture in the fourth-century controversies in Kannengiesser (1981).

Athanasius' approach to scriptural exegesis across the *Orationes* is clear and consistent. All passages that refer to the Son and His Incarnation are understood within the absolute ontological division between the divine and creation. The Son is fully God, and His divinity was not lessened or compromised by becoming Incarnate in a human body. Properties appropriate to creatures, such as suffering or ignorance and the very state of being created or made, cannot apply to the divine Son. Athanasius therefore sees in the Scriptures a 'double proclamation' of the Incarnate Christ. When Christ is said to be in the Father or one with the Father, these passages apply to the divine Word. When Christ is said to be exalted or anointed or to express ignorance, these passages apply to His human body. Proverbs 8:22, which the early Church regarded as an allusion to the Son, must similarly refer to Christ's body when it uses the term 'created'. With modern eyes, this exegetical approach has sometimes been seen as artificial and contrived. For Athanasius, his exegesis of each contested passage was in accordance with the overall message of the Scriptures:

The scope and character of Holy Scripture, as we have often said, is as follows. It contains a double account of the Saviour, that He was ever God, and is the Son, being the Father's Word and Radiance and Wisdom; and that afterwards for us He took flesh of a virgin, Mary Bearer of God [*Theotokos*], and was made man. And this scope is to be found throughout inspired Scripture, as the Lord Himself has said, 'Search the Scriptures, for it is they that testify of Me' [John 5:39]. (III.29)

This conception of the scriptural message underlay Athanasius' theological vision of the divine Son who became Incarnate as man to bridge the gulf that divided humanity from God. It was precisely that vision of revelation and salvation that Athanasius felt compelled to defend against the threat of 'Arianism'.

'ATHANASIAN ARIANISM'

The theology of Athanasius has struck a chord in the hearts of believers right down to the present day. His teachings helped to define what would be recognized as Christian orthodoxy by later generations, and he was remembered as the champion who preserved that orthodox faith through the turmoil of the 'Arian Controversy'. In the light of this reputation, it is hardly surprising that until relatively recently few challenged Athanasius' interpretation of the doctrinal debates of his time. The numerous anti-'Arian' works that Athanasius composed, from the *Orationes contra Arianos* to the *De Synodis*, were accepted as a guide to the teachings of his opponents, whose errors Athanasius contrasted to the orthodoxy that he represented.

Yet deep respect for Athanasius' theology does not require that we adopt at face value his presentation of men whom he regarded as enemies and whose teachings he set out to condemn.[31] Modern scholars have become increasingly aware of how Athanasius' polemical writings may have influenced our knowledge of the fourth-century controversies. The following pages will trace the development of Athanasius' anti-'Arian' polemic and its implications. By doing so we are able to gain a new appreciation of the context in which he wrote and the teachings of those he branded as 'Arians'. But no less importantly, we also gain a better understanding of Athanasius' own theology, his awareness of the issues that were at stake, and his long-term achievement.[32]

There is no reference to 'Arianism' in any Athanasian work written before 335, including the *Contra Gentes–De Incarnatione*. As we saw in the previous chapter, the earliest statement that his opponents were motivated by heresy occurs in the documents from the Council of Tyre in 335 preserved in the *Apologia contra Arianos*. The same argument then appears in the *Epistula Encyclica* of 339 after Athanasius' flight into his second exile. It was at this time that he began to compose the *Orationes contra Arianos*, which laid down in detail his construction of the 'Arian heresy'.

Instead of Christ for them is Arius, as for the Manichees Manichaeus...When the blessed Alexander cast out Arius, those who remained with Alexander remained Christians; but those who went out with Arius abandoned the Saviour's Name to us who were with Alexander, and they were henceforth called Arians. Behold then, after the death of Alexander, those who are in communion with his successor Athanasius, and with whom the same Athanasius communicates, are instances of the same rule; neither do any of them bear his name, nor is he named from them, but all again and customarily are called Christians. For though we have a succession of teachers and become their disciples, yet, because we are taught by them the teachings of Christ, we are and are called Christians and nothing else. But those who

---

[31] 'To an extraordinary degree, the faith of Athanasius has become the faith of the Church, and to criticize him must look as if we wished to shatter the rock from which we were hewn. Nevertheless I have come to think that the methods used by Athanasius in defending his faith will not serve to commend eternal truths to the present age; and it is for the Church's ultimate good that we seek to show where their weakness lies' (Stead 1976: 136–7).

[32] For a fuller discussion of Athanasius' construction of 'Arianism', on which the summary here is based, see Gwynn (2007: 169–244).

follow the heretics, though they have countless successors, yet in every respect they
bear the name of the founder of their heresy. While Arius is dead, and many of his
followers have succeeded him, nevertheless those who hold the doctrines of that
man, as being known from Arius, are called Arians. (I.2–3)

The introduction to the first *Oratio contra Arianos* sums up Athanasius'
construction of the entire 'Arian Controversy'. Arius is the founder of the
heresy, just as Mani founded Manichaeism, and those whom Athanasius
condemns as 'Arian' must share Arius' errors. Against their heresy is set the
true faith of the Christian Church, to which Athanasius has succeeded from
Alexander. Throughout his anti-'Arian' writings Athanasius maintains this
polarized contrast of manifest heresy and traditional orthodoxy. In *Oratio
contra Arianos* I, Athanasius continues on from his introductory rhetoric to
define the teachings that he attributes to 'Arianism'. After a lengthy denunciation of Arius' *Thalia* (I.5–6), he summarizes those teachings as follows:

What can they bring forward to us from the infamous *Thalia*?...That not always
was God a father, but later He became so. Not always was the Son, for He was not
until He was begotten. He is not from the Father, but He also came into existence
out of nothing. He is not proper to the *ousia* of the Father, for He is a creature
[*ktisma*] and a thing made [*poiēma*]. Christ is not true God, but He also by participation was made God. The Son does not know the Father exactly, nor may the Word
see the Father perfectly, and the Word does not understand nor know the Father
exactly. He is not the true and only Word of the Father, but by name only is called
Word and Wisdom, and by grace is called Son and Power. He is not unchangeable,
like the Father, but is changeable by nature, like the creatures. (I.9)

Athanasius' definition of the 'Arian heresy' has been extremely influential.[33] It therefore has to be emphasized that no one in the fourth century
actually taught all the doctrines that Athanasius condemns. This holds true
for Arius himself, and even more so for Eusebius of Nicomedia and Asterius 'the Sophist', the two other men named as 'Arian' in the *Orationes contra
Arianos*.[34] Athanasius' definition is in fact a polemical construct, which is
perhaps best described as 'Athanasian Arianism'. Like his predecessor Alexander in the latter's *Encyclical Letter*, Athanasius certainly drew upon Arius'
original teachings, but extracted from those teachings implications that
Arius would never have accepted.

---

[33] Athanasius' polemic is the basis for the model of 'Arianism' in Hanson (1988: 19–23),
which is influenced in turn by that of Lorenz (1979: 37–49).
[34] For their theologies, which are known primarily from the writings of their opponents,
see Bardy (1936), Luibheid (1976), Lienhard (1999), and Gwynn (2007).

Arius did deny the eternity of the Son. He described the Son as a creature (*ktisma*), explicitly rejected that He could be proper to the *ousia* of the Father, and at least in one letter referred to the Son as coming into existence 'out of nothing'. Similarly, Arius refused to call the Son 'true God', denied in a sense that He was the only Word and Wisdom of God (for the Father also had His own Word and Wisdom), and taught that the Son could not fully know the Father. Yet alongside the genuine teachings of Arius that Athanasius condemns stand an equally significant number of alleged 'Arian' principles that derive from Athanasius' polemical interpretation. These include the assertion that Arius taught that the Son was God only by participation and Word and Wisdom only by name and grace, and most importantly the repeated charge that Arius rendered the Son mutable and reduced Him to the level of all other created beings.

Eusebius of Nicomedia and Asterius 'the Sophist' are the two best-known 'Arians' after Arius of the early fourth century. Eusebius was the highly influential bishop of the imperial capital when Arius first clashed with Alexander. He was regarded by Athanasius as the leader of *hoi peri Eusebion* ('the Eusebians'), the 'Arian party' that conspired to send him into exile.[35] Asterius was not a cleric (he was barred from ordination, as he had offered pagan sacrifice during the Great Persecution) but was an important theologian and preacher, whose treatise the *Syntagmation* now survives only in fragments.[36] Both men shared Arius' refusal to describe the Son as eternal or from the Father's *ousia*, and believed that the Son must be a *ktisma* and a product of the Father's will. Like Arius, they held that the Father alone is eternal and unbegotten, and that to name the Son co-eternal or co-essential with the Father was to teach two unbegotten beings or impose material or Sabellian ideas upon God. Unlike Arius, they did not refer to the Son as 'out of nothing' or teach that He did not fully know the Father. They also placed a greater emphasis upon the unique divinity of the Son, whom Asterius is reported to have described as 'the exact Image of His [the Father's] Essence and Will and Power and Glory'.[37]

There is thus a considerable basis of truth in Athanasius' interpretation of the theologies of these three men in the *Orationes contra Arianos*. There

[35] Our best source for Eusebius' theology is his *Letter to Paulinus of Tyre* in c.323 (Theodoret, I.6).
[36] The fragments of Asterius' works were collected by Bardy (1936: 339–54), and re-edited with further additions by Vinzent (1993: 82–141).
[37] Asterius, fragment XXIa (Bardy), 10 (Vinzent).

is a still greater degree of distortion, however, and it is the nature of that distortion that is of particular interest. In his construction of 'Arianism', Athanasius interpreted his opponents' doctrines in the light of his own theological assumptions. The historical value of Athanasius' anti-'Arian' polemic is not as a source for the teachings of those opponents. Instead, the polemic sheds further light on Athanasius' theology and on the issues that he believed were at stake in the fourth-century controversies.

Fundamental to Athanasius' conception of Christianity, as we have already seen, was the ontological separation of God and creation. Only if the Son is truly God, eternally and essentially the Son of the Father, can He fulfil the promised revelation of God and deification of humanity. The same ontological argument underlies Athanasius' construction of 'Arianism'. Either the Son is eternal and immutable God, the true and essential offspring of the Father, or He is a creature like any other, coming into existence from nothing and mutable by nature. And, if only a Son who is truly God can be the source for our revelation and deification, then a Son who is a creature cannot be our Saviour, for He cannot bridge the gulf that separates God from the created order to which He too belongs. The 'created Son' of Arius compromised Athanasius' entire understanding of salvation and represented a heresy that had to be opposed.

For Athanasius, and for later generations, the reduction of the Son to a creature (*ktisma*) would become the essential characteristic of 'Arianism'.[38] But the implications of this 'Arian' doctrine, which Athanasius develops at great length in the *Orationes contra Arianos*, derive almost exclusively from his own principles. It is Athanasius who believes that, if the Son is said to be a creature, then He is no different from all other creatures whose attributes He shares. On these grounds, he can repeatedly claim that the 'Arians' make the Son mutable[39] and teach that the Son was created in time (*Oratio* I.11) and was not the creative Word of the Father (*Oratio* II.21). None of these alleged doctrines was ever taught by any of the men whom

[38] 'Athanasius called "Arian" anyone who could be understood to mean that the Son is a creature' (Anatolios 1998: 96). For the continuity of this attitude in later centuries, see Slusser (1993) and Wiles (1996).

[39] See esp. *Oratio* I.35–52, in which Athanasius develops in full his argument that the 'Arians' attribute changeability, ethical advancement, and suffering to the divine Son. It is these passages above all that underlie the reconstructions of 'Arianism' proposed by Gregg and Groh (1981) and Hanson (1985, 1988). A new translation of the text in question has been produced by Anatolios (2004: 91–110), although the accompanying commentary is somewhat uncritical, primarily because Anatolios accepts at face value Athanasius' polemical assertion that Arius made the Son mutable (89–91).

Athanasius condemns. Moreover, Athanasius obviously knew that his opponents denied that the created Son was no different from other created beings. In *De Synodis* 16, he quoted Arius' explicit insistence in his *Letter to Alexander* that the Son is a creature, but not as one of the creatures. Within Athanasius' polarized ontology, however, such a distinction is meaningless. His denunciation of this 'Arian' argument in *Oratio contra Arianos* II is most enlightening:

Let us behold what it was that they replied to the blessed Alexander in the beginning, when their heresy was formed. They wrote then saying that, 'He is a creature [*ktisma*], but not as one of the creatures, He is a thing made [*poiēma*], but not as one of the things made, He is an offspring [*gennēma*], but not as one of the offsprings'...[Yet] this so great sophism of yours is shown to be foolish. For once again you still say that He is one of the creatures, and the things that someone might say about the other creatures, you also attribute to the Son, being truly foolish and blind. (II.9)

Either the Son is a *ktisma* like any other or He is proper offspring of the *ousia* of the Father. Such a conclusion is the inevitable and logical consequence of Athanasius' ontology. It is also a colossal distortion of the actual theology of the men whom Athanasius wishes to condemn. The very words that he here attributes to the 'Arians' are a product of the polemic. What Arius actually wrote in his *Letter to Alexander* was that the Son is 'the perfect creature [*teleion ktisma*] of God, but not as one of the creatures, offspring [*gennēma*], but not as one of the offsprings'. Athanasius cites the final clause correctly. But he inserts the line 'a thing made [*poiēma*], but not as one of the things made', and he omits the term perfect (*teleion*), with which Arius qualified his description of the Son as a *ktisma*. In effect, Athanasius has rewritten the words of Arius according to his own theology. He imposes his definition of *ktisma* and *poiēma* as synonyms,[40] whereas Arius used *ktisma* alone as this word gained scriptural support from Proverbs 8:22. And Athanasius ignores the concept of a 'perfect' creature, an irrelevant distinction if one assumes (as he did) that all created beings are alike by nature.

Yet the doctrine that the Son was 'a perfect creature, not like other creatures' was not empty rhetoric. It was an essential component of a widespread eastern theology that understood the Son as a unique and divine *ktisma*, an immutable mediator separate by *ousia* and *physis* both from the unbegotten Father and from the created order. This theology bridged the

---

[40] 'Once it has been shown that the Word is not a *poiēma*, it is also shown that He is not a *ktisma*. For it is the same to speak of a *poiēma* and a *ktisma*, so that indeed the proof that He is not a *poiēma* is proof also that He is not a *ktisma*' (*Oratio* II.18).

gulf between God and creation, not through the Incarnation of an onto-
logically divine Son, but through a mediator who was both a *ktisma* and
God. Athanasius' theology was to prove the more enduring, and it can be
strongly argued that his position is the more compelling. But, contrary
to his polemic, the men whom he condemned as 'Arian' did uphold the
existence of a divine unchangeable Son through whom the creation and
salvation of humanity was achieved.

Throughout the *Orationes contra Arianos*, Athanasius constructs an 'Arian
heresy' that every Christian had to condemn. Just as he preserved the
fundamental principles of his theology essentially unchanged across his
career, so too his definition of 'Athanasian Arianism' altered very little in his
later polemical writings. When he wrote the *De Decretis Nicaenae Synodi* in
the early 350s he revised his argument to incorporate the new prominence
that he accorded to the Nicene Creed, a shift to which we will turn shortly.
A similar revision occurred in the *De Sententia Dionysii*, a work devoted
to denying the 'Arians' any support from earlier Christian tradition, here
represented by Athanasius' predecessor Dionysius of Alexandria. Nevertheless, the presentation of 'Arianism' in these two works (*De Decretis* 6, *De
Sententia Dionysii* 2) is derived directly from the first *Oratio contra Arianos*.
This is equally true for the *Life of Antony* (69–70) and the *Encyclical Letter to
the Bishops of Egypt and Libya* in 356 (12).

The last of these texts contains a particularly striking application of
Athanasius' polemical method. One of his aims in the *Encyclical Letter* of
356 was to urge his audience not to subscribe to a creed that the 'Arians'
were then intending to circulate within the Egyptian Church.[41] According
to Athanasius, the 'Arians' hoped that through this creed 'they may seem
to remove the evil repute of Arius, and to escape notice themselves as if
not holding Arius' doctrines; and on the other hand, so that by writing
these things they might seem again to hide the Nicene Council and the
faith established there against the Arian heresy' (5). The creed itself, Athanasius acknowledges, is scriptural and not obviously in error. 'If these
writings were from the orthodox...then nothing in them would be suspect' (8). But, as the creed comes from men Athanasius had condemned as
'Arian', he dismisses their scriptural language as mere heretical deceit. 'If
they have written other words apart from the aforementioned doctrines

---

[41] The exact identity of the 'Arian' creed in question is uncertain, although Barnes (1993:
122) suggests that this is a reference to the Sirmium Creed of 351.

of Arius, then condemn them as hypocrites who conceal the venom of their thought' (19). The actual doctrines of the creed under dispute have become irrelevant. Athanasius has named the authors 'Arians', and 'Arians' they must be.

The culmination of Athanasius' anti-'Arian' polemic is the *De Synodis Arimini et Seleuciae* (359–61). For his account of the joint councils of Ariminum and Seleucia in 359, Athanasius traces a line of 'Arian' succession from the *Thalia* of Arius and the writings of the 'Eusebians' through the eastern creedal statements of the 330s and 340s. He represents every one of these diverse theological statements, down to and including the so-called Dated Creed presented to the councils of 359, as the products of a single 'Arian tradition'. The many differences between the various statements are denounced as 'Arian' deceit and inconsistency. Once again Athanasius polarizes the fourth-century controversies between the two alternatives of orthodoxy (the Nicene Creed) and heresy. In reality, the documents contained in the *De Synodis* provide some of our best evidence for the wide spectrum of doctrinal views that existed within eastern Christianity at this time.

Perhaps the most important text with which to illustrate the impact of Athanasius' polemic is the Dedication Creed of 341.[42] At some point between January and September in that year, some ninety or so eastern bishops gathered in Antioch with the eastern emperor Constantius to dedicate the 'Golden Church' built by Constantine. Those in attendance included Eusebius of Nicomedia (now bishop of Constantinople) and almost every other living bishop whom Athanasius named as a 'Eusebian'. Two major documents are associated with the council. The wrongly named 'First Creed' of Antioch is actually the council's letter to Julius of Rome, notable for the authors' insistence (most likely in response to the influence of Athanasius' polemic) that 'we have not been followers of Arius, for how could we, who are bishops, follow a presbyter?' (quoted in *De Synodis* 22). The true creedal statement of the council is the Second or Dedication Creed, preserved in *De Synodis* 23.

The Dedication Creed explicitly rejects the more extreme elements of 'Athanasian Arianism', but is far from being compatible with the theology of Athanasius. The Son is 'God from God, whole from whole, sole from sole, perfect from perfect, King from King, Lord from Lord, living Word,

---

[42] On the evidence for the council, see Bardy (1936: 85–132) and particularly Schneemelcher (1977).

living Wisdom, true Light, Way, Truth, Resurrection, Shepherd, Door'. However, He does not hold these titles by His own essential nature. Instead, as Asterius had already taught, He is the 'exact Image of the Essence, Will, Power, and Glory of the Godhead of the Father'. The Son is 'immutable and unchangeable', and any suggestion that 'time or season or age is or has been before the generation of the Son' is anathematized, but He is not said to be eternal. A second anathema condemns the idea that the Son might be 'a creature [*ktisma*] as one of the creatures, an offspring [*gennēma*] as one of the offsprings, or a thing made [*poiēma*] as one of the things made'. This doctrine excludes Athanasius' allegation that the 'Arians' reduced the Son to the level of all mutable creatures, while still admitting the possibility that the Son is Himself a 'perfect creature'. The declaration that '[we believe] in the Holy Spirit, who is given to those who have faith for comfort and sanctification and perfection' might further suggest a conception of salvation through deification.

Judged by the standards of later orthodoxy, there are evident flaws in the theology expressed in the Dedication Creed. '*Homoousios*', 'from the *ousia* of the Father', and 'true God from true God' are omitted; the eternity of the Son is left unspoken; and the doctrine of the Trinity is openly subordinationist. The identities of the Father, Son, and Holy Spirit 'denote accurately the peculiar subsistence [*hypostasis*], rank, and glory of each that is named'. But the creed cannot be described in any meaningful way as 'Arian'.[43] The Council of 341 comprised a considerable bloc of the eastern Church, and its creedal statement represented a theology that was widely influential in the east for much of the fourth century.[44] This theological tradition was reluctant to describe the Son as eternal, or to speak of Him as *homoousios* to or from the *ousia* of the Father. The Son is God, and the Word, Wisdom, and Power of God, but He possesses His divinity through the will of the Father, of whom He is the Image. Thus the union of the Father and the Son is not ontological, and great emphasis is placed on the distinct identities of the individual *hypostases* of the Trinity. This emphasis

---

[43] Hilary of Poitiers described the Council of 341 as a '*sanctorum synodus*' (Hilary, *De Synodis* 32).

[44] For a survey of the subsequent history of the Dedication Creed in the fourth-century controversies, see Bardy (1936: 96–119). At the Council of Seleucia in 359, it was this creed and not Nicaea that those eastern bishops now usually known as the 'Homoiousians' invoked as the traditional faith of the Church (Socrates, II.39–40; Sozomen, IV.22), and some eastern bishops still held to this creed in 381 (Socrates IV.4, V.8; Sozomen IV.7, IV.12, VII.7).

was apparently aroused by fears of the Sabellian implications of *homoousios*, especially as revealed in the theology of Marcellus of Ancyra.[45]

The Dedication Creed highlights the difficulties raised by Athanasius' polarized vision of the 'Arian Controversy'. Not only did those he branded as 'Arian' not hold the doctrines that he attributed to them, but in the 340s and 350s his own theology was not the universal orthodox faith that he wished to claim. The doctrinal questions that were dividing the eastern Church centred not upon whether the Son was divine, which all agreed, but on how that divinity could be expressed. Athanasius' insistence on the ontological unity of Father and Son was still regarded with suspicion by those in the east who saw such teachings as compromising the unique authority of the Father and the individual identities of the Trinity.

In the longer term, however, recognizing the tensions beneath Athanasius' anti-'Arian' polemic reaffirms the magnitude of his theological achievement. Despite his rhetoric, Athanasius was not simply defending the established orthodoxy of the Christian faith. He had to demonstrate that the doctrines that he taught were the truth that the Church should adopt. And over time he succeeded. Whatever the distortions inherent in his construction of 'Arianism', Athanasius was completely sincere in his conviction that any theology that denied the ontological unity of Father and Son must lead to the errors that he condemned. Against such heresy, the co-eternal and co-essential Son of God was the only safeguard for Christian revelation and salvation, symbolized in Athanasius' writings from the 350s onwards by the Nicene Creed.

THE COUNCIL OF NICAEA AND THE HOLY SPIRIT

The fundamental principles of Athanasius' theology and his construction of 'Arianism' remained consistent across the middle decades of the fourth century. Nevertheless, the controversies in which he was embroiled continued to evolve. New issues emerged and new opponents challenged

[45] On the influence of Marcellus upon the Dedication Council, see Hanson (1988: 285–92), Tetz (1989), and Lienhard (1999: 167–71). The emphasis upon the three distinct *hypostases* of the Trinity in the creed rejected the Sabellianism that Marcellus' teaching was alleged to imply. So did the creed's concluding statement (again paralleled in the extant fragments of Asterius) that there must be 'a Father who is truly Father, and a Son who is truly Son, and the Holy Spirit who is truly Holy Spirit... so that they are three in subsistence (*hypostasei*) and one in agreement'.

the orthodoxy that he represented. Athanasius therefore did not cease to refine his doctrines and the language through which they were expressed. Two themes in particular emerged in his writings during the 350s that had not previously received close attention: the importance of the Nicene Creed and the full divinity of the Holy Spirit. Neither theme was entirely new to Athanasius, nor did either represent a dramatic shift in his theological thinking. Rather, Athanasius incorporated both Nicaea and the Holy Spirit within his existing teachings and interpreted their contribution to his orthodox faith accordingly.

In the years following the Council of Nicaea, the voice of the original Nicene Creed was conspicuous only by its silence. Even for those who had gathered at the council in 325, the creed and its unscriptural watchword *homoousios* had raised uncomfortable questions. During the reign of Constantine no one challenged Nicaea directly. But the vast majority of eastern bishops would seem to have viewed the creed with distrust and emphatically did not regard it as an authoritative statement of orthodoxy. After Constantine's death, alternative creeds swiftly appeared, most notably the Dedication Creed of 341 and the Macrostich Creed of 344. These creeds avoided the more contentious expressions used at Nicaea and better reflected the concerns prevalent in much of the eastern Church during this time.

Athanasius shared the prevailing silence on Nicaea in his early theological writings, if not perhaps feeling the same distrust. The term *homoousios* occurs just once in the three *Orationes contra Arianos* (I.9), and the Council of Nicaea is accorded no deep significance. Yet, when he wrote the *De Decretis Nicaenae Synodi* in *c.*350–5, his position had changed. Now the Nicene Creed had become the essential safeguard against the 'Arian heresy'. The cause of the change can only be speculated. Athanasius offered no explanation and maintained that he continued to defend the traditional orthodox faith. It is possible that he responded to the increasing circulation of the Dedication and Macrostich Creeds, which he attributed to men whom he regarded as 'Eusebians' and 'Arians'. He may also have reacted against the religious policies of the emperor Constantius in the early 350s, although here it is difficult to separate cause and effect. Constantius in the west demanded that the bishops renounce both Athanasius and the Nicene Creed, and the *De Decretis* may have been written for a western audience. Certainly when Athanasius wrote he felt under threat. The 'Arians' were presently passive but 'in a little while they will turn to outrage' (2), and the doctrines that he upheld had only limited eastern support outside Egypt. The Council of Nicaea, still remembered as one of the great events of Constantine's reign, held authority to which he could appeal and a special attraction as the council that had condemned Arius and his heresy.

Perhaps the most striking feature of Athanasius' decision to endorse the Nicene Creed as the orthodox symbol is that neither his theology nor his construction of 'Arianism' underwent any significant change. In his subsequent works *homoousios* rather than 'proper offspring of the *ousia* of the Father' became his preferred expression for the ontological unity of the Father and the Son. And in his polarized vision of the 'Arian Controversy' Nicaea now represented orthodoxy, for 'He who does not hold the doctrines of Arius necessarily holds and intends the doctrines of the [Nicene] Council' (*De Decretis* 20). But Athanasius did not reinterpret his beliefs in the light of the Nicene Creed. On the contrary, he redefined Nicaea according to his theological principles.[46]

The *De Decretis* is addressed to an unnamed friend of Athanasius to whom the 'Arians' had complained about the use of unscriptural language at Nicaea (1). Athanasius likens the 'Arians' to Jews in their falsity and lack of understanding, and declares that they should have learned from the example of their fathers the 'Eusebians'. At the council the 'Eusebians' had convicted themselves with their impiety and contradictions. But even they had finally subscribed to the creed, as is attested by Eusebius of Caesarea's *Letter to His See* (1–5).[47] This is followed by a restatement of Athanasius' understanding of the true divinity of the Son against the errors of the 'Arians' drawn directly from the *Orationes contra Arianos* (6–17). The Son is God by nature, co-eternal and co-essential with the Father. He is the Creator not one of the creatures, and when He is said to have been created in Proverbs 8:22 this refers to His humanity taken on for our sake in the Incarnation.

It is against the background of this theological argument that Athanasius turns to the Council of Nicaea itself and the composition and meaning of the creed. After a further denunciation of the 'Arians' for themselves employing unscriptural phrases such as 'out of nothing' and 'once He was not' (18), Athanasius blames their evasions for the language adopted in 325:

[46] For a very similar argument, see Ayres (2004a).

[47] Despite Athanasius' attempt to claim that Eusebius' *Letter* confirmed his own interpretation of the Nicene Creed, the bishop of Caesarea in fact understood *homoousios* and *ek tēs ousias* in much vaguer terms. For the parallels between the arguments of Eusebius and Athanasius over the definition of Nicaea, see Ayres (2004a: 350–3).

The Council wished to banish the impious statements of the Arians and to write the confessed language of the Scriptures, that the Son is not out of nothing but from God, and is Word and Wisdom and neither a creature [*ktisma*] nor a thing made [*poiēma*], but proper offspring from the Father. But the Eusebians, compelled by their inveterate heterodoxy, understood His being from God to be in common with us... The fathers, perceiving their treachery and the cunning of their impiety, were then forced to express more clearly the sense of the words 'from God', and to write 'the Son is from the essence [*ek tēs ousias*] of God', in order that 'from God' might not be thought to apply in common and equally to the Son and to generated beings, but that it may be confessed that everything else is a creature and the Word alone is from the Father. For though all things are said to be from God, yet this is not in the sense in which the Son is from Him. (19)

The same explanation is offered for the inclusion of *homoousios*:

When the bishops said that the Word must be described as true Power and Image of the Father, in all things exact and like the Father, and as unalterable and always and in Him without division (for never was the Word not, but He was always, existing everlastingly with the Father, as the radiance of light), the Eusebians endured indeed, as not daring to contradict, being put to shame by the arguments which were urged against them. But they were caught whispering to each other and winking with their eyes, that 'like' and 'always' and 'power' and 'in Him' were, as before, common to us and the Son, and that it was no difficulty to agree to these... The bishops, discerning in this too their dissimulation, and whereas it is written 'Deceit is in the heart of the impious that imagine evil' [Proverbs 12:20], were again compelled on their part to collect the sense of the Scriptures, and to re-say and re-write what they had said before, more distinctly still, namely, that the Son is 'of one essence [*homoousios*]' with the Father. (20)

Finally, the gathered bishops made it explicit that the terms used were chosen to condemn the 'Arian heresy':

They immediately added, 'But those who say that the Son of God is out of nothing, or created, or alterable, or a thing made, or from another essence, these the holy and catholic Church anathematizes'. By saying this, they showed clearly that *ek tēs ousias* and *homoousion* are destructive of the catchwords of the impiety, that He is a creature and a thing made and a generated being and changeable and that He was not before he was begotten. (20)

Athanasius' account is a crucial source for our knowledge of the Council of Nicaea and its proceedings, but it must be handled with caution. The distinction that he draws between the 'Nicene bishops' and the 'Eusebians' is a product of his polemical rhetoric, for at the council no such distinct blocs existed. Nor did the so-called 'Eusebians' actually hold the heretical ideas for which Athanasius has made them spokesmen. Most importantly, Athanasius has interpreted the Nicene Creed according to his own theological definitions. If the Son is *homoousios* to the Father, then He is the 'proper offspring' of the Father and neither a creature nor something made but separate by nature from all created beings. This is the language of Athanasius, not of Nicaea. The terms offspring (*gennēma*) and nature (*physis*) do not appear in the Nicene Creed, and nor does the word creature (*ktisma*). Although the Nicene anathemas appear to condemn the teaching that the Son was created (*ktiston*), this is true only of those versions of the Nicene Creed 'quoted' by Athanasius. In every other version of the text, particularly those that derive directly from Eusebius of Caesarea, this anathema is absent.[48] Athanasius has made the interpolation in order to impose his condemnation of the 'Arian' created Son.

In the closing sections of the *De Decretis* Athanasius sought to reinforce his presentation of Nicaea as the traditional faith of the Church. He argued that the unscriptural words used in the creed 'contain the sense of the Scriptures' (21), and cited supporting passages from earlier Fathers: Theognostus (25), Dionysius of Alexandria and his namesake of Rome (26–7), and Origen (27). These passages were not entirely convincing.[49] Theognostus, a third-century head of the catechetical school of Alexandria, was a somewhat controversial figure. Origen, as we have seen, could be cited in support of all sides of the fourth-century debates. And Athanasius' presentation of the two Dionysii aroused sufficient opposition to require him to compose a further work in defence of his judgement (the *De Sententia Dionysii*). From this evidence Athanasius felt able to conclude that the Nicene Creed preserved the teachings 'which from the beginning those who were eyewitnesses and ministers of the Word have handed down to us' (27). The final pages of the *De Decretis* then denounce the 'Arians' for their misuse of the term 'unbegotten' (28–32), another argument lifted straight from the *Orationes contra Arianos*.

Later generations would remember Athanasius as the 'champion of Nicaea'. He was said to have been a leading protagonist at the council, although Athanasius himself makes no such claim. His eventual triumph should not blind us to the struggle he faced in bringing the Nicene Creed

---

[48] Wiles (1993).

[49] There is an assessment of Athanasius' presentation of the Nicene fathers and his appeals to patristic tradition in the *De Decretis* in Graumann (2002: 119–41).

out of the shadows and into the forefront of debate. Athanasius wrote the
De Decretis not just to uphold the authority of Nicaea but to define how
Nicaea was to be interpreted. In the early 350s neither his interpretation
nor the creed itself was widely accepted across the eastern Church.[50] That
the Nicene Creed would indeed become the acknowledged symbol of
fourth-century orthodoxy, and understood according to Athanasius' teachings, was a remarkable achievement.

One subject on which the original Nicene Creed offered merely the briefest passing reference was the status of the third person of the Trinity. The
initial debate between Arius and Alexander before Nicaea had not involved
the Holy Spirit, and the relationship of the Spirit to Father and Son was recognized but left undefined. The first creed to contain an extended statement
on the Spirit was the Dedication Creed of 341. Only in the 350s, however,
do the Spirit's nature and place within the Trinity seem to have become
a focus for controversy.[51] In *c*.357, during Athanasius' third exile, he was
informed by Serapion of Thmuis that there were Christians who accepted
the full divinity of the Son but denied that of the Spirit. Athanasius replied
in a long letter, later supplemented by shorter summaries.[52] He denounced
those who had fallen into this error as the 'Tropici' (as they reduced the
Spirit to a figure or trope). He then compiled the earliest detailed defence
of the Spirit's divinity and Trinitarian status.

The 'Tropici' appear to have believed that the Spirit had to be a creature,
for otherwise He would be the Son's own brother or son and compromise
the Son's title as only-begotten.[53] In his first and most important *Letter on
the Holy Spirit*, Athanasius compares this teaching to that of the 'Arians',
who degraded the Son to the level of creation. Here as elsewhere he rejects
those who seek to understand the Godhead on human terms, and draws
on the same arguments that he had employed against the 'Arian' Son in the
Orationes contra Arianos. Humanity is created and sanctified through the
Spirit, who therefore cannot Himself require creation or sanctification. 'It
is in the Spirit that the Word glorifies creation and presents it to the Father
by divinizing it and granting it adoption. But the one who binds creation

---

[50] This diversity is well demonstrated by Ayres (2004b: 85–92).

[51] On these debates, see Hauschild (1967), Haykin (1994), and Ayres (2004b: 211–18).

[52] The manuscript transmission of the *Letters to Serapion on the Holy Spirit* is complex. Traditionally there are four letters, but the second and third form a single whole, and much of
the fourth appears to be an independent composition. There is a partial translation of the first
letter with introduction and notes in Anatolios (2004: 212–33).

[53] For an assessment of the theology of the 'Tropici', see Heron (1974).

to the Word could not be among the creatures and the one who bestows sonship upon creation could not be foreign to the Son' (I.25). The deification of humanity through the Incarnation, rooted in turn in the complete ontological separation of God and creation, underlies Athanasius' vision of the Spirit no less than of the Son.

A more difficult question was how to express the Trinity as three persons and yet one God. This conceptual and terminological problem repeatedly troubled Christians during the fourth century. In the first *Letter on the Holy Spirit* Athanasius initially denounced those who investigated such matters too closely:

If one were to enquire and ask again: How can it be that when the Spirit is in us, the Son is said to be in us, and when the Son is in us, the Father is said to be in us? Or how is it really a Trinity if the three are depicted as one? Or how is it that when one is in us, the Trinity is said to be in us? Let such an enquirer begin by separating the radiance from the light, or wisdom from the one who is wise, or else let him say himself how these things can be. But if this cannot be done, then how much more is it the presumption of insane people to enquire into these things with respect to God? (I.20)

Further on in the letter, he returned to the problem in greater depth. The Spirit 'is one and belongs [*idion*] to the one Word, and accordingly belongs [*idion*] to the one God and is of the same essence [*homoousion*]' (I.27). This is the only occasion on which Athanasius uses the Nicene term *homoousios* for the Spirit as well as the Son. To support his argument, which cannot be proven explicitly from Scripture, he appeals to 'the tradition and teaching and faith of the catholic Church from the beginning, that which the Lord has given, the Apostles preached, and the Fathers guarded' (I.28). According to that traditional faith:

The Trinity is holy and perfect, confessed as God in Father, Son, and Holy Spirit, having nothing foreign or extrinsic mingled with it, nor compounded of creator and created, but is wholly Creator and Maker. It is identical with itself and indivisible in nature, and its activity is one. For the Father does all things through the Word and in the Holy Spirit. Thus the oneness of the Holy Trinity is preserved and thus is the one God 'who is over all and through all and in all' [Ephesians 4:6] preached in the Church—'over all', as Father, who is beginning and fountain; 'through all', through the Son; and 'in all' in the Holy Spirit. It is Trinity not only in name and linguistic expression, but Trinity in reality and truth. Just as the Father is the 'One who is' [Exodus 3:14], so likewise is His Word the 'One who is, God over all' [Romans 9:5]. Nor is the Holy Spirit non-existent, but truly exists and subsists.

The catholic Church does not think of less than these three, lest it fall in with Sabellius and with the present-day Jews who follow Caiaphas, nor does it invent any

more than these three, lest it be dragged into the polytheism of the Greeks. Let
them learn that this is indeed the faith of the Church by considering how the Lord,
when He sent the Apostles, exhorted them to establish this as a foundation for the
Church, saying: 'Go and make disciples of all nations, baptizing them in the name
of the Father and the Son and the Holy Spirit' [Matthew 28:19]. (I.28)

Athanasius' primary concern throughout the first *Letter on the Holy Spirit*
is to maintain the unity of the Trinity in a single Godhead, one in nature
and one in activity. Yet he is no less determined to maintain the individual
identities of the Father, Son, and Spirit, a Trinity in truth not just in language. To focus exclusively on the unity is to fall into Sabellian Modalism,
which Arius had suspected in Alexander of Alexandria, while to exceed
the Trinity is pagan polytheism. The difficulty that Athanasius faced was
how to express his conception of the Trinity as three in one. He lacked the
clarity of language that would subsequently be achieved by the Cappadocian Fathers, particularly Basil of Caesarea in his *De Spiritu Sanctu*. Nevertheless, Athanasius exerted a powerful influence. As we will see when we
turn to Athanasius' later writings, he and the Cappadocians shared the
same fundamental theological values, and their differences lie in terminology more than in understanding.

One Athanasian argument in support of the full divinity of the Spirit
that would reappear in the Cappadocians was the appeal to the liturgical
custom of baptism. As an expression of Christian faith in the work of the
Spirit, the liturgy was ahead of theology in the mid-fourth century. Athanasius' invocation of Matthew 28:19 underlined the role of the Spirit in every
Christian's life. In doing so he also hammered home the pastoral significance of the issue at stake. Baptism for the forgiveness of sins, Athanasius
insisted, could not be achieved unless Father, Son, and Spirit were equally
divine. Thus he warned the 'Tropici': 'Where is your hope? For who will
join you to God if you do not have the Spirit of God Himself but one that
belongs to creation?' (I.29). Only the orthodox may hope to receive God's
promise of salvation.

The gift and the grace that is given are given in the Trinity: from the Father, through
the Son, in the Holy Spirit. Just as the grace that is given is from the Father and
through the Son, so there would be among us no communion in the gift except in
the Holy Spirit. For it is by our participation in the Spirit that we have the love of the
Father and the grace of the Son and the communion of the Spirit itself. (I.30)

In the fullness of time Athanasius' doctrine of the Holy Spirit, like his
interpretation of Nicaea, would acquire great authority in Christian thought.
Whatever slight deficiencies he may have had in language were more than

absolved by his insight into the mind of the Church. Through his emphasis on the role of the Spirit in salvation and baptism, Athanasius appealed not only to intellectuals debating the nature of the Trinity but to the faith of the ordinary Christian. Just as he had in the *Contra Gentes–De Incarnatione*, Athanasius captured the concerns of all those who looked to Christianity for support in this life and hope for the world to come. His triumph, however, lay in the future. In the late 350s his teachings were deeply controversial. The Spirit's full divinity remained disputed, particularly by those whom tradition would name *Pneumatomachoi* ('fighters against the Spirit').[54] Further councils contested the status of Nicaea. And new questions were emerging to challenge Athanasius and the fourth-century Church.

ATHANASIUS' LATER WRITINGS: RECONCILIATIONS AND NEW CONTROVERSIES

By the close of the 350s Athanasius had reason to feel increasing isolation. His followers in Egypt were persecuted while he was forced to remain in concealment. His supporters in the west had been driven into exile for their defence of him and the Nicene Creed. In the east the prevailing theology was still dominated by men whom he regarded as 'Arian' and who questioned that the Son was co-eternal and co-essential with the Father. In these difficult times Athanasius stayed true to his principles. The Son must share the full divinity of the Father for the Incarnation to achieve the promise of salvation that God had given to humanity. This emphasis remained constant not only in Athanasius' doctrinal treatises but in the ascetic and pastoral works discussed in the following chapters. Yet Athanasius' theological understanding was never static. In his later writings a momentous shift took place. Without compromising his teachings or his opposition to heresy, Athanasius recognized that those who held views other than his own did not therefore necessarily share the errors of 'Arianism'. It was a shift that played a crucial role in the reunification of the wider eastern Church and the eventual triumph of what became the Nicene orthodox faith.

The years on either side of Athanasius' flight into his third exile in 356 witnessed important developments in theology as well as ecclesiastical

---

[54] Athanasius coined this term against the 'Tropici' in his *Letter on the Holy Spirit* I.32. It would become a standard label for all those who challenged the Spirit's full divinity.

politics. Whatever consensus had existed among the eastern bishops broke
apart after Eusebius of Nicomedia's death in 341/2. Distrust of Nicaea
and *homoousios* was widespread, as was opposition to the teachings attributed to Marcellus of Ancyra. His disciple Photinus of Sirmium was condemned by a council held in that city in 351 led by Basil of Ancyra, himself
the replacement for the condemned Marcellus. The Council of 351 also
issued a creed that included anathemas against the materialistic use of *ousia*
language and anyone teaching that Father and Son were co-eternal Gods. A
further Council of Sirmium in 357 went further in condemning all use of
ousia language, a decree immortalized in later tradition as the 'Blasphemy
of Sirmium'.[55]

Yet the question of how to express the relationship between the Father
and Son remained. A wide spectrum of theological views emerged, many
of which could trace connections back to the diverse men whom Athanasius had branded as 'Eusebians'. There were a few, represented notably by
Aetius and Eunomius, who taught that the Father and Son were entirely
unlike (*anomoios*) according to *ousia*. Less extreme were those, perhaps
the majority of eastern Christians in the 350s, who preferred to describe
the Son simply as 'like' (*homoios*) to the Father and avoided the term *ousia*.
Basil of Ancyra came to favour the more precise expression 'like in essence'
(*homoios kat' ousian*). These three theologies are often known in scholarship
as Anomoian (or 'Neo-Arian'), Homoian, and Homoiousian, although to
what extent they represented specific doctrinal positions or parties is difficult to determine.[56]

Amid the shifting creeds and controversies, the emperor Constantius
struggled to bring about the unity of the Church. In 359 he summoned
the joint councils of Ariminum in the west and Seleucia in the east.
Under imperial pressure, both councils were encouraged to endorse the
so-called Dated Creed, which defined the Son as 'like the Father in all
respects' but declared that *ousia* language must be avoided as unscriptural
and causing disturbance. At Ariminum the western bishops preferred to
uphold the Nicene Creed. In the east a considerable bloc likewise resisted,
although their chosen symbol was the Dedication Creed of 341. Eventually, after much manœuvring, a modified version of the Dated Creed was

---

[55] For more detailed narratives of the complex events of these years, see Barnes (1993),
D. H. Williams (1995*b*), Ayres (2004*b*), and Beckwith (2008).
[56] See, among other studies, Kopecek (1979), Brennecke (1984, 1988), Löhr (1986, 1993),
and Vaggione (2000).

proclaimed for east and west by a small Council of Constantinople in early 360. The Son was 'like to the Father who generated Him'. The qualification 'in all respects' was dropped, but the ban on *ousia* language was repeated. According to the later words of Jerome, 'the whole world groaned, and was astonished to find itself Arian' (*Against the Luciferians* 19).

Athanasius began to compose his *De Synodis Arimini et Seleuciae* before the business of the twin councils of 359 had even been concluded. He wrote the bulk of the work after the Council of Seleucia had broken up (1 October), but before he had learned that Constantius had forced the western envoys of Ariminum to accept a new creed (10 October).[57] The westerners were praised for their defence of Nicaea. More significant is Athanasius' recognition of the eastern opposition at Seleucia as fundamentally orthodox. His argument here is a little disingenuous. Athanasius at no point admits that he had condemned Basil of Ancyra only three years before in his *Encyclical Letter to the Bishops of Egypt and Libya*.[58] Nor does he refer to the eastern support for the Dedication Creed, which even in 359 he still condemned as 'Arian'. Nevertheless, this is the first indication of Athanasius' desire for reconciliation, and an important step towards possible rapprochement.

The opening two-thirds of the *De Synodis*, as we saw previously, construct the councils of Ariminum and Seleucia as the continuation of a single heretical tradition that began with Arius himself. When he turns from polemic to reconciliation, Athanasius explicitly separates those he now accepts as orthodox from these 'Arians':

Those who deny the Council altogether, are sufficiently exposed by these brief remarks [against the 'Arian heresy']; those, however, who accept everything else that was defined at Nicaea, and doubt only about the *homoousion*, must not be treated as enemies. For indeed we do not attack them here as Ariomaniacs, nor as opponents of the Fathers, but we discuss the matter with them as brothers with brothers, who share our meaning and dispute only about the word. For, confessing that the Son is from the essence [*ousia*] of the Father, and not from other subsistence [*hypostasis*], and that He is not a creature nor a thing made, but His genuine and natural offspring, and that He is eternally with the Father as being His Word and Wisdom, they are not far from accepting even the term *homoousios*. (41).

---

[57] Athanasius added in a postscript that he heard of Ariminum's aftermath when he had finished writing (*De Synodis* 55). He also inserted chapters 30 and 31 into the work after Constantius' death in 361.

[58] This abrupt shift is not due to any sudden change in Basil's own theology or attitude towards *homoousios* in the period 356–9: see Steenson (1985).

Basil of Ancyra is immediately identified as one of those who may be recognized as orthodox, though Athanasius' summary of Basil's teachings is not entirely accurate.[59] Nor is his argument addressed directly to Basil or his eastern supporters. Athanasius' immediate purpose is to appeal to those who already uphold Nicaea to receive these eastern bishops as friends not enemies. In the final pages of the *De Synodis* he repeatedly insists on the superiority of the Nicene Creed and reaffirms once more that this is the traditional faith of the Church (42–54). He then concludes with an evocation of his hopes for Christian unity:

> Remaining on the foundation of the Apostles and holding fast the traditions of the Fathers, pray that now at length all strife and rivalry may cease, and the futile questions of the heretics may be condemned and all logomachy; and the guilty and murderous heresy of the Arians may disappear and the truth may shine again in the hearts of all, so that all everywhere may 'say the same thing' [1 Corinthians 1:10], and think the same thing, and that, no Arian contumelies remaining, it may be said and confessed in every church, 'One Lord, one faith, one baptism' [Ephesians 4:5], in Christ Jesus our Lord, through whom to the Father be the glory and the strength, unto ages of ages. Amen. (54)

A similar tone of defiant reconciliation pervades the first writings to which Athanasius contributed following his restoration in February 362 after Constantius' death in 361. Two documents are preserved from the council that met in Alexandria shortly after Athanasius' return. The *Epistula Catholica*, part of the council's encyclical letter, requires that bishops who had acknowledged the councils of 359–60 must subscribe to Nicaea and the full divinity of the Holy Spirit if they are to be accepted into communion. The second document is the *Tomus ad Antiochenos*, addressed to the divided Christians of Antioch. The failure of this appeal for Antiochene unity was discussed in the preceding chapter. However, the *Tomus* also holds significance for Athanasius' growing campaign for theological reconciliation.[60] The opening sections repeat the argument of the *Epistula Catholica* that those who renounce 'Arianism' must confess the Nicene Creed and anathematize those who degrade the Holy Spirit (3). The *Tomus* then turns to the major doctrinal question under dispute in Antioch: whether it is appropriate to speak of one *hypostasis* or three *hypostases* in the Trinity. The creed

---

[59] Basil's strongest theological statement, the letter that he wrote on behalf of the Council of Ancyra he summoned in 358, is quoted in Epiphanius, *Panarion* 73.2. See Lienhard (1985).

[60] See Tetz (1975), Pettersen (1990), and, more recently, Gemeinhardt (2006) and Karmann (2009).

attributed to the Western Council of Serdica in 343, which insisted upon one *hypostasis*, is dismissed as a draft that the bishops at Serdica rejected and so should not be read.[61] Each alternative is now examined more carefully:

As to those whom some were blaming for speaking of three *hypostases*, on the grounds that the term is unscriptural and therefore suspicious, we thought it right indeed to require nothing beyond the confession of Nicaea. But on account of the contention we made enquiry of them, whether they meant, like the Arian mad-men, *hypostases* foreign and strange, and alien in *ousia* from one another, and that each *hypostasis* was divided apart by itself, as is the case with creatures in general and in particular with those begotten of men, or like different substances, such as gold, silver, or brass; or whether, like other heretics, they meant three beginnings and three Gods, by speaking of three *hypostases*. They assured us in reply that they neither meant this nor had ever held it. But upon our asking them, 'what then do you mean by it, or why do you use such expressions?', they replied, because they believed in a Holy Trinity, not a Trinity in name only, but existing and subsisting in truth. (5)

Following this:

We made enquiry of those blamed by them for speaking of one *hypostasis*, whether they use the expression in the sense of Sabellius, to the negation of the Son and the Holy Spirit, or as though the Son were non-substantial or the Holy Person imper-sonal. But they in their turn assured us that they neither meant this nor had ever held it, but 'we use the word *hypostasis* thinking it the same thing to say *hypostasis* or *ousia*'; 'but we hold that there is one because the Son is of the *ousia* of the Father, and because of the identity of nature'. For we believe that there is one Godhead, and that it has one nature [*physis*], and not that there is one nature of the Father, from which that of the Son and of the Holy Spirit are distinct. (6)

Athanasius himself had always preferred the latter interpretation. He consistently used *hypostasis* as a synonym for *ousia*, as he did in the *De Synodis* 41 passage quoted earlier. By acknowledging that those who taught three *hypostases* could also represent the Nicene faith, the *Tomus ad Antiochenos* thus marks a significant development. Each group recognized the orthodoxy of the other, although it is claimed that 'all, by God's grace, and after the above explanations, agree together that the faith confessed by the fathers at Nicaea is better than the said phrases, and that for the future they would prefer to be content to use its language' (6). Slightly later in the

---

[61] This claim is more than a little suspect. The 'draft' creed circulated in both east and west, and is quoted in Theodoret, II.8.

Tomus, this theme of language is raised again. In the interests of peace, only those who refuse to explain their words should be condemned. All others should be warned 'not to enquire further into each other's opinions, nor to fight about words to no useful purpose, nor to go on contending with the above phrases, but to agree in the mind of piety' (8). It is shared belief that is important rather than the precise terminology used.

Did Athanasius' arguments in favour of doctrinal reconciliation have any practical effect? This is difficult to assess. We cannot prove that the *De Synodis* appeal had any immediate impact, and unity in Antioch remained elusive. Despite the confidence of the *Tomus*, the language of the original Nicene Creed would prove insufficient to define the emerging orthodox faith. The divinity of the Holy Spirit required stronger expression within the Trinity than the single verse at Nicaea, which appeared to confirm the Spirit's subordination to the Father and Son. On an even more fundamental level, no adequate language existed to express the nature of the Trinity itself as both three persons and one God. There were still those who feared that words like *homoousios* preserved the unity of the Godhead only at the cost of undermining the individual identities of Father, Son, and Spirit. The terms *hypostasis* and *ousia* would have to be separated and reinterpreted to mean respectively identity and unity before a formula could be found to venerate the Trinity as three in one: three *hypostases* in one *ousia*.

For the solution to these challenges we must turn not to Athanasius but to the Cappadocian Fathers.[62] Their teachings influenced all subsequent interpretations of the revised Nicene Creed adopted by the Council of Constantinople in 381 and used in modern churches today. The Cappadocian understanding of the Trinity as three *hypostases* in one *ousia* was not a formula that Athanasius ever used or would have wished to use. And yet, as the *Tomus ad Antiochenos* concluded, agreement in faith is more important than agreement in language. In faith Athanasius and the Cappadocians came very close, and Athanasius' efforts to resolve the divisions of the early 360s helped to pave the way for the Cappadocian achievement.

There was another theological issue debated in the *Tomus* that raised rather similar questions and also became the focus of major debate in the eastern Church in the 360s and 370s. The different Antiochene groups were examined on their understanding of the Incarnation:

---

[62] On the development of what has become known as 'Neo-Nicene' theology, see Vaggione (2000) and Ayres (2004b).

They confessed that the Saviour had not a body without a soul, nor without sense or intelligence; for it was not possible, when the Lord had become man for us, that His body should be without intelligence, nor was the salvation effected in the Word Himself a salvation of body only, but of soul also. And being Son of God in truth, He became also Son of Man. (7)

The place of Jesus' human soul had never previously been a focus of attention in Athanasius' doctrine of the Incarnation or his refutation of 'Arianism'. It is probable that Arius, like a number of his contemporaries, did omit Christ's soul in his theology. But there is little sign that he or Athanasius considered this to be a matter of any great significance.[63] In the second half of the fourth century, the soul of Christ gained a new importance. Apollinaris of Laodicea was a strong supporter of Nicaea and a one-time associate of Athanasius. Seeking a means to express the unity of the divine Christ with the human Jesus, Apollinaris proposed that in the Incarnation the Logos took the place of the soul. His concern for the status of the divinity and the humanity in the Incarnation prefigured the great Christological controversies that divided the Church in the fifth century. But Apollinaris' teachings compromised too far the full humanity of Jesus, and he was condemned at the Council of Constantinople in 381.

Athanasius' relationship with Apollinaris is complex.[64] The *Tomus ad Antiochenos* is the first work in which Athanasius addresses the question of Christ's soul directly, and the context and framing of the argument suggest that the chief concern is with 'Arianism' not the teachings of Apollinaris.[65] There are works against Apollinaris attributed to Athanasius, but they are generally believed to be pseudonymous.[66] Refutation of Apollinaris was left once more to the Cappadocian Fathers, whose Christological language developed beyond that which Athanasius and Apollinaris shared. Nevertheless, here again the beliefs that the Cappadocians held in common with Athanasius outweigh the differences of expression, and Athanasius fully shared their insistence that the Incarnation required that the Son be united with a complete human being of body and soul.

These new controversies over Trinitarian terminology and the soul of Christ dominated doctrinal debate in the 360s and 370s. It has on occasion

[63] The conclusion of a number of modern scholars is that Athanasius neither emphasizes nor denies Christ's soul: Wiles (1965), Louth (1985), and Anatolios (1998: 77–8).
[64] Lienhard (2006).
[65] Pettersen (1990: 193–8), although I would question his belief that Christ's '*soma apsychon*' was an established 'Arian' doctrine.
[66] For a rare contrary view, see Dragas (2005: 133–50).

been argued that Athanasius, in the final stage of his life, increasingly lost touch with the questions dividing the contemporary eastern Church. As the Cappadocians advanced Greek theological understanding, it is said, Athanasius remained rooted in earlier debates and anti-'Arian' polemic. There is a partial degree of truth to such claims. Athanasius was now an old man, entering the seventh decade of an extremely active life. His writings from these last years naturally draw on previous arguments and long-held beliefs. They also demonstrate that Athanasius continued to adapt those arguments as contexts and audiences changed, reformulating his principles for the benefit of another generation of Christians.

Shortly after the Council of Alexandria that despatched the *Tomus ad Antiochenos*, Athanasius was sent into exile by the pagan emperor Julian 'the Apostate'. Julian's death in 363 allowed his return and brought to the throne the Christian Jovian, whom Athanasius hastened to meet. His *Letter to Jovian* (*Letter* LVI) advised the emperor to follow the Nicene faith and condemn the 'Arians', who reduce the Son to a mutable creature and blaspheme the Spirit as created in turn by the Son. Nicaea represented the orthodox truth, and, with the exception of a few heretics, 'the whole world holds the apostolic faith' (LVI.2). This is more than a slight exaggeration, and there is little in the anti-'Arian' rhetoric of real relevance to the issues that divided the eastern Church in the late 350s and early 360s. But Athanasius achieved his primary aim to rally Jovian in support of the Nicene Creed. And the closing words of the *Letter* reinterpret Nicaea in the light of current debate:

They [the Nicene fathers] have not merely said that the Son is like the Father, lest He should be believed merely like God, instead of very God from God; but they wrote *homoousios*, which was peculiar to a genuine and true Son, truly and naturally from the Father. Nor yet did they make the Holy Spirit alien from the Father and the Son, but rather glorified Him together with the Father and the Son, in the one faith of the Holy Triad, because there is in the Holy Triad also one Godhead. (LVI.4)

Much the same approach is adopted in the *Epistula ad Afros*, despatched to the west by Athanasius in 367. Here he upholds the supremacy of the Council of Nicaea over that of Ariminum championed by western 'Homoian' bishops like Auxentius of Milan. The content is lifted almost verbatim from the *De Decretis* and *De Synodis*, with little concession to developments during the 360s. Athanasius also reverts to his older usage of *hypostasis* and *ousia* as synonyms (4), ignoring those who speak of multiple *hypostases*. His argument would not have impressed contemporary eastern opinion, but was appropriate when addressed to a western audience where the two controversial terms were both traditionally translated by the Latin *substantia*.

Perhaps the most significant of the later theological writings of Athanasius are two letters addressed to bishops who had appealed to him for doctrinal advice. The first was written to the Egyptian Adelphius of Onuphis in *c*.370. The second in *c*.372 was a response to an appeal from Epictetus of Corinth. In each case Athanasius was asked for his judgement on controversial interpretations of the Incarnation. Athanasius' condemnation of the offending interpretations as 'Arian' reflects his automatic assumptions and his now very familiar polemical rhetoric. But the understanding of the humanity and divinity of Christ that Athanasius then presents draws upon principles that he had held since the *Contra Gentes–De Incarnatione* while at the same time prefiguring the Christological debates of the following century.

The *Letter to Adelphius* opens with a refutation of those who deny that the true Word became human or who assert that to worship the Incarnate Son is to worship His created body.[67] Athanasius insists that the orthodox do not worship a creature, but nor do they decline worship of the Word because of His created body:

For the flesh did not detract from the glory of the Word. Far from it! Rather, it is the flesh which was glorified by the Word. Nor was the Son's divinity diminished because He who is in the form of God received the form of a servant. Rather, He became the liberator of all flesh and of all creation. And if God sent His Son born of a woman, this is not a deed that brings us shame but glory and great grace. He became a human being that we might be divinized in Him; He came to be in a woman and was begotten of a virgin in order to transport our errant race into Himself and in order that from then on we may become a holy race and 'partakers of the divine nature' [2 Peter 1:4]. (4)

Athanasius' conception of human salvation, deified through the grace of the Incarnation, remained as strong in the *Letter to Adelphius* as in his earliest works. Where his emphasis had changed, if only by degree, was in a greater insistence upon the unity of the divinity and humanity in Christ. 'Those who do not want to worship the Word who has become flesh show no gratitude for His humanization. And those who separate the Word from the flesh negate the belief that there is one redemption from sin and one destruction of death' (5). The divinity and humanity cannot be separated,

---

[67] Translation, introduction, and notes in Anatolios (2004: 234–42).

and yet retain their independent identities. This was a theme to which Athanasius returned in greater depth in his *Letter to Epictetus* in *c.372*.

Epictetus had sent to Athanasius memoranda containing the questions then under debate in the Corinthian church. These questions raised issues that would recur in the Christological debates of the next century. Is the body of the Incarnate Christ *homoousios* with the Word? Should we count that body within the Trinity and so make a Tetrad? Did the Word change in His nature through the Incarnation? Did He experience the suffering of Christ in His divinity? Interestingly, one question that was not included in this catalogue is whether the Word took the place of the human soul in the Incarnate Christ. The argument of Apollinaris is not discussed in the *Letter to Epictetus*, although it is stated that salvation extends to the whole human being, body and soul (7).

There was little difficulty in disposing of some of these questions. As Nicaea taught, Athanasius declares, the Word is *homoousios* with the Father but not with His body, which is by nature from Mary. The Christian faith teaches a Trinity not a Tetrad, and the divine Word cannot change in His nature or suffer directly. The real issue at stake, however, could not be resolved so easily. What is the relationship between the divinity and humanity of the Incarnate Christ? How can we express that relationship without compromising the distinct human and divine natures of the Incarnation or the single identity of Christ?

Athanasius first emphasizes that Jesus' birth was real, against the docetic view that the Word only appeared to take on flesh, and that the events of his human life were real. The humanity grew, advanced, and endured. But 'in the body which was circumcised, and carried, and ate and drank, and was weary, and was nailed on the tree and suffered, there was the impassible and incorporeal Word of God' (5). At some level, the experiences of Jesus' body were also experienced by the Word, for the sake of our salvation:

What the human body of the Word suffered, this the Word, dwelling in the body, ascribed to Himself, in order that we might be enabled to be partakers of the God-head of the Word. And truly it is strange that He it was who suffered and yet suffered not. Suffered, because His own body suffered, and He was in it, which thus suffered; suffered not, because the Word, being by nature God, is impassible. (6)

And through the Word, the body in turn was deified:

The Son, being God and Lord of glory, was in the body which was ingloriously nailed and dishonoured; but the body, while it suffered, being pierced on the tree, and water and blood flowed from its side, yet because it was a temple of the Word was filled full of the Godhead. (10)

Human language and knowledge are insufficient to grasp the mysteries of the divine. Athanasius knew this as well as anyone. The *Letter to Epictetus* reaffirms his devout belief in the full humanity and full divinity of the Incarnate Christ. His belief in the unity of Christ in one person was no less sincere but more difficult to express. The humanity was deified by the divinity, and the Word was in the body when the body suffered. The old charge that Athanasius taught a 'spacesuit Christology' can, therefore, again be dismissed, for the Word is not separated from the experiences of the body. However, Athanasius still preferred to hold *hypostasis* and *ousia* as synonyms. He did not have the benefit of the Cappadocian redefinition of *hypostasis*, which in turn made possible the understanding of the Incarnation at the Council of Chalcedon in 451 as the hypostatic union of two natures in one person. Nor was he as adept as his great successor Cyril of Alexandria in his attribution of the properties of each of Christ's two natures to the other through the communication of idioms. Athanasius' fundamental vision of the Incarnation differs little if at all from that of Cyril and later orthodoxy, and the *Letter to Epictetus* was widely cited in the fifth-century debates. Yet those who did so frequently edited the letter to accord better with their contemporary usage.[68]

The theological writings of Athanasius have continued to be read down the long years to our own time. His influence on the history of Christian thought has been immense. In the formative fourth-century age of controversy and definition, the development of doctrine could have taken many different paths. Athanasius preserved his understanding of the fundamental principles of the faith across a lifetime in which he endured persecution and struggled against rival teachings that he believed undermined the very foundations of the Christian religion. From the *Contra Gentes–De Incarnatione* at the beginning to the *Letter to Epictetus* at the end, at the heart of his teachings stood the Incarnation of a true and divine Son and Word who took on a body so that humanity might be deified. As we will see in the next two chapters, this conviction of salvation through divine grace underlies equally Athanasius' devotion to asceticism and the pastoral guidance that he offered to those who followed him. His Trinitarian and Christological doctrines would require further expression by subsequent generations. But his status as a Father of orthodoxy was recognized by all in the controversies to come, and Athanasius' theology still strikes a chord for every Christian believer in the present day.

---

[68] On the complex later history of the *Letter to Epictetus*, see Ch. 6.

4

Ascetic

The fourth century was a formative age for Christianity and the Roman Empire in many different ways. Constantine's conversion and the corresponding expansion in the scale and prestige of the Church accelerated the formalization of Christian organization and doctrine. Athanasius, as we have already seen, played a crucial role in that process. The dramatic rise of the ascetic movement must be set within the same context, and Athanasius was once again a central figure. Asceticism had a long history in antiquity before Christianity, and had influenced the early Christians from the very beginnings of the new religion. But only in the fourth century did the lives of individual ascetics become the subject of widespread attention and organized monasticism emerge. Athanasius' writings are a key source for the development of asceticism, while he was also a man of deep personal ascetic convictions who encouraged others to adopt those values.[1]

Two issues need to be addressed immediately when we assess Athanasius and his relationship with the ascetic movement. The first concerns Athanasius' ascetic writings. Considerable doubt surrounds the authorship of a number of ascetic texts transmitted to us under Athanasius' name. The most famous such work, the *Life of Antony*, is still widely accepted as Athanasian, although this has been challenged.[2] Several of his letters to monks have likewise been preserved, perhaps most notably the *Letter to Amoun*, which discusses bodily emissions and the value of marriage and celibacy, and the *Letter to Dracontius* asking that monk to accept appointment to the episcopate.[3] These letters are preserved in Athanasius' original Greek, but many of his ascetic writings are transmitted through Coptic, Syriac, and Armenian.[4] This includes several treatises on virginity and fragments

---

[1] For different perspectives on the importance of asceticism within Athanasius' life and thought, see Brakke (1995), Kannengiesser (1998), and Ng (2001). For general introductions to the rise of Christian asceticism and monasticism in Late Antiquity, see, among many others, Chitty (1966), Brown (1988), Elm (1994), Shaw (1998), Clark (1999), Dunn (2000), and the articles collected in Wimbush and Valantasis (1998).

[2] See Ch. 1, n. 26.

[3] The Greek letters are translated with a short introduction by Barnard (1994).

[4] There is a survey of these writings and their relative authenticity in Brakke (1994a).

of various other works, not all of which are authentic. The existence of pseudonymous works attests to the status attached to Athanasius' name by later generations of ascetics, but does complicate analysis. Yet it is important that we look beyond the *Life of Antony* and embrace the broader ascetic content of the Athanasian corpus.

The second issue that must be raised is the close interrelationship between Athanasius' commitment to asceticism and his wider life and writings. Athanasius' undoubted ascetic principles and his contribution to the ascetic movement cannot be studied in isolation. The theological doctrines that he taught had a direct impact on how he understood the ascetic life. So too did the fluctuations of his episcopal standing, for his following among the ascetics of Egypt played an important part in maintaining his authority as bishop of Alexandria. This is not to suggest that Athanasius' promotion of asceticism should be interpreted purely as a form of ecclesiastical politics. But equally we cannot deny that Athanasius actively sought ascetic support for his position, particularly through the ordination of monk-bishops and the composition of the *Life of Antony*. Here, as throughout, the ecclesiastical, theological, and ascetic elements of Athanasius' career and thought combine.

THE GOLDEN AGE OF EGYPTIAN ASCETICISM

In our generation in Egypt I see three chapter-heads given increase by God for profit of all who understand—the bishop Athanasius, Christ's champion for the Faith even unto death; and the holy Abba Antony, perfect pattern of the anchoretic life; and this Community, which is the type for all who desire to gather souls according to God, to take care of them until they be made perfect. (Pachomius, quoted in the *Vita Prima Pachomii* 136)

The practice of *askesis*, the life of austerity and self-discipline in pursuit of spiritual growth, traces its roots back to the dawn of antiquity. Our historical understanding of asceticism has inevitably been influenced by the Christian lens that dominates so many of our sources, but Christian ascetic ideals emerged against a background of Graeco-Roman philosophy and Jewish teachings.[5] Those ideals are already visible in the Gospel accounts of John the Baptist and Jesus, and remained prominent across the early

[5] For an introduction to pagan and Jewish asceticism, see respectively Francis (1995) and Diamond (2004), and also the articles collected in Wimbush (1990) and in Wimbush and Valantasis (1998).

Christian centuries. The ascetic movement of the fourth century was therefore a continuation rather than a break from previous tradition. Nevertheless, Athanasius' lifetime witnessed a dramatic transformation in the status and influence of asceticism within Christianity. As persecution of the Church faded into memory, the ascetic lifestyle provided a new expression of faith and dedication to take the place of martyrdom.[6] At the same time, the growth of Christianity following Constantine's conversion led some men and women to seek a deeper religious experience through their ascetic commitment, whether as individual hermits or in communal monasteries. A new ascetic elite began to appear, to whom other Christians looked for guidance and inspiration.[7]

Christian asceticism and monasticism could take many different forms. The conventional classification of late-antique monasticism distinguishes two essential types, the eremitic monasticism of the solitary hermit, best exemplified by the Egyptian monk Antony (c.251–356), and collective cenobitic monasticism, originally associated in Egypt with Antony's younger contemporary Pachomius (292–346). There were other types of ascetic practices that flourished in Late Antiquity, and both eremitic and cenobitic monasticism varied significantly in different regions and periods.[8] It is important to emphasize this diversity here, as the following pages will naturally focus specifically on Egypt. Athanasius met Antony in person and wrote his biography, and, while he did not apparently meet Pachomius, he certainly had close associations with Pachomian monasticism.[9] An outline account of Antony and Pachomius and their respective contributions to the ascetic movement provides the setting within which to understand Athanasius' own ascetic values and the importance of asceticism to his episcopate and theology.

If tradition is to be believed, Antony of Egypt was born in c.251 and died in 356. For our knowledge we depend heavily on Athanasius' *Life*, written shortly after the hermit's death. The *Life* is by no means a straightforward narrative, as will be discussed further below, but it allows us to sketch the major events of Antony's career. We also possess a number of letters preserved

---

[6] Antony had sought martyrdom in the Great Persecution, but he was preserved by God, and his ascetic discipline took the place of the martyr's crown (*Life of Antony* 46–7).

[7] The modern literature on the late-antique holy man is vast. For an introduction, see in particular Brown (1971, 1995, 1998) and Cox Miller (1983).

[8] For a discussion of one such divergent tradition, see Caner (2002).

[9] Athanasius' sole reference to Pachomius by name occurs in his highly fragmentary first *Letter to Horsiesius*, written in early 363. His second *Letter to Horsiesius* in c.368 is a eulogy to Theodore, Pachomius' favourite disciple. These letters reflect Athanasius' respect for the Pachomian monastic network, and also suggest that his influence on the Pachomian communities increased after Pachomius' death: see further Goehring (1986).

in Coptic whose attribution to Antony is increasingly accepted as genuine.[10] Those letters provide valuable insight into Antony's personal ascetic ideals, although they do not entirely reconcile with the image of the hermit laid down in his *Life*.

Born into a moderately wealthy Christian family, Antony lost his parents when he was around the age of 20, leaving him to care for his home and his sister. Attending church a few months after their deaths, he heard the Gospel reading to which he would devote his life: 'If you wish to be perfect, go and sell everything you possess and give it to the poor and come, follow me and you will have treasure in heaven' (Matthew 19:21–2).

Leaving the church, Antony heeded the Saviour's call. He sold his property and gave the money to the poor, reserving just a little for his sister's needs. He then committed her to the care of faithful virgins, and sought the ascetic life. Antony was obviously not the first. There was a house of virgins in his village where his sister could live,[11] and when Antony embarked on his new lifestyle he immediately sought the guidance of a hermit who lived in the next village and had practised asceticism for many decades. Antony also sought out other teachers, just as he would become a teacher in his turn. At that time, 'no monk at all knew of the distant desert; but all who wished to give heed to themselves practiced the discipline in solitude near their own village' (*Life of Antony* 3). Through Antony, this was going to change.[12]

Initially, Antony too remained on the fringes of civilization. He dedicated himself to prayer while keeping his hands busy with work, and struggled with the temptations of the Devil. This period culminated in Antony living in the tombs set some distance from the village, where with God's aid he overcame the Devil's lures and assaults. Finally, after some fifteen years, Antony elected to travel deeper into the wilderness. Crossing the Nile, he came to an abandoned fortress and there remained in solitude, visited only by acquaintances who brought him bread twice a year and lowered the loaves to him as he refused to allow them to enter. He remained within the fortress for two decades, emerging at last in *c*.305, when increasing numbers of those who wished to become his disciples began to break their way inside.

---

[10] Seven letters in Coptic are attributed to Antony by Jerome, *De Viris Illustribus* 88. The standard work on the letters is Rubenson (1995), although his arguments in favour of their authenticity remain under debate: for a recent discussion, see Bumazhnov (2007).

[11] Antony later learnt that his sister had preserved her life of virginity and become a guide for other virgins (*Life of Antony* 54).

[12] On the importance of geography in the *Life* and the relationship between literary construction and reality, see Wipszycka (2004).

These were the years of the Great Persecution, with the conversion of Constantine still in the future. But Antony was already spreading the ascetic call. Although he did not face martyrdom himself, he ministered to the confessors, before withdrawing back into solitude after the persecution ceased. Unable to avoid the throngs who sought him out, in *c*.313 Antony decided to pass on into the upper Thebaid, where he was less well known. As he looked for a boat to transport him along the river, he heard a heavenly voice calling him to the inner desert. In the company of a Saracen caravan, he set out for three days and nights until he came to the mountain where he settled until his death some forty years later. Aside from brief visits to other hermits, Antony made only one major journey, to Alexandria in 338 to denounce the 'Arians'. He continued to teach and follow his chosen way of life, and died in 356 at a reported age of over 100.[13]

Not least through the efforts of Athanasius, Antony would become the model for anchoretic or eremitic monasticism in Egypt and beyond. He lived a solitary life, although disciples and petitioners ensured that he was rarely truly alone. Pachomius, the second founding figure in this golden age, espoused a more communal conception of asceticism.[14] Our sources for Pachomius' life and teachings pose similar problems to those for Antony. There are a number of *Lives* of Pachomius that survive in Coptic, Greek, and Arabic, although their manuscript transmission is highly complex. Some of these *Lives*, notably the *Vita Prima Pachomii*, which is the earliest Greek *Life*, were written some decades after Pachomius' death and were influenced in part by Athanasius' *Life of Antony*. But the *Lives* also draw on oral material from those who had known Pachomius, probably originally preserved in Coptic. We further possess the *Rules* of Pachomius translated into Latin by Jerome in 404, although these *Rules* appear to reflect the Pachomian tradition as it existed a generation after Pachomius rather than the monastic organization that Pachomius personally laid down.

Born a generation after Antony, Pachomius was a pagan who around the age of 20 was conscripted into the army during the civil war between Licinius and Maximin Daia in 312 / 13. Impressed by the charity of Christians who brought the recruits food and drink, he prayed that he would serve God if God would release him from his plight. Maximin's defeat freed

---

[13] The monastery founded on Antony's mountain, which already existed by the time of Athanasius' death, is brought to life in Bolman (2002).

[14] A thorough introduction to Pachomius and Pachomian Monasticism is provided by Rousseau (1999); see also Brakke (1995: 111–29), Goehring (1986, 1996), and Harmless (2004: 115–50).

Pachomius from the military, and he kept his promise, receiving baptism in the village of Chenoboscia (Coptic Šeneset) and committing himself to his new faith.

Pachomius served within the local Christian community, but was swiftly attracted to an ascetic lifestyle. Like Antony, he looked to a local hermit for guidance during the early years of his ascetic career, the anchorite Palamon, and like Antony was aided by a divine voice in finding his true calling. Unlike Antony, Pachomius' call was to found a collective monastery, which he did at the deserted village of Tabennesi in perhaps *c.320*. As he attracted more followers, Pachomius evolved a communal structure based on mutual support. Over time regulations were developed to cover food, clothing, and sleeping patterns, and an organized monastery began to appear.

Exactly how great a break from previous practices Pachomius' first community actually was is difficult to determine. Gatherings of ascetics were not unknown at this time, and Pachomius visited or entertained members of other groups. What does appear to be different is that Pachomius and his disciples founded a series of monasteries, which remained united with each other. This is not to imply that all the first Pachomian communities shared a uniform organization, for what would be preserved as the *Rules* of Pachomius were not fully refined until after his death. Nevertheless, by *c.330* Pachomius had founded a further monastery not far from Tabennesi at Phbow, which became his headquarters in *c.337*, and other foundations followed, including a women's convent. Existing communities could likewise apply to join the Pachomian network. The scale of that network cannot be precisely determined from the existing evidence, but Tabennesi and Phbow may each have supported 1,000 monks or more, and by the end of the fourth century the Pachomian communities have been estimated at some 7,000 members.[15]

When Pachomius died in May 346, his movement had spread through much of the Thebaid, following the Nile north to Panopolis and south past Thebes to Latopolis. Athanasius was evidently aware of the importance of Pachomian monasticism upon his election as bishop in 328. One of his first actions was to set out on a tour of the Thebaid in 329–30, during which, according to later tradition, Pachomius watched him from among the crowds of monks.[16] There are claims that Athanasius even considered ordaining Pachomius but the latter fled into hiding.[17] Athanasius would

---

[15] For the evidence, see Rousseau (1999: 74–5).

[16] *Vita Prima Pachomii* 30. This is Athanasius' journey recorded in *Festal Index* 2.

[17] Bohairic *Life of Pachomius* 28.

eventually succeed in drawing a number of Pachomian monks into the episcopate as part of his efforts to integrate the ascetics more closely into the Egyptian Church.

Antony and Pachomius were by no means the only ascetics in early fourth-century Egypt.[18] There were hermits living outside villages and gatherings of male and female virgins in Alexandria and other urban centres. All would have a part to play in Athanasius' episcopate. Yet the three 'chapter-heads' of their age, as Pachomius is said to have described them, represent forces fundamental to shaping Egyptian Christianity. Antony became the ideal for the solitary holy man, offering inspiration and spiritual support to those who turned to him, including Athanasius. The Pachomian foundations fulfilled a different need among those who sought a communal monastic lifestyle and aided Athanasius with practical organization and material resources, particularly during his third exile in the desert. Across his episcopate Athanasius maintained a close association with the thriving ascetic movement. This in turn was made possible by the powerful influence that ascetic ideals exerted on Athanasius' own life and thought.

ATHANASIAN ASCETICISM

According to the Coptic tradition preserved in the *History of the Patriarchs*, Athanasius was drawn to the ascetic life even as a youth before his baptism.[19] We may not accept the historical accuracy of this later tradition, but it is beyond question that Athanasius was powerfully influenced by the ascetic movement from an early stage. His conception of asceticism was rooted in his theology. The deification of humanity achieved through the Incarnation enabled living men and women to draw closer to the divine through their ascetic discipline. Athanasius never ceased to emphasize that chastity, fasting, and other ascetic practices, while important, were not an end in themselves but a means towards spiritual growth. Moreover, ascetic virtues were not the preserve of a special elite, but could be pursued in different measure by all Christians in town, country, and desert alike. In the

---

[18] This diversity, which I cannot attempt to do justice to here, has been rightly emphasized in a number of articles by Wipszycka (1996) and Goehring (1999a, 2007).

[19] See the quotation at the head of Ch. 1, and the discussion of the *History of the Patriarchs* in Ch. 6.

following pages these cardinal themes will be traced through Athanasius' wide-ranging ascetic writings. The next chapter will consider his applica-tion of his ascetic arguments in the pastoral context of the *Festal Letters*.

Athanasius' first *Letter to Virgins*, a work that survives only in Coptic, has been provisionally dated to 337–9 between his first and second exiles.[20] It is an appropriate work with which to begin an assessment of the ascetic programme of Athanasius, who placed great weight on the ideal of female virginity.[21] The extant text of the partially fragmentary letter opens with a comparison of virginity to marriage (2–3). The state of marriage is natural to humanity and governed by God's law. But virgins transcend the law and come closer to the divine. 'Virginity, having surpassed human nature and imitating the angels, hastens and endeavours to cleave to the Lord' (3). Athanasius then launches into a polemical attack on the pagans who falsely call some of their women virgins just as they falsely call their idols gods (4–6). This paves the way for the celebration of Mary as the true virgin. She preserved her virginity after Christ's birth and had no other children in order that she should remain the pattern for later virgins (9–11). The vision of Mary's lifestyle that Athanasius presents (12–17) owes more to his ideals than to scriptural evidence, and encapsulates the values and behaviour that he wished contemporary Egyptian virgins to follow:

Mary was a holy virgin, having the disposition of her soul balanced and doubly increasing. For she desired good works, doing what is proper, having true thoughts in faith and purity. And she did not desire to be seen by people; rather, she prayed that God would be her judge. Nor did she have an eagerness to leave her house, nor was she at all acquainted with the streets; rather, she remained in her house being calm, imitating the fly in honey. She virtuously spent the excess of her manual labour on the poor. And she did not acquire eagerness to look out the window, rather to look at the Scriptures. And she would pray to God privately, taking care about these two things: that she not let evil thoughts dwell in her heart, and also that she not acquire curiosity or learn hardness of heart. (13)

The virgin must be modest and humble, pursuing good works while avoid-ing the dangers of pride and envy and shunning the temptations of worldly life. Mary likewise showed the same balance with regard to her bodily needs:

The desire of the belly did not overcome her, only up to the measure of the body's necessity. For she ate and drank, not luxuriously, but so that she might not neglect

---

[20] Translation in Brakke (1995: 274–91).
[21] Elm (1994: 331–72); Brakke (1995: 17–79). On virginity in late-antique Christianity, see, in addition to these works and the general books cited in n. 1, Cloke (1995) and Cooper (1996).

her body and it die contrary to its time. Moreover, she did not sleep beyond measure, but so that the body alone might rest, and afterwards she would be awake for
her work and the Scriptures. (14)

Athanasius does not wish virgins to follow the extreme asceticism of the
desert hermits. Instead, his advice is more practical, urging them to maintain their strength and devote themselves to working with their hands and
scriptural study. The female ascetics to whom he writes live within towns,
although they should avoid going out in public except to attend church.
Mary lived with her parents and walked to the temple with them. Obedience is no less a virtue for virgins than chastity and humility, and Mary
again represents the ideal: 'First she would pray to God, and afterwards she
would submit to her parents. But as for fighting with her father or mother,
she considered it an abomination to God. And she had this desire before
her eyes: to submit to her parents more than like a slave' (16).

Finally, the virgin Mary obviously had no association with male slaves or
men of any other social class. This, Athanasius explains, is why she reacted
with fear when she was hailed by the archangel Gabriel, for she was unfa-
miliar with male voices. But she kept her courage and proved worthy of
God's favour. 'This is the image of virginity, for holy Mary was like this.
Let her who wishes to be a virgin look to her, for on account of things like
this the Word chose her so that He might receive this flesh through her and
become human for our sake' (17).

The core virtues that Athanasius requires from those who pursue the life
of virginity are traditional virtues of the Christian religion. The ideal that
he presents in the first *Letter to Virgins* closely parallels the models found
elsewhere in fourth-century asceticism, and Athanasius' arguments influenced a number of later writers.[22] Still, there are certain elements that are
characteristic of Athanasius and reflect his specific concerns. The practical
guidance and desire to discourage extreme displays of asceticism is one
feature of Athanasius' advice to virgins.[23] Another is the emphasis that a
virgin follows her path through her own free will, aided by divine grace.
Virginity is not required by God's law, and virgins must heed the pattern
laid down by Mary and devote themselves fully if they are to remain on
their chosen road.[24]

[22] For two western examples, see Ambrose of Milan and Jerome in Ch. 6.
[23] One of the miracles achieved by Antony was to heal a virgin whose suffering had been
caused by her extreme discipline (*Life of Antony* 61).
[24] In this regard Athanasius held virgins and martyrs in the same respect (*De Incarnatione*
48.2–3), and this attitude is also attributed to Antony (*Life of Antony* 79).

Perhaps most importantly, Athanasius' conception of the ascetic life in the first *Letter to Virgins* is inseparably intertwined with his theology of the Incarnation. According to Athanasius, ascetic chastity did exist among the Jews before Christ, but this was very rare and limited to prophets such as Elijah and Elisha, Jeremiah, and John the Baptist. This changed with the Incarnation. 'When the Lord came into the world, having taken flesh from a virgin and become human, at that time what used to be difficult became easy for people, and what was impossible became possible' (8). Through Christ and His sacrifice, those who uphold virginity may draw closer to God. Athanasius returns to this theme at length towards the end of the letter. He reports that a group of virgins once approached his predecessor Alexander for guidance (36). Alexander then addressed them regarding Christ (37–45), and Athanasius presents his theological argument through Alexander's voice.

Virgins who wish to draw near to Christ, Alexander declares, must learn who Christ is. He is the Word, Wisdom, Power, and Image of the Father, and He and the Father are one. He took flesh through the virgin Mary so that He might destroy sin, and although He became human He was not weakened as God. For the virgin He is the bridegroom. 'And if it used to be impossible for a human being to join with God, He has made it possible by having become human' (40). The understanding of salvation through deification that runs throughout Athanasius' theology is here restated, in Alexander's words, in the specific context of asceticism.[25] And, just as Athanasius believed that the 'Arian' view of the Son denied the possibility of salvation, so Alexander goes on to warn the virgins to avoid those who insult their bridegroom, a polemic to which I will return later in this chapter.

The final characteristically Athanasian argument of the first *Letter to Virgins* is pastoral more than doctrinal, and addresses one of the major tensions that emerged with asceticism among Christian congregations. Athanasius insists repeatedly that, while virginity is superior to marriage, on no account should marriage itself be degraded. This argument appears at the beginning of the extant text, when it is stated that virginity transcends the law but marriage is lawful and appropriate to human nature (2). Following his invocation of Mary as the pattern for virginity, Athanasius repeats this point. Virginity was not commanded by the law, 'so that we would not think that marriage, which is in accordance with nature, were contrary to the law or acting as a constraint, hindering people from virginity, and so

---

[25] The doctrine that it was through the Incarnation that virginity became fully attainable for all humanity is also maintained in *De Incarnatione* 51.1 and *Apologia ad Constantium* 33.

that the person who was not a virgin would not be condemned as having not performed a commandment' (18). As Paul wrote (1 Corinthians 7:38), marriage is good even if virginity is better (19).

All the ascetic, theological, and pastoral themes that emerge from reading the first *Letter to Virgins* appear in different forms across Athanasius' other ascetic writings. The second *Letter to Virgins*, written after 346 and possibly near the end of his episcopate, survived in a Syriac manuscript.[26] It is framed as a letter to a group of virgins who have gone on pilgrimage to Jerusalem, consoling them on having to leave the holy places. The virtues of humility, modesty, and obedience are reaffirmed, with emphasis once more that ascetic practices must be combined with pious devotion. 'It is not holiness of the body alone that is required, but also that of the spirit' (4). A virgin must similarly beware the vices of worldly life, and be careful to walk and dress soberly and to eat and bathe only enough for health. One should pray and not talk in church (10), and public baths are a particular danger and may lead others into corruption, as Bathsheba led David (17). These again are standard ascetic ideas but adapted to Athanasius' purposes. He criticizes virgins who live in 'spiritual marriage' together with celibate men as devaluing their devotion.[27] And he repeats his insistence that virgins are not compelled by law or threat, but take their lifestyle upon themselves. 'By your own will you became a virgin: you presented a willing sacrifice' (23).

A third Athanasian work, known simply as *On Virginity*, exists in both Syriac and Armenian versions.[28] The work cannot be precisely dated, but the arguments presented are very familiar. Virgins must be obedient to the Lord, even more than women of the world must obey their husbands. Orthodoxy and purity of thought are as important as bodily purity, and vigilance is required to avoid falling into shame and error. Do not envy or plot against others, and 'watch, so that you who are continent never condemn those who are chaste in marriage and so bring sin upon yourself' (10). The true virgin whose life and faith are worthy of her status will be rewarded in heaven:

---

[26] Translation in Brakke (1995: 292–302). On this letter, see also Frank (2000: 108–11).

[27] As Brakke (1995: 20–9) has observed, such 'spiritual marriages' were not a concern in Athanasius' first *Letter to Virgins*, and may reveal a custom that has increased in the years between the two letters.

[28] Translation in Brakke (1995: 303–9). Note that this authentic work must be distinguished from the Pseudo-Athanasian text, also entitled *On Virginity*, which survived only in Syriac and is edited in Brakke (2002).

Then you will dwell with Christ. Then you will see your bridegroom, your brother, your father, your lord, your king, your Lord God Sabaoth, Adonai, El, who is, was, and always will be. Then He will appear to you, He who established heaven and spread forth the earth among the waters. To the virgin alone belongs this right, this heritage, this rank, this station, such glory, because she has hated the day of humanity, because she has rejected all uncleanness. Then she will rejoice in repose; then she will exult. (17)

It is not only in treatises dedicated to virginity that Athanasius expounds his ascetic ideas. Some extensive Coptic fragments survive of an otherwise unknown Athanasian text on the moral life.[29] Once again we find the praise of those who make the decision to turn to asceticism. 'The people who walk angelically according to their free will and practice discipline in the life of the angels remove themselves completely from the desires of the flesh' (2). They avoid meat and wine, consuming sparsely only vegetables and water, and keep vigils and nights of prayer rather than sleep. But not all can achieve such a higher state. Those who cannot should still seek to distance themselves from worldly vices and not be condemned for their efforts. Marriage is good, as long as sexual relations are for procreation and not for pleasure. Drinking a little wine is not a sin, but excess is to be avoided. This pastoral emphasis that all Christians should live by such ideals to the limits of their ability is here extended even to those not yet full members of the Church. 'I am not saying these things only to the person who has received the light, baptism, but I am commanding also the one who is going to receive' (7). Catechumens too must prepare themselves for a Christian life. In this aim, humanity is aided once more by Christ through the Incarnation. 'As for us, brothers, let us obey the teaching of our Lord and suffer for Him so that we might be glorified with Him and we too might be a single body in Christ Jesus' (10).

Athanasius expresses the same ideals in his correspondence with the leading monks of the Egyptian desert. One of his best-known letters, probably written during Athanasius' golden decade (346–56), was addressed to Amoun, the founder of an ascetic community in Nitria.[30] Some of Amoun's monks, possibly including Amoun himself, were concerned that bodily emissions were sinful and unclean. Athanasius insists that all things created by God are good and pure. Bodily emissions are a part of nature independent of the human will, and cannot be evidence of sin. To debate such a question, Athanasius argues, is futile and the work of the Devil, who seeks always to distract ascetics from their meditations.

[29] Translation in Brakke (1995: 314–19).
[30] In *Life of Antony* 60, Antony saw the soul of Amoun carried to heaven by angels.

From emissions, Athanasius then passes on to the wider issue of sexuality. Again he rebukes those in Amoun's community who regard marriage as defilement. Honourable marriage for procreation is not sinful, just as killing in war is lawful and praised even though to kill is in itself wrong. 'There are two ways of life in these matters—one, marriage, more moderate and ordinary; the other, virginity, angelic and more perfect. Now if a person chooses the worldly way, that is, marriage, he is indeed not to blame; but he will not receive such graces as the other way.' Athanasius concludes by urging Amoun to strengthen his community according to these warnings, and silence those who raise such questions.

Throughout the writings summarized here Athanasius expresses a sincere respect for ascetic values and the men and women who pursued such a vocation. His criticism is reserved for the most extreme practices and for ascetics who exalt themselves and disparage those who live an ordinary pious Christian life. In the next chapter we will see Athanasius maintain the same principles in the more explicitly pastoral context of his *Festal Letters*. But there remains one outstanding Athanasian ascetic work that requires attention: the *Life of Antony*. Dedication and renown made Antony unique. As Athanasius declared in the conclusion to his famous biography, Antony was an example from whom all 'may learn what the life of the monks ought to be' (94). The ideals that Antony represents provide a further demonstration of the principles of Athanasius' wider ascetic programme, now expressed through a model whom every monk and virgin should admire and imitate.[31]

Like the virgins to whom Athanasius addressed several of his letters, Antony devoted himself to asceticism of his own free will. He received the aid of divine grace, upon which all must depend, but he held to his commitment and resisted the temptations of demons. Although unlearned,[32] he was able to dispute with philosophers and interpret the Scriptures, while in his conviction and the strength of his bodily discipline and spiritual knowledge Antony rose above his contemporaries. Yet the ascetic values that he embraced were the universal values that Athanasius insisted every Christian could aspire to attain in their measure. Fasting and celibacy were

---

[31] How far the Athanasian ideals that I am concerned with here can be reconciled with the historical Antony remains controversial. For comparisons between the *Life of Antony* and our other evidence (Antony's *Letters* and his sayings in the *Apophthegmata Patrum*), see Dörries (1949), Rubenson (1995), and Harmless (2004).

[32] It is here that we encounter the most obvious contrast between the Antony of the *Life* and the Antony of the *Letters*, for the latter reveal a strongly Origenist theology and an emphasis on knowledge (*gnōsis*): Rubenson (1995).

balanced by prayer and contemplation of Scripture, while the work of his hands supported him and gave him the means for charity. These were the virtues Antony in turn encouraged in others, and he warned of the corresponding vices: greed for money and glory, desire for food, sexual lust, and false belief. His struggles differed from those of others in depth but not in nature.

There are themes prominent in the *Life of Antony* that do not find such close parallels in Athanasius' other ascetic works. This is true of the demons whose trials Antony continually endured.[33] From the very beginning of his ascetic devotion Antony faced temptations, threats, and physical abuse at demonic hands. He possessed the gift of discernment of evil spirits, and instructed others on how to recognize and defeat them. The conflict with demons was a recurring motif of late-antique asceticism, especially for those who followed Antony out into the deeper desert, but is not a subject that Athanasius places any significance upon elsewhere. This silence may reflect the character of his writings, for we have no reason to think that he did not share the contemporary belief in demons. The *Life of Antony* reports that Antony gave a discourse 'in the Egyptian tongue' (16) to a group of monks, in which demons are said to oppose all Christians but particularly monks. For even demons fear the ideals of the ascetic life:

They are afraid of the ascetics on several counts—for their fasting, the vigils, the prayers, the meekness and gentleness, the contempt for money, the lack of vanity, the humility, the love of the poor, the almsgiving, the freedom from wrath, and most of all their devotion to Christ. It is for this reason that they do all they do—in order not to have those monks trampling them underfoot. For they know the grace that has been given to the faithful for combat against them by the Saviour. (30).

In addition to restating once more the virtues of asceticism, these words attributed to Antony recall another fundamental Athanasian principle: the dependence of the ascetic upon the grace given to humanity through the Incarnation. Antony did not achieve his many miracles by his own greatness. Instead, he gave thanks to God, who worked through him, and insisted that those who sought to venerate him should do likewise. At the onset of his ascetic career he was thus able to defeat the Devil. For 'working with Antony was the Lord, who bore flesh for us, and gave to the body the victory over the Devil, so that each of those who truly struggle can say, it is "not I, but the grace of God which is in me" [1 Corinthians 15:10]' (5).

---

[33] On the importance of demons in Late Antiquity, see the classic article of Brown (1970) and now Brakke (2006).

Later in his life, when he had retired to his mountain, the hermit would be challenged to debate by pagan philosophers. In his condemnation of their errors, Antony offered a concise statement of the doctrine of deification that underlay Athanasius' theology and his understanding of asceticism. 'The Word of God was not changed, but remaining the same He assumed a human body for the salvation and benefit of humanity—so that sharing in the human birth He might enable humanity to share the divine and spiritual nature' (74).[34]

Antony addressed monks and philosophers, he received and wrote letters to emperors, gave to the poor, and aided any who sought him out. Despite his desire for solitude and his anchoretic reputation, the hermit was rarely truly alone. From his abandoned fortress or desert mountain, Antony remained engaged with the world around him. He therefore contributed in his way to bridging the potential gulf between the ascetic and the 'ordinary' Christian. The pastoral achievements he wrought were greater than those of many bishops and represented Athanasius' ideal model, inspiring through spiritual leadership those who could not reach the same degree of perfection.

It was as if he were a physician given to Egypt by God. For who went to him grieving and did not return rejoicing? Who went in lamentation over his dead, and did not immediately put aside his sorrow? Who visited while angered and was not changed to affection? What poor person met him in exhaustion who did not, after hearing and seeing him, despise wealth and console himself in his poverty? What monk, coming to him in discouragement, did not become all the stronger? What young man, coming to the mountain and looking at Antony, did not at once renounce pleasures and love moderation? Who came to him tempted by a demon and did not gain relief? And who came to him distressed in his thoughts and did not find his mind calmed?' (87)

By word, deed, and example, Antony spread the ascetic vocation across Egyptian Christianity and beyond. Athanasius immortalized Antony's achievement in making 'the desert a city'.

When he spoke and urged them to keep in mind the future goods and the affection in which we are held by God, 'who did not spare His own Son, but gave Him up for us all' [Romans 8:32], he persuaded many to take up the solitary life. And so, from then on, there were monasteries in the mountains and the desert was made a city by monks, who left their own people and registered themselves for the citizenship in the heavens. (14).

[34] The place of the *Life of Antony* within Athanasius' theology has been discussed further by Gregg and Groh (1981: ch. 4), Brakke (1995: 216–44), and Anatolios (1998: 165–95).

THE BISHOP AND THE MONKS: ATHANASIUS AND THE 'POLITICS' OF ASCETICISM

We must hold Athanasius' conception of the ascetic movement and his personal ascetic principles firmly in mind when we turn to the role that asceticism played in the course of his episcopate. There is no doubt that the support of a considerable bloc of the Egyptian ascetic community was an important factor in maintaining Athanasius' influence over the Egyptian Church and his hold on the Alexandrian see. Whether it is correct to speak of the 'politics' of asceticism is more open to debate.[35] As Athanasius' entire career attests, politics and piety are not mutually exclusive categories. To dismiss Athanasius' alliance with the monks and virgins of Alexandria and Egypt as merely political manipulation is to do Athanasius and the ascetics alike a grave disservice. Yet Athanasius did gain practical as well as spiritual aid from his relationship with the ascetics, to their lasting mutual benefit. Moreover, the ascetic movement within Egypt as elsewhere took a myriad of different forms. Athanasius sought to impose a degree of unity, establishing models of behaviour that reflected both his ascetic ideals and the demands of episcopal power. This inevitably brought him into conflict with others who had their own alternative visions for the course of Egyptian asceticism.

The relationship between the bishop of Alexandria and the Egyptian ascetics raised a further underlying question with serious implications for Christianity as a whole. The ascetic movement was arguably the greatest potential challenge to episcopal authority over the late-antique Church.[36] There had always been those within the early Church who had questioned whether the worldly concerns required of the clergy were truly compatible with Christian moral and spiritual leadership. The gradual emergence of the monarchical episcopate in the second and third centuries AD united spiritual and administrative authority in a single figure. But tensions still remained, and the rise of ascetic holy men and women brought those tensions into renewed focus. An anchorite like Antony derived his status from

---

[35] Taken from Brakke (1995), although his view is more nuanced than his title might suggest.

[36] On the much-debated relationship between ascetic and episcopal authority in Late Antiquity, see, among many, Rousseau (1978), Chadwick (1993), Leyser (2000), Sterk (2004), Rapp (2005: 137–52), and the articles of Martin and others collected in Camplani and Filoramo (2007). Here one might still note Weber's famous classification of the three pure types of legitimate authority: legal, traditional, and charismatic (Weber 1978: 212–54, esp. 246–54 'The Routinization of Charisma').

personal holiness and charisma, not from clerical office. The separation between cleric and monk only increased with the social prominence and privileges that came to the Church with imperial patronage. The ascetic renunciation of society in order to follow a life in Christ threatened to create an alternative Christian elite, one that might undermine or supersede the bishop in offering guidance to the Christian community.

John Cassian, a generation after Athanasius' death, wrote that 'monks should flee bishops' (*Institutes* XI.18).[37] Cassian was by no means alone in his judgement, and monastic reluctance to face ordination became a recurring hagiographical theme. In truth, asceticism was never necessarily incompatible with ecclesiastical office, and over time the ascetic movement strengthened rather than weakened episcopal leadership. Yet this was far from being an inevitable conclusion. Athanasius played a fundamental role both in incorporating ascetic values more closely within the roles expected of the bishop and in integrating monks and clergy. The mutual bond between the ascetic movement and the hierarchical Church that Athanasius forged in Egypt has lasted down to the present day and created a reservoir of strength upon which he and later Alexandrian bishops would draw.

The prominence of asceticism within Egyptian Christianity had created issues for the bishops of Alexandria long before Athanasius' election. Tensions between charismatic and ecclesiastical authority helped to cause the conflicts between bishop Demetrius and Origen that led to the latter's departure from the city in the 230s. The influence that Arius attained as a presbyter before his condemnation by Alexander was in no small measure due to his reputation for ascetic austerity.[38] Perhaps most significantly within Egypt, the rigorous attitude of Melitius of Lycopolis, which led to his break with Peter of Alexandria during the Great Persecution, appealed to a considerable number of Egyptian ascetics. The Melitian Schism took a strong root among the monks and monasteries of Upper Egypt, which endured to the end of Athanasius' life and beyond.[39] From the beginning of his episcopate Athanasius therefore faced an ongoing struggle for leadership over Egyptian asceticism as well as the wider Egyptian Church.

It is hardly surprising that Athanasius took immediate steps upon his election to secure closer relations with the ascetic communities. His

---

[37] For the context of Cassian's oft-quoted warning, see Rapp (2005: 137–9).

[38] See Epiphanius, *Panarion* 68.4, 69.3. Arius' early followers reportedly included some 700 virgins.

[39] On the importance of monasticism to the Melitian movement, see Bell (1924: 38–99) and Hauben (1998: 339–41).

opening *Festal Letter* for Easter 329, as we shall see in the next chapter, contains an exhortation both to those committed to virginity and to those who might adopt an ascetic lifestyle only for the Easter celebration. His trip to the Thebaid recorded in *Festal Index* 2 for 329–30 must have been motivated in part by the concentration of monasticism in Upper Egypt and the strong Melitian presence there. As tensions mounted in the years before Athanasius' condemnation in 335, ascetics on different sides could be drawn into conflict. This may be reflected in the anti-Melitian attacks of the early 330s revealed by *Papyrus London* 1914, while the earliest claim of violence against Athanasius' ascetic supporters is attributed to the Mareotis Commission despatched by the Council of Tyre (in the *Encyclical Letter* of the Council of Alexandria in 338, quoted in *Apologia contra Arianos* 15).

When Athanasius returned from his initial exile in the west in 337, the tensions intensified. His episcopal position remained vulnerable, and the need for unity was even more pressing. Rival movements within Egyptian asceticism threatened both his leadership and his ascetic ideals. Antony's famous visit to Alexandria to denounce the 'Arians', discussed further below, took place in 338. Nor were the 'Arians' the only opponents whom Athanasius regarded as a danger. This is visible from the first *Letter to Virgins*, roughly contemporary to Antony's visit. Athanasius laid down his model of virginity in that letter not only to promote his ideals but to rally his audience to a particular vision of asceticism, one that recognized his authority and rejected the alternatives that he condemned.[40]

Two rival visions were singled out for special attention in the first *Letter to Virgins*. One is that of the early fourth-century Egyptian ascetic Hieracas.[41] We know relatively little of his teachings, but he is denounced by Athanasius for saying 'that marriage is evil inasmuch as virginity is good' (24). This hardline argument seems to have won support among a number of ascetics in Egypt, possibly including the Melitians. For Athanasius such ideas directly opposed his inclusive pastoral approach to asceticism, which maintained the value of marriage even while praising the superiority of virginity.

The second focus of Athanasius' polemic is inevitably the danger of 'Arianism'. Speaking through the voice of Alexander, Athanasius unites virginity with orthodoxy and requires that proper virgins must hold a correct

---

[40] One Egyptian ascetic leader who does appear to have shared Athanasius' vision was Didymus the Blind, whose surviving works defend Nicene orthodoxy and support Athanasius' emphasis on ecclesiastical authority and the virtue of marriage. See further Layton (2004).

[41] Epiphanius, *Panarion* 67; Goehring (1999*b*).

doctrinal understanding of the Son's divinity. 'Watch out, O my daughters, let no one lie and speak against your bridegroom in your presence, envying your noble and holy union and the thinking about Him that you have, desiring to separate you from His love' (42). Some say that the Word is created and did not exist before He was begotten. 'These are not the words of truth; rather, they belong to the deceitful people who falsely say against the noble one that He is a creature and make Him foreign to the substance of the Father in order to deceive you, his brides' (42).

The errors that Athanasius invariably attributes to the 'Arians' are here given a specifically ascetic interpretation. Those who follow this heresy not only insult the Son of God but reject the life of virginity that is made possible through the Incarnation. Athanasius urges his audience to rally behind what he preaches as the orthodox faith. There can be no true ascetics among the 'Arians' who believe that the Son was weakened when He became man.

They talk about the works of the Lord's humanity because they envy the vow of virginity and do not recognize God's love for humanity in it. If the Word had not become flesh, how would you now be joined with Him and cling to Him? But when the Lord bore the body of humanity, the body became acceptable to the Word. Therefore, you have now become virgins and brides of Christ. (43)

Athanasius' efforts to unite Egyptian asceticism suffered a setback with his second flight into exile and the appointment of Gregory as his replacement in Alexandria. Gregory's arrival into the city in 339 was accompanied by the abuse of loyal virgins and monks, according to Athanasius' *Epistula Encyclica*. Stories of such abuse are a recurring feature of his polemic, and the factual basis of the rhetoric is very difficult to assess. But Athanasius clearly had established a strong ascetic following through his efforts in the first decade of his episcopate. He worked hard to keep that following from exile, and continued to attack his rivals for the hearts of the Egyptian ascetics. It is in this context that we should probably set the *Ad Monachos*, Athanasius' first *Letter to the Monks*.[42]

The first *Letter to the Monks* is addressed 'to those everywhere who are living a monastic life, who are established in the faith of God, and sanctified in Christ'. Its content provides no precise indication of its date. Athanasius states that he has written for the monks, 'a brief account of the sufferings that we and the Church have endured, refuting as best I could the accursed heresy of the Arian madmen and showing how it is wholly hostile to the

---

[42] Translation in Barnard (1994: 10–11).

truth'. This was long interpreted as an allusion to the *Historia Arianorum*, and so the letter was traditionally placed in the late 350s during Athanasius' third exile. But the *Historia Arianorum* is hardly a brief account, and nor does it provide a theological refutation of 'Arianism'. On the other hand, the letter refers to the death of Arius as proof of his impiety, and when Athanasius wrote his *De Morte Arii* he informed Serapion that 'I have despatched to your piety what I wrote to the monks'. We may therefore place the first *Letter to the Monks* alongside the *De Morte Arii* early in Athanasius' second exile.[43] The work that he sent to the monks and Serapion appears to be lost, which is in keeping with his unusual request in the letter that the monks read that work and then return it uncopied. Athanasius' concern in this correspondence from exile is above all to denounce the 'Arians' and ensure that his ascetic followers remain apart from them and loyal to the orthodox Church that he represents.

The same theme pervades Athanasius' second *Letter to the Monks*.[44] The chronology of this letter is again disputed, and it can be set plausibly at any point from the late 330s to the early 360s.[45] In any case, the thrust of the argument is a universal theme of Athanasius' ascetic polemic. 'There are certain people who think like Arius, and travel about the monasteries with the sole object of pretending to come from us to visit you in order to deceive the simple. There are also certain people who, while affirming that they do not hold with Arius, yet compromise themselves and worship with his group.' Athanasius warns the monks not to associate with such people, shunning both the 'Arians' and those who worship with them.[46] The polarization that underlies his theological construction of the 'Arian Controversy' also shapes his vision of Egyptian asceticism, separating the true monks and virgins who follow his leadership from those who fall into disobedience and error.

Upon his glorious return in 346, Athanasius set out to restore his position among the Egyptian ascetics just as he did among the clergy and bishops. The *Letter to Amoun* continues Athanasius' campaign against alternative ascetic ideals. He criticizes the extremism of those who regard bodily emissions as

[43] This argument has been revised from Kannengiesser (1982: 992).

[44] Translation in Barnard (1994: 12–13).

[45] Part of the text of this letter was preserved inscribed on the wall of an Egyptian tomb used as a monastic cell (*CIG* iv. 8607).

[46] Athanasius' warning corresponds to the story in *Vita Prima Pachomii* 137–8 when the *dux* Artemius led a party searching for Athanasius to the monastery of Phbow in the Thebaid. The *dux* asked the monks to pray with him, but they refused as he had with him an 'Arian' bishop. The *dux* then fell asleep, and awoke terrified by a vision that caused him to give up his search.

sinful, as well as those who challenge the sanctity of marriage. There may have been concern that such extreme views revealed the influence of Manichaeism, a highly ascetic movement that was prominent in Egypt and is attacked elsewhere in Athanasius' writings and by his colleague Serapion.[47] Amoun is urged to keep his flock on the correct path.

The *Letter to Amoun*, like the first *Letter to Virgins* and the two *Letters to the Monks*, reveals Athanasius' determination to mould the ascetic movement in Egypt under his leadership. His success was crucial to his ecclesiastical position. Yet, here again, this 'political' aim cannot be separated from his sincere ascetic, theological, and pastoral principles. Athanasius believed implicitly in the importance of the ascetic lifestyle, just as he believed that 'Arianism' compromised human salvation and deprived ascetics of the proximity to God granted through the Incarnation. Extreme practices likewise led to error and threatened the pastoral inclusivity that was integral to his ascetic vision. All these concerns draw together when we consider one of Athanasius' most lasting contributions to the history of asceticism: his desire to incorporate monks within the episcopal hierarchy.[48]

In 353/4 the monk Dracontius, raised against his will into the episcopate, refused to fulfil his office and returned to his monastery. Athanasius' *Letter to Dracontius*, written shortly before the Easter celebration for 354, rebukes him and those who advised his course of action. The see in question was itself of considerable importance, for Hermopolis Parva was the bishopric that oversaw the ascetic mountain of Nitria. A Melitian bishop had been based there when the *Breviarium Melitii* was compiled, and Athanasius was at pains to maintain his influence in the region. Nevertheless, there were deeper principles at stake. Athanasius appealed to Dracontius to do his duty and heed the pastoral needs of his congregation, and in doing so composed an influential defence of the compatibility of asceticism with clerical office.

'What you have done is blameworthy, beloved Dracontius.' One who has received grace should not flee or give others reason to flee. Athanasius fears that this will open the way for Melitians and other opponents, and warns Dracontius that 'the episcopal oversight of the district will be sought by numbers of people, many of them, as you know, unfit'. But

---

[47] For an introduction to Manichaeism, see Lieu (1992). Athanasius particularly singles out the *dux* Sebastianus, a Manichee who led the persecutions in Egypt during his third exile (*Apologia de Fuga* 6; *Historia Arianorum* 55, 59, 61). Athanasius also condemned the Manichees for lack of compassion and charity (*Historia Arianorum* 61). For Serapion's attacks on Manichaeism, see Fitschen (1992).

[48] See Brakke (1995: 99–110) and the works cited above (n. 36).

Athanasius is more concerned for those Dracontius has abandoned. 'Whereas before your election you lived for yourself, after it you live for your flock.' They look to their bishop for the food of the Scriptures and have been left hungry. How will Dracontius defend himself before Christ? If he has acted from fear, then he should have shown zeal. Athanasius now turns to the true cause of Dracontius' flight.

If you find the administration of the churches distasteful and the ministry of the episcopate unrewarding, then you despise the Saviour who made these arrangements. I urge you, dismiss these thoughts, and do not tolerate those who give such advice, for it is unworthy of Dracontius. The order established by the Lord through the Apostles remains good and firm; but the cowardice of the brethren will not endure.

Dracontius was by no means the only monk to enter the episcopate in fourth-century Egypt. Later in his letter Athanasius repeats his pastoral warning, that Dracontius is responsible before God for those placed in his care. He then reminds him of those monks who have followed the clerical path before him. Their number includes Athanasius' close friend Serapion, and Ammonius who accompanied Serapion on his mission to Constantius in 353.

They did not despise the ministry and were not more severe towards themselves, but rather looked for the reward of their work, making progress themselves and guiding others onwards. How many have they turned away from idols? How many have ceased from their intimacy with their demons because of their warning? How many servants have they brought to the Lord, to the amazement of those who saw such marvels?

These are the blessings that the ascetic bishop may bring for his flock. Therefore, Athanasius concludes, 'do not say, or believe those who say, that the episcopal office is a valid excuse for sin, nor that it provides a pretext for sin'. A monk need not fall into spiritual decline when he becomes a bishop and involved in worldly affairs. 'We know both bishops who fast, and monks who eat. We know bishops who drink no wine, and monks who drink. And we know bishops who perform marvels, and monks who do not.' Such behaviour is not the exclusive preserve of the monk nor denied to the bishop. Athanasius' argument to Dracontius is a practical application of his conviction that all Christians could pursue asceticism, each to their own measure. He ends the letter by calling Dracontius to return to his church to preach the Easter sermon and proclaim the day of Resurrection. His appeal evidently succeeded. Dracontius still belonged to the episcopate when he was exiled in 356 as persecution of Athanasius' followers resumed, and when the persecution ended he joined Athanasius at the Council of Alexandria in 362.[49]

By the end of his golden decade in 356 Athanasius had secured the loyalty of the majority of the Egyptian ascetic population. He was to reap the benefits of that loyalty many times during the six years of his third exile, inspiring countless later stories that I will not recount here. His ascetic followers also bore the brunt of the violence of his foes, although here again we face the difficulties posed by polemical rhetoric. Athanasius' earliest account of this violence, in the closing chapters added to the *Apologia ad Constantium* in 357, opens with a brief panegyric on the state of virginity. Athanasius repeats his emphasis that the life of virginity was made possible through the Incarnation, and condemns the 'Arians' for stripping and scourging the innocent women. 'Such wickedness belongs only to heretics, to blaspheme the Son of God and to do violence to His holy virgins' (33). Nor did the 'Arians' permit the virgins to bury their dead, for which Athanasius consoled them in an otherwise unknown work quoted in Theodoret's *Ecclesiastical History* (II.11).

Similar condemnation of the 'Arian' abuse of virgins and monks at this time recurs in the *Historia Arianorum*. One passage in particular deserves attention:

Many virgins who condemned their impiety and professed the truth, they [the 'Arians'] brought out from the houses; others they insulted as they walked along the streets and caused their heads to be uncovered by their young men. They also gave permission to the women with them to insult whom they wished; and although the holy and faithful women stepped aside and gave them the way, yet they gathered around them like Maenads and Furies, and thought it a misfortune not to find a way to injure them. (59)

There seems little reason to doubt that supporters of Athanasius did suffer at the hands of his enemies, and his loyal virgins were among his most recognizable and vulnerable supporters. However, the 'Arian' women whom he condemns as Maenads and Furies were almost certainly virgins and holy women themselves. Athanasius refused to acknowledge their status, as in his eyes their allegiance invalidated their ascetic lifestyle. In reality, the separation between 'orthodox' and 'heretical' women was never as clear-cut

---

[49] Athanasius' last reference to Dracontius is at the end of *Festal Letter* XL (368), where in an announcement of new appointments to Egyptian sees he is succeeded as bishop of Hermopolis Parva by Isidore. Athanasius emphasizes at the end of this announcement that 'all these men are ascetics, being in the life of monasticism'.

as Athanasius would like us to believe.[50] There is much we will never know of the Egyptian ascetics whom Athanasius branded as 'Arians' or 'Melitians' and whose writings (with the exception of a few scattered Melitian papyri) are lost to us. Athanasius did not secure universal support, and, as is true of his theology, we should be wary of assuming that his ascetic programme was as influential among his contemporaries as later tradition might suggest.

The most influential work of Athanasius' programme was once more the *Life of Antony*.[51] By the very act of writing the biography, Athanasius was making a claim to represent the Egyptian ascetics who admired Antony's commitment and example. The *Life* also provided Athanasius with the ideal vehicle to construct the image of Antony that he wished others to heed. In his preface Athanasius addresses an audience outside Egypt, but he can hardly have excluded a local readership, and the *Life* represents a further statement of his campaign to unify the Egyptian ascetic movement behind his leadership. His sincere respect for Antony reinforced his appeal to Antony's authority in support of his own. Athanasius' Antony shunned Melitians and 'Arians' and obeyed the clergy and the bishop of Alexandria. Thus Antony became a model for the close bond that Athanasius sought to build between the organized Church and the monasteries and hermits of the desert.

It would be a gross exaggeration to suggest that ecclesiastical politics or the condemnation of heresy were Athanasius' chief motive when he wrote the *Life*. The main body of the work concentrates upon Antony's ascetic achievements, and only towards the end does Athanasius turn to other concerns. Antony, it is said, remained always tolerant and humble. 'Though the sort of man he was, he honoured the rule of the Church with extreme care, and he wanted every cleric to be held in higher regard than himself. He felt no shame at bowing the head to the bishops and presbyters' (67).[52] Antony, however, reserved that obedience solely for representatives of the true faith.

In things having to do with belief, he was truly wonderful and orthodox. Perceiving their wickedness and apostasy from the outset, he never held communion with the Melitian schismatics. And neither toward the Manichaeans nor toward any other

---

[50] Burrus (1991); Elm (1994: 348–53); cf. Brakke (1995: 63–75).

[51] On the ecclesiastical importance of the *Life*, see again Brakke (1995).

[52] Later in the *Life*, when Antony opposed the Egyptian practice of honouring the bodies of the dead, he 'frequently asked a bishop to instruct the people on this matter' (90).

heretics did he profess friendship, except to the extent of urging the change to right belief, for he held and taught that friendship and association with them led to injury and destruction of the soul. So in the same way he abhorred the heresy of the Arians, and he ordered everyone neither to go near them nor to share their erroneous belief. Once when some of the Ariomaniacs came to him, sounding them out and learning that they were impious, he chased them from the mountain, saying that their doctrines were worse than serpents. (68)

On another occasion when the Arians falsely claimed that he held the same view as they, he was quite irritated and angry at them. Then, summoned both by the bishops and all the brothers, he came down from the mountain, and entering into Alexandria, he publicly renounced the Arians, saying that theirs was the last heresy and the forerunner of the Antichrist. He taught the people that the Son of God is not a creature, and that He did not come into existence from nonbeing, but rather that He is eternal Word and Wisdom from the essence of the Father. 'So', he asserted, 'it is sacrilegious to say "there was when He was not" for the Word coexisted with the Father always. Therefore you are to have no fellowship with the most ungodly Arians, for there is no "fellowship of light with darkness" [2 Corinthians 6:14]. You are God-fearing Christians, but they, in saying that the Son and Word of God the Father is a creature, differ in no way from the pagans, who "serve the creature rather than the Creator" [Romans 1:25]. Be assured that the whole creation itself is angered at them, because they number among the creatures the Creator and Lord of all, in whom all things were made.' (69)

The denunciation of 'Arianism' placed in the mouth of Antony directly echoes the polemic of Athanasius' theological works.[53] So too does the description of the 'Arians' as precursors of the Antichrist and the warning not to associate with the heretics (the theme of Athanasius' second *Letter to the Monks*). Antony's visit to Alexandria took place in 338, during the short interlude between Athanasius' first and second exile.[54] It is entirely plausible that he did speak on Athanasius' behalf, although whether Antony's attitude towards 'Arians' and 'Melitians' was as clear-cut as Athanasius would have liked remains uncertain. The *Life of Antony* is vehement on the hermit's hostility to 'Arianism'. Antony foretold the 'current assault of the Arians' (82), a reference that places the *Life* during Athanasius' third exile,

---

[53] In one of his *Letters*, Antony also condemns the 'Arians', who teach that the Son is mutable, exists in time, and has an end (*Letter* IV.17).

[54] 'Antony, the great leader, came to Alexandria, and though he remained there only two days, showed himself wonderful in many things, and healed many' (*Festal Index* 10 for 338). This may have been the one occasion Athanasius and Antony met, as Athanasius states 'we were escorting him' (*Life of Antony* 71) at the time of a miracle just before his departure, although the meaning of this passage is far from clear.

and predicted the death of the *dux* Balacius, who had been responsible for violence towards virgins in the earlier days of Gregory of Alexandria (86).[55] The warning to avoid all contact with the 'Arians' is repeated twice more in Antony's last advice to his monks (89) and in his final words to his disciples (91). There is a strong suspicion that Athanasius wished to claim Antony for his own position, against rivals (like the 'Arians' in passage 69) who saw the great monk in a rather different light.[56]

Antony died at the reported age of 105 in AD 356. By the time of his death, his reputation had already reached across the Mediterranean to Spain and Gaul (93). The *Life of Antony* would dramatically accelerate the spread of his fame in east and west. A crude Latin translation was available by the late 360s, and the polished Latin text of Evagrius (later bishop of Antioch and a friend of Jerome) was circulated in *c*.371 and in 386 was read by Augustine of Hippo in Milan. Over time the *Life* would be translated into every major Christian language and played no small part in preserving Athanasius' legacy. His association with Antony, which authorship of the *Life* reinforced, enhanced Athanasius' spiritual standing and his carefully nurtured relationship with the Egyptian ascetic communities. The bond he forged between the ascetics and the episcopate of Alexandria was to prove an invaluable source of strength to his successors Theophilus and Cyril. Yet that relationship could never have flourished if Athanasius had not shared the convictions of those monks and virgins and fought so hard to keep the ascetic movement within the Church he represented. He had earned the gift that Antony bestowed upon him with his final words:

'Distribute my clothing. To Bishop Athanasius give the one sheepskin and the cloak on which I lie, which he gave to me new, but I have by now worn out. And to Bishop Serapion give the other sheepskin, and you keep the hair garment. And now God preserve you, children, for Antony is leaving and is with you no longer.' (91)

Each of those who received the blessed Antony's sheepskin, and the cloak worn out by him, keeps it safe like some great treasure. For even seeing these is like beholding Antony, and wearing them is like bearing his admonitions with joy. (92)

---

[55] In *Historia Arianorum* 14, Athanasius retells the same episode but reworks the details to condemn more explicitly his former rival Gregory.

[56] For discussion of some of these competing claims to Antony and his legacy, see Gregg and Groh (1981: ch. 4) and Brennan (1985).

5

Father

Athanasius held the Alexandrian see for forty-five years. His name is for ever associated with the ecclesiastical and theological conflicts that divided the fourth-century Church and with the rise of asceticism. He spent long periods in exile, attended councils and imperial courts, and addressed his numerous writings to emperors, bishops, and hermits alike. But Athanasius did not seek a career in politics or academic theology and nor did he go out into the desert as a monk. The vast majority of his life was devoted to the vocation that according to tradition he entered as a child performing rituals by the seaside: that of the spiritual father of the Christian communities of Alexandria and Egypt who looked to him for guidance and pastoral care.[1]

That Athanasius dedicated himself to the pastoral duties required of a bishop is, one would have thought, a statement of the obvious. It is a statement, however, that needs to be made. The pastoral obligations that Athanasius faced and his commitment to meeting those expectations reveal an essential dimension to his character that is all too easily forgotten or ignored. Conventionally, as in the preceding chapters, Athanasius' career has been approached primarily through his great apologetic, doctrinal, and ascetic writings. The day-to-day life of the bishop is difficult to reconstruct from that evidence and seems buried beneath Athanasius' more earth-shaking activities. Yet without an appreciation of his pastoral context we cannot fully understand Athanasius' motivations or actions. It is in his pastoral role that we see how the ecclesiastical, theological, and ascetic elements of his career come together. We also gain a clearer insight into the achievement of Athanasius and his true greatness. Despite years of conflict and exile, Athanasius through his pastoral dedication won and retained the love and support of his church, of the monks, and of the people of Alexandria and Egypt.

---

[1] Scholarship on the pastoral and spiritual teachings of Athanasius has been limited. For some approaches, see Merendino (1965), Kannengiesser (1989), Ng (2001), and Demacopoulos (2007: 21–49).

Throughout this chapter our chief source will be Athanasius' *Festal Letters*.[2] Sadly, although he must have preached on hundreds if not thousands of occasions down the years, no authentic example of a complete Athanasian sermon survives.[3] There are passing references to his episcopal duties in his apologetic writings and in his correspondence with Egyptian monks and clergy. But only in the *Festal Letters* can we examine Athanasius' pastoral work in detail. Some of the difficulties raised by these letters were discussed in Chapter 1, notably the loss of the original Greek texts and their complex manuscript transmission in Syriac and Coptic. We should also remember that, as the letters were circulated for the celebration of Easter, they inevitably focus on certain themes, which may not always be representative of Athanasius' wider pastoral programme. Nevertheless, they have immense value for our knowledge of Athanasius as a pastoral bishop.

The *Festal Letters* were, in effect, sermons delivered by correspondence.[4] They were circulated to all Christian communities that acknowledged Athanasius' authority and are believed to have been read aloud by the leaders of those communities. The famous *Festal Letter* XXXIX on the canon of Scripture, to which I will return at the end of this chapter, was read out and then posted in the Pachomian monasteries of Egypt.[5] Composition of the *Festal Letters* was a statement of Athanasius' position at the head of the Egyptian Church and provided the ideal opportunity to communicate and promote his theological, moral, and ascetic values. This we see immediately from the very first Athanasian *Festal Letter*, written for the Easter of 329.

IN THE BEGINNING: THE FIRST *FESTAL LETTER*

'Come, my beloved, the season calls us to keep the feast. Again, the Sun of Righteousness, causing His divine beams to rise upon us, proclaims beforehand the time of the feast, in which, obeying Him, we ought to celebrate it, so

---

[2] In the words of Frances Young (1983: 80), the letters 'are full of scriptural quotations, traditional typology and simple piety. They make up, to some extent, for the loss of his sermons.' Kannengiesser (1989) offers an important study of the *Festal Letters* as a source for Athanasius' pastoral activities, although he at times underestimates the ecclesiastical and polemic elements contained in the letters. See also Wahba (1998).

[3] On the importance of preaching in the early Church, see Dunn-Wilson (2005) and the articles collected in Hunter (1989) and Cunningham and Allen (1998). Scholarship has particularly focused on the extensive sermons of John Chrysostom, as in the study by Maxwell (2007). For Athanasius we possess only the pseudonymous Athanasian homiletic cycle preserved in Coptic, which is translated into Italian with commentary in Orlandi (1981).

[4] A comment made by Burgess (1854: 118a).   [5] Bohairic *Life of Pachomius* 189.

that when the time has passed by, gladness likewise may not leave us.' (*Festal Letter* I.1)

These lines have a special resonance for any student of Athanasius. They are the opening words of his episcopate, or more accurately the opening words of the earliest work now extant that Athanasius composed as the bishop of Alexandria. The exhortation to obey the Lord and celebrate with joy the feast of Easter would recur throughout the many *Festal Letters* that Athanasius would write for the Egyptian Church across the next half-century. But that call had particular significance for Athanasius in 329 as he prepared for the first Easter following his controversial election. The great feast offered a focus of devotion around which all Christian Egypt could unite, while the traditional *Festal Letter* gave the new bishop the opportunity to proclaim his message to the far-flung communities to whom at this time he was little more than a name. *Festal Letter* I thus repays careful reading and sheds valuable light on Athanasius' conception of his pastoral role.

After the opening exhortation, Athanasius draws on an array of scriptural texts to hail the importance of correct faith and observance in every time and season. The doctrinal and moral lessons that he teaches reflect the same principles that will drive his later theological and ascetic writings. Salvation comes through Christ and His Incarnation according to the divine plan for all humanity. Athanasius calls on his congregations to heed the underlying message of the Scriptures, which sometimes summons the believer to spiritual battles and sometimes challenges all to live according to their chosen path.

Let us, having recourse to our understanding and henceforth leaving the figures at a distance, come to the truth and look upon the priestly trumpets of our Saviour, which cry and call us, at one time to war, as the blessed Paul says: 'We wrestle not with flesh and blood, but with principalities, with powers, with the rulers of this dark world, with wicked spirits in heaven' [Ephesians 6:12]. At another time the call is made to virginity and lowliness and conjugal unanimity, saying, to virgins, the things of virgins; and to those bound by a course of abstinence, the things of abstinence; and to those who are married, the things of an honourable marriage; thus assigning to each domestic virtues and honourable recompense. (*Festal Letter* I.3)

Two characteristic elements of Athanasius' pastoral teaching are strongly in evidence here. All the *Festal Letters* draw heavily on the words of Scripture, and in his exegesis Athanasius constantly seeks to make the Scriptures relevant to the lives of his audience. This is not to suggest that his language is necessarily simple, for some of the images that he conjures are highly complex.[6] But even his most mystical exegesis always has a pastoral purpose, to teach practical lessons that everyone may follow. In the same vein, Athanasius addresses himself to the entire Egyptian Church, not only the most devout or ascetic. Virgins are honoured, but so are those who find happiness in virtuous marriage. Athanasius' concern is for all the faithful who share the feast to which they are now summoned.

Before the Easter feast it is necessary to fast, both with the body and no less with the soul. Athanasius cautions that, 'when we fast, we should hallow the fast. For not all those who call upon God, hallow God, since there are some who defile Him; yet not Him—that is impossible—but their own conscience concerning Him' (*Festal Letter* I.4). Those who pollute the fast include those who do evil to their neighbours and those who exalt themselves. The soul must be nourished with the virtues of righteousness, temperance, meekness, and fortitude and with Christ, who is the heavenly bread of the saints. Otherwise the soul will feed on the sins and vices of the Devil. Athanasius sets before his audience the miraculous examples of Moses, Elijah, and Daniel, who during their fasts received the divine word. 'Because the length of the fast of these men was wonderful, and the days prolonged, let no man lightly fall into unbelief on that account. But rather let him believe and know that the contemplation of God, and the Word which is from Him, suffice to nourish those who hear and stand to them in place of food' (*Festal Letter* I.6).

It has already been observed that, despite the controversial environment in which Athanasius took office, there is no reference to his election or to contemporary debates in this opening *Festal Letter*. The theme throughout is moral exhortation and the wisdom of Scripture. Yet this does not mean that there is no polemical element. Immediately following his call to emulate the Old Testament prophets, Athanasius contrasts those who heed the truth of Easter with those who have failed to understand.

Wherefore, my beloved, having our souls nourished with divine food, with the Word, and according to the will of God, and fasting bodily in things external, let us keep this great and saving feast as becomes us. Even the foolish Jews received indeed this divine food, through the type, when they ate a lamb in the Passover. But not understanding the type, even to this day they eat the lamb, erring in that they are without a city and the truth. (*Festal Letter* I.7)

The Jewish Passover is merely a 'shadow' of the true Passover, which is the Christian Easter. Athanasius' condemnation of the ignorance of the Jews, which commences with this passage, is in fact relatively mild in

---

[6] On the Origenist theological language of this and other *Festal Letters*, see again Kannengiesser (1989).

comparison to some of his later *Festal Letters*. This anti-Jewish tone has to be acknowledged as another recurring feature of these epistles and one that has caused modern scholars certain embarrassment. It is true that hostility towards the Jews is hardly surprising in a fourth-century Christian text dedicated to Easter, and represented a cause around which Christians could unite. But, while it may be tempting to dismiss such polemic as no more than conventional rhetoric, Athanasius' repeated contrast of faithful Christians and ignorant Jews must at the least have hardened such divisions in the minds of his audience. Not every element of Athanasius' Easter summons must necessarily meet with our approval today.

The fundamental driving force of this first *Festal Letter*, however, is pastoral not polemical. The letter is a homily, an epistolary sermon. Athanasius reaches out across the broad sweep of the Egyptian Christian community, his message encapsulated in his exhortatory conclusion.

Let us remember the poor, and not forget kindness to strangers; above all, let us love God with all our soul and might and strength, and our neighbour as ourselves. So may we receive those things which the eye has not seen nor the ear heard, and which have not entered into the heart of man, which God has prepared for those that love Him through His only Son, our Lord and Saviour, Jesus Christ; through Whom, to the Father alone, by the Holy Spirit, be glory and dominion for ever and ever, Amen. Salute one another with a kiss. All the brethren who are with me salute you. (*Festal Letter* I.11)

THE PASTORAL BISHOP

A fourth-century bishop, as we saw in Chapter 2, had a variety of roles to play. In his church he was a preacher and teacher, responsible for the celebration of the liturgy and the spiritual and charitable care of his congregation. As a prominent social leader within his city, the bishop was also a central figure in civic administration and an important source of wealth and patronage. He represented the local community in the great councils and before imperial officials and even the emperor. Many of these roles had their origins in the evolution of the episcopal office in the first three Christian centuries preceding the conversion of Constantine. But, as imperial support flowed into the Church from Constantine onwards, the range and scale of the duties expected of the bishop expanded dramatically. This in turn raised new questions over the nature of episcopal leadership and how it should be held and exercised.[7]

[7] For bibliography on the changing roles of the fourth-century bishop, see Ch. 2, n. 2.

Athanasius played a central role in redefining the place of the bishop in the late-antique world. He was held up as an ideal for future generations a few short years after his death by Gregory of Nazianzus in his *Oration XXI*. Yet it is one of the great tragedies for modern Athanasian studies that we know so little of the bishop's daily routine. The account of his episcopal career offered earlier in this book is a story of ecclesiastical politics. In comparison to what we know about John Chrysostom or Augustine of Hippo, we gain only the briefest insights into Athanasius' clerical life, and many of his activities are known only from polemical contexts, which can easily conceal their pastoral significance.

For an example, we might consider Athanasius' fourth *Festal Letter*, written for the Easter of 332. This is the earliest *Festal Letter* to contain a direct reference to contemporary events. As Athanasius declared in his opening words, the circulation of his Easter announcement had been delayed.

I send unto you, my beloved, late and beyond the accustomed time; yet I trust you will forgive the delay, on account of my far journey, and because I have been tried with protracted illness. Being then hindered by these two causes, and unusually severe storms having occurred, I have deferred writing to you. But notwithstanding my far travelling, and my grievous sickness, I have not forgotten to give you the festal notification, and, in discharge of my duties, I now announce to you the feast. For although the letter has been delayed beyond the accustomed period of the proclamation, yet it should not be considered as ill-timed, inasmuch as, since the enemies have been put to shame and reproved by the Church, because they persecuted us without a cause, we may now sing a festal song of praise, uttering the triumphant hymn against Pharaoh: 'We will sing unto the Lord, for He is to be gloriously praised; the horse and his rider He has cast into the sea' [Exodus 15:1]. (*Festal Letter* IV.1)

Slightly later in this letter, Athanasius states that he was summoned to the court of Constantine to answer his enemies' accusations. He identifies those enemies as the Melitian schismatics, which, as we have previously seen, is a point of some importance, because in his subsequent writings he attributed his trial before Constantine to the 'Arian' conspiracy of the 'Eusebians'. Athanasius presents himself as the persecuted representative of the Church (although we assume he is not here likening Constantine to the Pharaoh of Exodus). The *Festal Letter* gave him the opportunity to explain his situation to the Egyptian Christians in his own words, while the action of writing a *Festal Letter* was itself a statement of Athanasius' claim to remain the true bishop of Alexandria despite his tribulations.

Nevertheless, to read the fourth *Festal Letter* purely as an exercise in ecclesiastical apologetic is to do Athanasius a grave injustice. As he rightly

insists, under the circumstances he faced it was a considerable achievement
to have fulfilled his duty and provided the festal notification to the Egyptian
churches. Athanasius then draws on his experiences to offer inspiration and
exegetical instruction to his congregations. Like those who suffered in the
Scriptures, they too must overcome their adversaries and approach the
feast with virtue. And so the force of this letter is once again moral and
spiritual exhortation:

> We need in this to put on our Lord Jesus, that we may be able to celebrate the feast
> with Him. Now we are clothed with Him when we love virtue and are enemies
> of wickedness; when we exercise ourselves in temperance and mortify lascivious-
> ness; when we love righteousness before iniquity; when we honour sufficiency
> and have strength of mind; when we do not forget the poor but open our doors to
> all men; when we assist humble-mindedness but hate pride. (*Festal Letter* IV.3)

Athanasius here repeats the call to remember the poor with which he
concluded his first *Festal Letter*. The importance of charity for the early
Christian Church has long been recognized.[8] Christian charity differed from
the welfare provided by the classical Graeco-Roman elite in its concern
for the very poor and its explicitly religious motivation. The care that the
early Christians offered to widows and orphans and for the sick and injured
played a major role in attracting converts to the new religion,[9] and over
time became one of the central obligations expected of a bishop. There is
no question that Athanasius met those expectations. Unfortunately, outside
the *Festal Letters*, this is another aspect of his pastoral duties that comes into
focus only at times of polemical conflict.

The charge that they deprived the poor of the expected charitable
distributions is levelled by Athanasius against both his Alexandrian rivals,
Gregory and George. But the abuse of charity was also alleged against
Athanasius himself, as the Council of Alexandria in 338 reported:

> A quantity of corn was given by the father of the Emperors [Constantine I] for the
> support of certain widows, partly of Libya and partly indeed out of Egypt. They
> have all received it up to this time, Athanasius getting nothing from this but the
> trouble of assisting them. But now, although the recipients themselves make no
> complaint but acknowledge that they have received it, Athanasius has been accused
> of selling all the corn and appropriating the profits to his own use. (*Encyclical Letter*
> of the Council of 338, quoted in *Apologia contra Arianos* 18)

---

[8] See, in general, Patlagean (1977); Brown (2002).
[9] This is a major theme of Stark (1996).

This accusation is dismissed by the Alexandrian council as an 'Arian calumny', under cover of which Athanasius' accusers seek 'to take away the corn from the Church and give it to the Arians'. After Gregory's entrance into Alexandria in 339, Athanasius took up the same theme, asserting that Gregory 'cut off the bread of the ministers and virgins' (*Epistula Encyclica* 4). The polemic culminates, as so often, in the *Historia Arianorum*, where Athanasius repeats his condemnation of Gregory and then charges George and the 'Arians' with going one stage further:

When the *dux* [Sebastianus] gave up the churches to the Arians, and the destitute persons and widows were unable to continue any longer in them, the widows sat down in places which the clergy entrusted with their care appointed. And when the Arians saw that the brethren readily ministered unto them and supported them, they persecuted the widows also, beating them on the feet, and accused those who gave to them before the *dux*. (*Historia Arianorum* 61)

The truth or otherwise of such claims is exceedingly difficult to assess. Athanasius, Gregory, and George all claimed the right to organize the distribution of charity, which was an important marker of the legitimate bishop of Alexandria, and in turn sought to discredit any rival.[10] But the biases of the polemic must not lead us to dismiss charity as no more than a tool for ecclesiastical leverage. Control over charity was important precisely because the early Church placed such great emphasis upon aiding the poor and disadvantaged. That Athanasius took this to heart in his pastoral mission, the *Festal Letters* make plain. Across his episcopate he continued to oversee charitable support for thousands of those in need and to urge others to do the same, even if our evidence preserves only a fraction of the works he wrought.

Charity, moral exhortation, and exegetical instruction were some of the roles that fell to Athanasius as the pastoral leader of the Christians of Alexandria and Egypt. The *Festal Letters* preserve some of his gifts as a teacher, although they cannot truly compensate for the loss of the sermons he preached. But preaching was only one of the bishop's responsibilities in the celebration of Christian worship. The rising numbers and greater social prominence that imperial patronage brought to the Church in the fourth century accelerated the ongoing formalization of early Christian liturgy and ceremonial.[11] Rituals of baptism (notably the growing practice

[10] This is rightly emphasized by Haas (1997: 248–56).
[11] On the history of the liturgy, see the older classics of Dix (1945) and Jungmann (1959), although Dix in particular exaggerates the impact of Constantine on Christian liturgical practice, and more recently Bradshaw (1996) and the articles collected in Jones et al. (1992).

of infant baptism) and the Eucharist became more standardized, although regional variations still remained. Increasing use was made of wider urban spaces with processions and festivals.[12] Local bishops like Athanasius were crucial in shaping these developments, overseeing the public life of their communities.

Sadly, our evidence once again offers only glimpses of Athanasius' liturgical and ceremonial contribution. The vast bulk of that evidence inevitably relates to Easter, which was the greatest festival of the Church and the focus of the *Festal Letters*. In his polemical writings Athanasius has few occasions to refer to such celebrations. The one notable exception concerns the controversy in *c*.351 when Easter was celebrated in the new and as yet undedicated church of the Caesareum. Athanasius' primary motive in the *Apologia ad Constantium* is to defend his actions, but behind the rhetoric his account sheds some light on the size of the Alexandrian Christian community and the importance of the Easter festival as an expression of their unity and faith.

It was the feast of Easter, and the multitude assembled together was exceedingly great, such as Christian kings would desire to see in all their cities. Now when the churches were found to be too few to contain them, there was no little stir among the people, who desired that they might be allowed to meet together in the great Church where they could all offer up their prayers for your [Constantius'] safety. And this they did. For although I exhorted them to wait awhile and to hold service in the other churches, with whatever inconvenience to themselves, they would not listen to me; but were ready to go out of the city and meet in desert places in the open air, thinking it better to endure the fatigue of the journey than to keep the feast in such a state of discomfort. (*Apologia ad Constantium* 14)

Athanasius goes on to explain that with the great multitude of worshippers the many children and older women suffered under the pressure of the crowds, although no one was killed. His predecessor Alexander had used the Church of Theonas before its completion under the same circumstances, and Athanasius now followed that precedent. The expanding Christian numbers in Alexandria were clearly outstripping the capacities of the older church buildings. Athanasius sought to maintain the togetherness of his community, and warned against allowing the people to go out beyond the city. 'The desert has no doors and all who choose may pass through it, but the Lord's house is enclosed with walls and doors and marks the difference between the pious and the profane' (*Apologia ad Constantium* 17).

[12] See Baldovin (1987); Bauer (1996).

Other brief glimpses of Athanasius' ceremonial leadership appear elsewhere in our sources. We have witnessed in previous chapters the great procession that welcomed him home to Alexandria in 346 and the vigil he led when the Church of Theonas came under attack on the night of 8/9 February 356. Further episodes were preserved in the Coptic Egyptian tradition, although the veracity of these later accounts is open to debate.[13] It is from scattered fragments such as these that we must seek to recapture the character of Athanasius' episcopal leadership and his impact upon his community. However, in one exceptional instance we can examine in some detail a significant change that Athanasius introduced into Egyptian Christian practice and his motives for doing so.

Here we turn once more to the *Festal Letters*. The controversy over the chronological order of the letters, discussed back in Chapter 1, is due in no small part to an important liturgical development in the Egyptian celebration of Easter during Athanasius' episcopate. When Athanasius became bishop, the custom in Egypt was for a six-day fast before Holy Week. This is the fast prescribed in the earliest *Festal Letters*, which make no attempt to explain what was evidently the standard Egyptian practice at this time. Yet only a few years after his election, Athanasius set out to replace the short fast with a longer forty-day Lenten fast, a break with local tradition he had to justify to his Egyptian audiences.

Modern scholars debate the precise moment at which the shift occurred, although a tentative date of 334 has plausibly been suggested.[14] It was once argued that Athanasius introduced the Lenten fast in *c*.336–7, after being influenced by practices that he witnessed during his first exile in the west. Athanasius is unlikely to have imposed such a change while he was in exile, however, and our key evidence is *Festal Letter* VI, which was most probably written in 334. This letter opens with the expected exhortation to honour the feast and give thanks to the Word, who became Incarnate for our salvation. The Jews are again condemned for their false Passover, and Abraham in offering to sacrifice his son Isaac is said to have worshipped the Son of God. These arguments are not new to Athanasius' Easter epistles. But when he comes to call his audience to the fast near the end of the letter, Athanasius declares:

As Israel, when going up to Jerusalem, was first purified in the wilderness, being trained to forget the customs of Egypt, the Word by this typifying to us the holy

---

[13] One such story, of the procession led by Athanasius to avert a tidal wave from Alexandria, is quoted from John of Nikiu at the end of the next chapter.

[14] For the arguments, see Brakke (2001: 457–61) and Camplani (2003: 178–81).

fast of forty days, let us first be purified and freed from defilement, so that when we depart hence, having been careful of fasting, we may be able to ascend to the upper chamber with the Lord, to sup with Him; and may be partakers of the joy which is in heaven. In no other manner is it possible to go up to Jerusalem, and to eat the Passover, except by observing the fast of forty days. (*Festal Letter* VI.12).

The need for a scriptural justification of the forty-day fast reflects the novelty of Athanasius' reform. And the stern warning in the final line suggests that he rightly anticipated resistance. In the light of the importance of the feast, any modification to traditional Easter worship would arouse alarm. We are, therefore, not surprised to learn that the new fast took time to become established. The *Festal Index* preserves as *Festal Letter* XII what is actually a personal letter that Athanasius wrote from exile in the west in *c*.337 or *c*.339/40 to his friend Serapion of Thmuis. Athanasius asks Serapion to circulate to the Egyptian churches the Easter message that he has enclosed. He then continues:

You should proclaim the fast of forty days to the brethren and persuade them to fast, lest, while all the world is fasting, we who are in Egypt should be derided as the only people who do not fast but take our pleasure in these days. For if, on account of the Letter [not] being yet read, we do not fast, we should take away this pretext, and it should be read before the fast of forty days, so that they may not make this an excuse for neglect or fasting. Also, when it is read, they may be able to learn about the fast. But O, my beloved, whether in this way or any other, persuade and teach them to fast the forty days. For it is a disgrace that when all the world does this, those alone who are in Egypt, instead of fasting, should find their pleasure. (*Letter to Serapion (Festal Letter* XII) 1)[15]

Athanasius obviously did face opposition to his introduction of the forty-day Lenten fast after 334. That opposition was difficult to overcome during his first two periods in exile, and still continued after his glorious return in 346. *Festal Letter* XIX for Easter 347 warns his audience once more that 'he who neglects to observe the fast of forty days, as one who rashly and impurely treads on holy things, cannot celebrate the Easter festival' (*Festal Letter* XIX.9). Acceptance of the forty-day fast had become one more marker of the true Christian and of those who recognized Athanasius' authority.

Why did Athanasius work so hard to impose the forty-day fast upon Egyptian Christianity, knowing full well the opposition he would arouse?

---

[15] The *Letter to Serapion* was once cited to support the argument that Athanasius' imposition of the forty-day fast was inspired by his time in the west. But this letter does not introduce the extended fast, but rather urges Serapion to enforce a practice that Athanasius has already imposed.

His *Letter to Serapion* emphasizes the need for Egypt to follow the practices of the wider Christian Church. The date and celebration of Easter had been a subject of discussion at the Council of Nicaea and Nicene canon 5 contains a reference to Lent.[16] This might indicate that Nicaea upheld a forty-day Lenten fast, which certainly existed in some churches by the early fourth century and which Athanasius wished Egypt to share. It has also been suggested that there was already an Alexandrian forty-day fast, which began at Epiphany (6 January) in imitation of Jesus' forty days in the wilderness and at the end of which catechumens were baptized. Athanasius may have moved this fast and associated it, not with Jesus' desert withdrawal, but with the Passover.[17]

Through the imposition of the forty-day fast, Athanasius therefore reinforced his leadership over the Egyptian Church and brought Egypt into line with orthodox Christian practice. Here again, however, to see this reform purely in terms of ecclesiastical authority is surely a mistake. The extended Easter fast served Athanasius' pastoral mission by promoting ascetic practices among the lay congregation for a longer duration and encouraging a greater focus of prayer on the Easter celebration. By the end of his episcopate, as far as we can judge, Athanasius had carried the argument. The forty-day Lenten fast has remained a period of the highest liturgical and spiritual importance for Christian worship in Egypt and by no means the least part of Athanasius' legacy.

PASTORAL THEOLOGY AND SALVATION

We have seen in an earlier chapter the importance that Athanasius placed on ensuring orthodox belief among his congregations at a time of theological controversy. This was not an 'academic' concern. The promise of Christian salvation rested upon the true understanding of the Incarnation and the relationship between God and humanity. In Athanasius' eyes it was this understanding that was threatened by the doctrines he regarded as 'Arian'. The fourth-century debates over how to define the Son and His divinity

---

[16] For an overview of the historical evolution of the Christian Easter and its liturgy, see Bertonière (1972) and the articles in Bradshaw and Hoffman (1999). There is a useful survey of the early evidence for the observance of Lent in Talley (1982), although unfortunately Talley is unaware of the problems involved with the numbering of Athanasius' *Festal Letters*.

[17] Brakke (2001: 460). This would explain why Athanasius in his scriptural justification for the forty-day fast in his *Festal Letters* never cites the apparently obvious example of Jesus' forty days in the desert.

raised very real pastoral concerns, which are reflected in the *Festal Letters* no less than in Athanasius' other writings.

The theology of Athanasius is most commonly studied through the detailed arguments presented in the great treatises, particularly *Contra Gentes–De Incarnatione* and the anti-'Arian' works. What we find in the *Festal Letters* are the same arguments reformulated for a pastoral context.[18] There is little explicit anti-'Arian' polemic, with a single notable exception to be discussed below. Athanasius' emphasis is rather on the positive call of faithful Christians to worship. The Incarnation and salvation through Christ are subjects highly appropriate to the Easter celebration that is the focus of the *Festal Letters* and are proclaimed in characteristically Athanasian terms. In the *Festal Letters* as elsewhere, Athanasius consistently upheld the full divinity of the Son, who took on our humanity as the fundamental guarantee for the Christian gift of salvation.

Examples of Athanasius' theological teachings can be drawn from throughout the surviving *Festal Letters*. The exhortation to the feast that opened Athanasius' first *Festal Letter* in 329 was immediately followed by the declaration that God sent His Word to aid us, 'saying "In an acceptable time have I heard thee, and on the day of salvation I have helped thee" [Isaiah 49:8]' (I.1). This theme is taken up at greater length in *Festal Letter* V for 333 as Athanasius praises the benevolence of God, which has made possible the Easter celebration:

He both brought about the slaying of His Son for salvation and gave us this reason for the holy feast, to which every year bears witness, as often as at this season the feast is proclaimed. This also leads us on from the cross through this world to that which is before us, and God produces even now from it the joy of glorious salvation, bringing us to the same assembly and in every place uniting all of us in spirit. (V.2)

Humanity by nature is unable to return a worthy recompense for the benefits given to us. Nevertheless, Athanasius calls on his congregations to show their thanks through piety and obedience to the Lord's commands and to keep the feast accordingly. Thus they will be separated from the pagans, Jews, schismatics, and heretics (V.3–4). Athanasius' vision of salvation in *Festal Letter* V closely parallels the argument of the *De Incarnatione*, which may be further evidence that the treatise was written at approximately this time.[19] *Festal Letter* VI, the letter that justified the forty-day Lenten fast and

---

[18] Merendino (1965); Anatolios (1998: 173–7).
[19] Kannengiesser (1989: 80).

was probably written for Easter 334, provides a further invocation of the Lord's sacrifice on our behalf:

The Lord died in those days, that we should no longer do the deeds of death. He gave His life, that we might preserve our own from the snares of the Devil. And, what is most wonderful, the Word became flesh, that we should no longer live in the flesh, but in spirit should worship God, who is Spirit. (VI.1)

The homiletic flavour of the theology that Athanasius presents in the *Festal Letters* is well represented in these passages. However, perhaps the most explicit and certainly the lengthiest theological statement preserved in Athanasius' Easter epistles is contained in *Festal Letter* X for 338. It has been observed previously that this letter is exceptional.[20] Composed in the tense period between Athanasius' first and second exiles, *Festal Letter* X opens with Athanasius' declaration that he has maintained the feast even when hindered by distance (X.1). This is followed by an extended meditation on scriptural examples of those who were persecuted for their faith (X.4–5). Athanasius uses his recent exile as a lesson for those under his pastoral care and teaches how Scripture helps Christians to self-understanding through trials. He also places himself within the tradition of the biblical patriarchs, reinforcing his own claim to orthodoxy and setting his foes alongside the Jews who killed Christ. *Festal Letter* X then culminates in one of the most powerful passages of theology and polemic anywhere in the Athanasian corpus:

The enemy draws near to us in afflictions and trials and labours, using every endeavour to ruin us. But the man who is in Christ, combating those things that are contrary and opposing wrath by long-suffering, contumely by meekness, and vice by virtue, obtains the victory and exclaims 'I can do all things through Christ who strengthens me' [Philippians 4:13] and 'In all these things we are conquerors through Christ who loved us' [Romans 8:37]. This is the grace of the Lord, and these are the Lord's means of restoration for the children of men. For He suffered to prepare freedom from suffering for those who suffer in Him; He descended that He might raise us up; He took on Him the trial of being born, that we might love Him who is unbegotten; He went down to corruption, that corruption might put on immortality; He became weak for us, that we might rise with power; He descended to death, that He might bestow on us immortality and give life to the dead. Finally, He became man, that we who die as men might live again, and that death should no more reign over us; for the apostolic word proclaims 'Death shall not have the dominion over us' [Romans 6:9, adapted].

---

[20] Ch. 2. As noted there (n. 30), *Festal Letter* X is the subject of an edition and monograph by Lorenz (1986).

Because they did not thus consider these matters, the Ariomaniacs,[21] being opponents of Christ and heretics, smite Him who is their Helper with their tongue, and blaspheme Him who set [them] free, and hold all manner of different opinions against the Saviour. Because of His coming down, which was on behalf of man, they have denied His essential Godhead; and seeing that He came forth from the Virgin, they doubt His being truly the Son of God; and considering Him as become incarnate in time, they deny His eternity; and looking upon Him as having suffered for us, they do not believe in Him as the incorruptible Son from the incorruptible Father. And finally, because He endured for our sakes, they deny the things which concern His essential eternity; allowing the deed of the unthankful, these despise the Saviour and offer Him insult instead of acknowledging His grace. (X.8–9)

Written for Easter 338, this is one of the earliest denunciations of the teachings attributed to 'Arianism' in Athanasius' writings. The construction of the heretics and the polarized contrast between their errors and the orthodoxy that Athanasius represents follow the same lines that we traced in his polemical treatises in Chapter 3. This is hardly surprising, for, when Athanasius circulated *Festal Letter* X, he had most probably begun to work on the *Orationes contra Arianos*. What we gain from the *Festal Letter* is a clearer appreciation of the pastoral issues at stake. The central theme of the letter's theological message is again the saving role of the Word through the Incarnation. Here we need to remember that none of those whom Athanasius condemned as 'Arian' would have disagreed with the praise of the Son offered in X.8. The question that was actually under debate, as we learn from X.9, was whether the Son had to share in the eternal and essential Godhead of the Father for the promise of salvation to be fulfilled. It was Athanasius' pastoral obligation to teach the true doctrine to the Egyptian churches and warn them against the 'Arian' errors. A similar still more concise description of 'Arianism' appeared in *Festal Letter* XI for the following year. The heretics have 'dug a pit of unbelief into which they themselves have been thrust…blaspheming the Son of God and saying that He is a creature and has His being from things which are not' (XI.10).[22]

No subsequent *Festal Letter* contains the same level of theological polemic as the letters written during the difficult years at the end of the 330s. But even in *Festal Letters* X and XI, Athanasius' chief aim was not to denounce 'Arianism'. His concern was rather the positive call that his people continue to celebrate Easter and praise God for the grace given to humanity through

[21] This characteristic Athanasian expression was miscopied in the Syriac manuscript transmission of the *Festal Letters* as 'Arius and Manetes'.

[22] *Festal Letter* XI.12 also contains the sole reference in any of the Easter epistles to the 'Eusebians', who encourage others to attack Athanasius.

the Incarnation. The arguments that he brought forward to achieve this purpose in the *Festal Letters* parallel closely those found in the more widely studied treatises like *De Incarnatione* and the *Orationes contra Arianos*. We are, therefore, reminded once more that the doctrinal controversies of the fourth century had very real pastoral implications for ordinary Christians. Athanasius never lost sight of the practical needs of his congregations. The emphasis on faith and correct belief in the *Festal Letters* is accompanied at all times with a corresponding emphasis on how a Christian should live, to which we must now turn.

PASTORAL ASCETICISM AND THE CHRISTIAN LIFE

Throughout Athanasius' writings the theological orthodoxy that he taught and the Christian lifestyle that he promoted are inseparably intertwined. This has already been explored in some detail in the preceding chapters, but is brought into particular focus through Athanasius' pastoral activity. In the *Festal Letters*, Athanasius placed just as much stress on correct action as he did on correct belief. The model of Christian behaviour that he encouraged his congregations to follow has been aptly described as an 'asceticism of everyday life'. The laymen and women of the Egyptian churches were urged to approach the Easter period as a time for fasting and prayer. In effect, they could adopt for Lent the principles that in his letters to monks and virgins Athanasius laid down as the basis of the ascetic commitment. By doing so they would narrow the growing gulf that threatened to separate ordinary Christians from the expanding ascetic movement. It is possible to see this at one level as a means for Athanasius to maintain the unity of the diverse communities under his leadership. But at the heart of Athanasius' pastoral mission was a deep conviction of the importance of ascetic principles to his vision of how a Christian should live in the world.

Athanasius recognized from the beginning of his episcopate the value of the *Festal Letters* as a means to preach a true Christian lifestyle. The significance of the Easter fast is a recurring theme of the first *Festal Letter*, as we have seen, and Athanasius addresses himself both to devout ascetics and to the lay population. Moreover, the fast is not merely an empty ritual to be performed without thought, but is intimately bound to the gift of salvation that the Easter celebration affirms. This is made explicit in *Festal Letter* V:

Let us eat the Passover of the Lord, who, by ordaining His holy laws, guided us towards virtue and counselled the abstinence of this feast. For the Passover is indeed abstinence from evil for exercise of virtue, and a departure from death unto life. This may be learnt even from the type of old time. For then they toiled earnestly to pass from Egypt to Jerusalem, but now we depart from death to life; they then passed from Pharaoh to Moses, but now we rise from the Devil to the Saviour. And as, at that time, the type of deliverance bore witness every year, so now we commemorate our salvation. We fast meditating on death, that we may be able to live. (V.4)

The introduction of the forty-day Lenten fast in *Festal Letter* VI gave further impetus to Athanasius' promotion of pastoral asceticism. Near the end of the letter, just before his warning that only those who celebrated the new forty-day fast could partake of the true Passover, Athanasius instructed his congregations on how they should conduct the fast. His exhortation draws on a series of scriptural examples, and Athanasius particularly singled out married couples and urged them to purify themselves for the feast.

Let us glorify the Lord by chastity, by righteousness, and other virtues. And let us rejoice, not in ourselves, but in the Lord, that we may be inheritors with the saints. Let us keep the feast then, as Moses. Let us watch like David, who rose seven times, and in the middle of the night gave thanks for the righteous judgements of God. Let us be early, as he said, 'In the morning I will stand before Thee, and Thou will look upon me; in the morning Thou will hear my voice' [Psalm 5:3]. Let us fast like Daniel; let us pray without ceasing as Paul commanded; all of us recognizing the season of prayer, but especially those who are honourably married; so that having borne witness to these things, and thus having kept the feast, we may be able to enter into the joy of Christ in the kingdom of heaven. (VI.12)

Here again we see Athanasius' fundamental emphasis that ascetic commitment is not the sole preserve of a spiritual elite. Every Christian man and woman, whatever his or her personal status, may aspire to share in the ascetic lifestyle. This universal vision runs throughout the Athanasian ascetica, and receives one of its strongest pastoral statements in the long tenth *Festal Letter* for Easter 338. The exceptional anti-'Arian' polemic at the end of this letter has already been discussed. But, earlier in *Festal Letter* X, Athanasius contrasted the persecution unleashed by his enemies to the goodness of God. The Lord knows well the weakness of humanity, and does not expect all to seek salvation in the same way. On the contrary, 'He varies Himself according to the individual capacity of each soul' (X.4). Athanasius divides the Christian community into three categories of perfection, illustrated by the Pauline Epistles and from the Gospels by the Parable of the Sower.

To those then who have not yet attained to the perfect way He becomes like a sheep giving milk, and this was administered by Paul, 'I have fed you with milk, not with meat' [1 Corinthians 3:2]. To those who have advanced beyond the full stature of childhood, but still are weak as regards perfection, He is their food according to their capacity, being again administered by Paul, 'Let him that is weak eat herbs' [Romans 14:2]. But as soon as ever a man begins to walk in the perfect way, he is no longer fed with the things before mentioned, but he has the Word for bread and flesh for food, for it is written, 'Strong meat is for those who are of full age, for those who, by reason of their capacity, have their senses exercised' [Hebrews 5:14].[23]

And further, when the word is sown it does not yield a uniform produce of fruit in this human life, but one various and rich. For it brings forth, some a hundred, and some sixty, and some thirty, as the Saviour teaches [Matthew 13:1–23, Mark 4:1–20, Luke 8:1–15]—that Sower of grace and Bestower of the Spirit. And this is no doubtful matter, nor one that admits no confirmation; but it is in our power to behold the field which is sown by Him, for in the Church the word is manifold and the produce rich. Not with virgins alone is such a field adorned, nor with monks alone, but also with honourable matrimony and the chastity of each one. For in sowing, He did not compel the will beyond the power. Nor is mercy confined to the perfect, but it is sent down also among those who occupy the middle and the third ranks, so that He might rescue all men generally to salvation. To this intent He has prepared many mansions with the Father, so that although the dwelling-place is various in proportion to the advance in moral attainment, yet all of us are within the wall and all of us enter within the same fence, the adversary being cast out and all his host expelled thence. For apart from light there is darkness, and apart from blessing there is a curse, the Devil also is apart from the saints, and sin far from virtue. (X.4)

In *Festal Letter* X Athanasius confronted the essential pastoral dilemma that the rise of the ascetic movement raised for the Christian community. The monks and virgins of the fourth century, like the martyrs and confessors of earlier times, exalted themselves to a higher spiritual level than their fellow believers. This threatened to create divisions that might provoke conflict and reduce 'ordinary' Christians to second-class citizens of the Church. Athanasius held true both to his respect for asceticism and to his pastoral mission. He paid due honour to those who followed an ascetic lifestyle and placed them in a higher category on the path to perfection. But he insisted that all true Christians would be saved and all could seek to progress towards perfection through their own free will. His interpretation of the Parable of the Sower in *Festal Letter* X echoes the first *Letter to*

---

[23] The passage quoted here from Hebrews is not attributed to Paul, as are those from 1 Corinthians and Romans. Athanasius was aware of the non-Pauline authorship of Hebrews, although, as we will see, he included Hebrews among the Pauline Epistles in *Festal Letter* XXXIX on the canon of Scripture.

Virgins (likewise dated to c.338) and the *Letter to Amoun*, confirming that he expressed such arguments in works intended for wider audiences than his specifically ascetic writings.[24] For Athanasius, the only division that mattered was the separation between faithful Christians and their adversaries, represented in *Festal Letter* X by the 'Arians'. His concern for ecclesiastical unity and theological orthodoxy, which also reinforced his disputed position as leader of the Egyptian Church in 338, came together with his ascetic programme in the pastoral context for which the letter was written.

Athanasius continued to promote ascetic practices among Egyptian Christians throughout his episcopate. The later *Festal Letters* provide fewer explicit statements on this theme, but this is due primarily to the fragmentary survival of the Easter epistles from the 350s and 360s. Certainly Athanasius' convictions did not waver, as his other writings make clear. He continued to preach the ascetic message to his congregations, urging his listeners to emulate their champions. One man at least took that message to heart. 'I heard the blessed Pope Athanasius in church, proclaiming the lifestyle of the monks and consecrated virgins and marveling at the hope laid up for them in heaven. And admiring their blessed life, I chose it for myself' (*Letter of Ammon* 2). The monk Ammon experienced his conversion to asceticism in c.351, and would later become a bishop and so join the increasing numbers of monks within the Egyptian episcopate.[25]

For a final example of Athanasius' pastoral vision of the Christian life, drawing again on theology and asceticism in concert, we will look beyond the *Festal Letters* to elsewhere in Athanasius' correspondence. The date when Athanasius wrote his *Letter to Marcellinus* is uncertain.[26] The text contains little specific historical content, and Marcellinus himself is unknown. He may have been a deacon of the Alexandrian church, or an urban Christian who had heeded Athanasius' call to adopt an ascetic life.[27] According to the letter, he had fallen ill, but had occupied his time by studying the Scriptures.

[24] A far more polemical approach to such questions, and to the Parable of the Sower, is exhibited by Jerome in 393 in his condemnation of Jovianus for teaching that virgins, married women, and widows are of equal merit in the eyes of God (*Contra Jovinianum* I.3).

[25] On Ammon's life and *Letter*, see further Goehring (1985).

[26] There is a translation with introduction and notes in Gregg (1980). See also Rondeau (1968), Anatolios (1998: 195–200), and Kolbet (2006).

[27] A deacon named Marcellinus signed the letter of protest against the Mareotis Commission in 335 (quoted in *Apologia contra Arianos* 73). The name was common, however, and there is no clear indication that Athanasius' addressee held clerical office. In the light of his illness, it is likewise possible but unproven that Marcellinus was also the recipient of Athanasius' fragmentary treatise *On Sickness and Health*.

He asked Athanasius for advice on the Psalms. Athanasius' response is a meditation on the Psalter as a guide for living a Christian life.

After congratulating Marcellinus on his enduring discipline (*askesis*) despite his sufferings, Athanasius commends him for studying the Psalms. 'I too have a great fondness for the same book—just as I have for all the Scripture. Indeed, it so happens that I had a conversation with a learned old man, and I wish to write you those things that old master of the Psalter told me' (1). Whether that old master was a real person or a rhetorical device remains unknown, but the Psalms were widely read in ascetic circles. In the *Life of Antony*, study of the Psalter is a crucial feature of the hermit's training, and the demons are said to have wailed when Antony would chant the Psalms.[28] To Marcellinus, Athanasius presents the Psalms as representative of the scope of scriptural wisdom and both a source of practical advice and a focus for prayer.

All the books of the Old Testament have a particular purpose, from the Pentateuch, which tells of creation, the patriarchs, and the Exodus, to the Prophets, who foretold the Saviour. 'Yet the Book of Psalms is like a garden containing things of all these kinds, and it sets them to music, but also exhibits things of its own that it gives in song along with them' (2). The themes of the other books are restated in the Psalms, especially the coming of the Saviour in the Incarnation (5–8). This uniformity proclaims the same Spirit, which speaks throughout the Scriptures (9–10). The Psalms, however, go further than the other books. Not only do they teach the need to repent, to bear sufferings, and to give thanks, but also how to do so and what one must say (10). Above all, Athanasius declares, the Psalms touch the reader more deeply than just inspiring emulation.

He who takes up this book—the Psalter—goes through the prophecies about the Saviour, as is customary in the other Scriptures, with admiration and adoration, but the other psalms he recognizes as being his own words. And the one who hears is deeply moved, as though he himself were speaking, and is affected by the words of the songs, as if they were his own songs. (11)

The Psalms guide us and inspire us, stirring emotion and leading us to self-reflection:

It seems to me that these words [the Psalms] become like a mirror to the person singing them, so that he might perceive himself and the emotions of his soul,

---

[28] *Life of Antony* 39–40. The importance of studying the Psalms is similarly emphasized in Athanasius' *Letter to Amoun*.

and thus affected, he might recite them. For in fact he who hears the one reading receives the song that is recited as being about him, and either, when he is convicted by his conscience, being pierced, he will repent, or hearing of the hope that resides in God and of the succour available to believers—how this kind of grace exists for him—he exults and begins to give thanks to God. (12)

These opening sections of the letter do not directly address Marcellinus and his request for advice. Athanasius' argument has a wider pastoral purpose, grounded in his conception of the Scriptures as a source of inspiration for all Christians, whatever their standing. Every man or woman who reads the Psalms may find guidance therein through divine grace. This grace is offered through the Saviour, for here, as throughout his teachings, Athanasius returns to the Incarnation as the foundation for the Christian faith and the model for the Christian life.

When He became man for us He offered His own body in dying for our sake, in order that He might set all free from death. And desiring to show us His own heavenly and well-pleasing life, He provided its type in Himself, to the end that some might no more easily be deceived by the enemy, having a pledge for protection—namely, the victory He won over the Devil for our sake. (13)

Against this background, the main body of the *Letter to Marcellinus* then turns to the individual psalms and their application to the human condition (14–26). Athanasius first catalogues the psalms by form and purpose, then identifies the different situations in which a person can turn to the Psalter for aid. Those who condemn the Jews for betraying the Saviour read Psalm 3; those who give thanks to the Lord for the vintage sing Psalms 8 and 83; those who see others doing evil say Psalm 36.[29] Charity to those in need is encouraged by Psalm 40, repentance by Psalm 50. Many psalms encourage thanksgiving and provide the words appropriate for praise: Psalms 104, 106, 134, 145, 146, 147, 148, and 150. And the Psalter offers particular support to those who suffer persecution, a theme of special significance for Athanasius himself, who may turn among others to Psalms 3, 17, 24, 26, 30, 39, 53, 55, 56, 58, 61, 76, 84, and 125.

The letter's concluding sections reaffirm Athanasius' vision of the Psalter. The Psalms are not musical to delight the ear, but for the benefit of

---

[29] Athanasius here warns against those who 'think that the evil is in their very nature, which is what the heretics assert' (18). This was a teaching held by some Gnostic groups and also by Manichaeism.

the soul and to govern the emotions to serve the will of God (27–9).[30] For those who recite the Psalms correctly, without artifice or profane addition, they are sufficient for all eventualities and will drive away demons (30–3). Athanasius closes the letter with an exhortation to Marcellinus that encapsulates his pastoral appeal to every Christian. The divine grace expressed through the words and deeds in the Scriptures can be attained by all who devote themselves to the spiritual life to the measure of their ability. 'You too, practicing these things and reciting the Psalms intelligently, in this way, are able to comprehend the meaning in each, being guided by the Spirit. And the kind of life the holy, God-bearing men possessed who spoke these things—this life you also shall imitate' (33).

THE CANON OF SCRIPTURE: *FESTAL LETTER XXXIX*

It seems appropriate to conclude this chapter with a consideration of what is perhaps Athanasius' best-known *Festal Letter* and one of his most frequently cited works. *Festal Letter* XXXIX, written for the Easter of 367, is a fundamental document for the evolution of the Christian Scriptures.[31] It contains the oldest extant list of New Testament books that duplicates the New Testament canon in the modern Bible. The importance of the letter was recognized early, for this is the only *Festal Letter* to survive substantially in Greek as well as in this case Coptic.[32] Because of its unique character, however, *Festal Letter* XXXIX has too often been read in isolation. Athanasius' emphasis upon the canon of Scripture cannot be understood properly unless we place this letter within its wider context. Once this is done, the letter becomes a valuable resource not only for scriptural history but for the theological and pastoral values that Athanasius still sought to promote in the closing years of his episcopate.

By 367 Athanasius' long struggle for the hearts and souls of the Christian communities of Egypt was almost at an end. He had returned from his fifth and final period of exile, and his authority and his reputation as the heroic defender of orthodoxy were firmly established. Opposition remained,

[30] According to Augustine (*Confessions* X.33), Athanasius was said to have insisted that lectors who recite the Psalms should avoid excessive modulation of voice and so appear to speak rather than to chant. See also P. Bright (1997).

[31] There is an overview of Athanasius' approach to the Scriptures in Ernest (2004). For a clear introduction to the formation of the Christian Bible, see McDonald (1995).

[32] For the text, see now Brakke (2010). On the letter, see also Brakke (1994b) and Demacopoulos (2007: 21–49).

but the pastoral labours of previous decades had secured him the devotion of the vast majority of the Egyptian Church. In *Festal Letter* XXXIX
we see Athanasius primarily as a teacher and exegete, educating his audience on reading the Scriptures and on which books they should regard as
canonical. But Athanasius' exegesis can never be separated from his concern for correct doctrine and practice, while his definition of the accepted
scriptural canon was also a statement of power addressed against those
whom he held to be in error. Here, as throughout the *Festal Letters*, Athanasius' pastoral convictions bring together the different strands that we have
traced across his life.

The opening lines of *Festal Letter* XXXIX are lost in both Greek and
Coptic. When our surviving text begins, Athanasius is already speaking
of God's revelation to man through the Word. 'For the teaching of piety
does not come from human beings; rather, it is the Lord who reveals His
Father to those whom He wills because it is He who knows Him [Matthew
11:27]' (7). The Lord taught Paul and the other Apostles, and so in turn
He is the one true Teacher who teaches all. 'The task of the teacher is to
teach, and that of the disciple is to learn. But even if these people teach,
they are still called "disciples", for it is not they who are the originators of
what they proclaim; rather, they are at the service of the words of the true
Teacher' (11). Athanasius reinforces his argument from theology, restating
the ontological gulf that separates humanity from the divine. Humanity is
part of the created order and therefore by nature must be taught, while the
Word by nature is a teacher who grants knowledge of the Spirit to those
who wish to become students of God.

In a manner familiar from his polemical writings, Athanasius immediately contrasts the faithful who have heeded the teachings of Christ with
those who have not. The Jews failed to understand Jesus and so persecuted
him, and they have been imitated by the heretics who in their ignorance
cannot celebrate the true Easter.

For the Jews gather together like Pontius Pilate, and the Arians and the Melitians
like Herod, not to celebrate the feast but to blaspheme the Lord, saying, 'What
is truth?' [John 18:38] and 'Take him away! Crucify him! Release to us Barabbas!'
[Luke 23:18]. For it is just like the request for Barabbas to say that the Son of God is
a creature and that there was a time when He was not. (14)

Only Athanasius and his churches keep the feast according to tradition and read the Holy Scriptures carefully and with a good conscience.
These twin arguments, exalting the divine revelation of the Word and
separating those who have received the truth from those in error, set the

scene for Athanasius to introduce his primary theme. The divine Scriptures are needed for salvation. But 'we are afraid that, as Paul wrote to the Corinthians [2 Corinthians 11:3], a few of the simple folk might be led astray from sincerity and purity through human deceit and might then begin to read other books, the so-called apocrypha, deceived by their having the same names as the genuine books' (15). Therefore:

It seemed good to me, because I have been urged by genuine brothers and sisters and instructed from the beginning, to set forth in order the books that are canonized, transmitted, and believed to be divine, so that those who have been deceived might condemn the persons who led them astray, and those who have remained pure might rejoice to be reminded [of these things]. (16)

According to Athanasius, the Old Testament books number twenty-two. This is, 'as I have heard' (17) (for Athanasius did not read Hebrew), the number of letters in the Hebrew alphabet. They begin with Genesis; Exodus; Leviticus; Numbers; Deuteronomy; Joshua; Judges; and Ruth. Then four books of Kings, the first two being reckoned as one book [1–2 Samuel] and the second two as one book [1–2 Kings]. There are first and second Chronicles, again reckoned as one book [1–2 Chronicles]; and first and second Esdras likewise [Ezra, Nehemiah]. Then Psalms; Proverbs; Ecclesiastes; the Song of Songs; Job; the Twelve Prophets counted together as one book; Isaiah; Jeremiah with Baruch, Lamentations, and the Letter; Ezekiel; and Daniel. The most notable omission here is the Book of Esther, which Athanasius later classes under non-canonical works, although he does include Baruch with Jeremiah.

The books of the New Testament follow. After Matthew; Mark; Luke; and John; there comes Acts of the Apostles; and the seven catholic letters: one by James; two by Peter; three by John; and one by Jude. Then there are fourteen letters by Paul, in order Romans; 1–2 Corinthians; Galatians; Ephesians; Philippians; Colossians; 1–2 Thessalonians; Hebrews; 1–2 Timothy; Titus; and Philemon. Finally, there is the Revelation of John. Athanasius places the catholic epistles before those of Paul, and includes Hebrews among the Pauline epistles.

'These are the springs of salvation, so that someone who thirsts may be satisfied by the words they contain. In these books alone the teaching of piety is proclaimed' (19). However, Athanasius acknowledges that 'there are other books, in addition to the preceding, which have not been canonized, but have been appointed by the ancestors to be read to those who newly join us and want to be instructed in the word of piety' (20). It is in this category that he includes the Wisdom of Solomon; the Wisdom of

Sirach; Esther; Judith; Tobit; Teaching of the Apostles; and the Shepherd of Hermas.[33] These works may be read, and are distinct from the true apocrypha, which are the invention of heretics. Athanasius refers to texts attributed falsely to Enoch, Isaiah, and Moses. Such works only spread discord. 'Therefore, it is fitting for us to decline such books. For even if a useful word is found in them, it is still not good to trust them' (23).

Athanasius continues his argument by emphasizing the theological sufficiency of the recognized scriptural books. 'If we seek the faith, it is possible for us to discover it through [the Scriptures], so that we might believe in the Father, the Son, and the Holy Spirit. If [we seek after] the subject of His humanity, John cries out, "The Word became flesh and lived among us" [John 1:14]' (24). Similarly the Scriptures confirm the resurrection of the dead and the coming judgement, with a further condemnation of the errors of the Manichaeans, Marcion, the Montanists, the Arians, and the Melitians. Thus the inspired works provide all that is required for instruction in the Christian faith:

Therefore, inasmuch as it is clear that the testimony from the apocryphal books is superfluous because it is unfounded—for the Scripture is perfect in every way—let the teacher teach from the words of Scripture, and let him place before those who desire to learn those things that are appropriate to their age. In the case of those who begin to study as catechumens, it is not right to proclaim the obscure texts of Scripture, because they are mysteries, but instead to place before them the teaching that they need: what will teach them how to hate sin and to abandon idolatry as an abomination. (28)

Athanasius here spells out the very real pastoral issue that underlies this *Festal Letter*. His interest in the canon of Scripture was not that of an academic scholar.[34] Teaching the faithful was one of the fundamental duties of a bishop, made still more important in the later fourth century by the rapid increase in Christian numbers. Scriptural study was crucial to the education of a Christian in Late Antiquity, as it is today, and Athanasius was not alone in emphasizing the need for careful instruction to ensure new converts did not fall into error.[35] *Festal Letter* XXXIX in 367 must be read in

[33] Much earlier, Athanasius had described the Shepherd of Hermas as a 'most helpful book' (*De Incarnatione* 3), although he had never regarded the work as part of the scriptural canon (see also *De Decretis* 18).
[34] For the argument that Athanasius sought to promote an episcopal parish-based spirituality over the authority of the teacher and martyr, see Brakke (1994*b*) and Watts (2006: 175–81).
[35] The finest extant examples of such instruction from the fourth century are the *Catechetical Lectures* of Cyril of Jerusalem. On Cyril, his teachings, and his context, see Drijvers (2004).

the light of this practical concern. Athanasius did not engage in exegesis or doctrinal debate unless those activities had a necessary pastoral purpose. This is summed up in the conclusion to the letter, when Athanasius states concisely why he had felt driven to write in the manner he had and the joyous ends that he hoped would be achieved:

I have not written these things as if I were teaching, for I have not attained such a rank. Rather, because I heard that the heretics, especially the wretched Melitians, were boasting about the books that they call 'apocryphal'. I thus have informed you of everything that I heard from my father [Alexander], as if I were with you and you with me in a single house, that is, 'the church of God, the pillar and strength of truth' [1 Timothy 3:15]. When we gather in a single place, let us purify it of every defilement, of double-heartedness, of fighting and childish arrogance. Let us be satisfied with only the Scripture inspired by God to instruct us. Its books we have set forth in the words above: which they are and how many their number. For in this way we now celebrate the feast as is fitting, 'not with old leaven nor with evil or wicked leaven, but with pure and true leaven' [1 Corinthians 5:8]. (32)

Pastoral duty is again a major emphasis here, the concern that Athanasius' congregation must not be led astray. He is also once more stamping his leadership on the Egyptian Church, seeking to ensure uniformity among his followers much as he had with the forty-day fast of Lent. In effect, the bishop of Alexandria has claimed the right not only to interpret Scripture but to determine what qualifies as Scripture, and has denounced any who hold alternative views as 'Melitian' or 'Arian'. Here, as throughout Athanasius' episcopal career, questions of ecclesiastical authority and sincere pastoral concern are inextricably intertwined.

Whether Athanasius succeeded in his ambitions, we do not know. As has already been mentioned, *Festal Letter* XXXIX is in fact the only Athanasian *Festal Letter* for which we have explicit testimony of its reception, when the letter was read out and then posted in Pachomian monasteries.[36] It has even been suggested that the famous collection of Gnostic codices discovered at Nag Hammadi were buried by nearby Pachomian monks after Athanasius condemned the use of such non-canonical works.[37] But the impact of pastoral care, like moral exhortation or spiritual guidance, has never been easy to gauge. What cannot be in doubt is Athanasius' conviction of his obligations and his desire to fulfil them. There are polemical themes

---

[36] Bohairic *Life of Pachomius* 189.
[37] Robinson (1996: 19–20).

in Athanasius' writings that do not always sit well with a modern audience, and he faced a constant struggle to maintain his position, which inevitably influenced his words and actions. Nevertheless, the motivating force behind *Festal Letter* XXXIX and all the *Festal Letters* was first and foremost pastoral. Athanasius was rightly remembered in Egyptian tradition as a great spiritual leader of the Christian Church.

6

Death and Legacy

The duties of his office he discharged in the same spirit as that in which he had been preferred to it...He was sublime in action, lowly in mind; inaccessible in virtue, most accessible in intercourse; gentle, free from anger, sympathetic, sweet in words, sweeter in disposition; angelic in appearance, more angelic in mind; calm in rebuke, persuasive in praise, without spoiling the good effect of either by excess, but rebuking with the tenderness of a father, praising with the dignity of a ruler, his tenderness was not dissipated, nor his severity sour; for the one was reasonable, the other prudent, and both truly wise; his disposition sufficed for the training of his spiritual children, with very little need of words; his words with very little need of the rod, and his moderate use of the rod with still less for the knife. (Gregory of Nazianzus, *Oration* XXI.9)

The people assembled and took counsel, and appointed the Father Athanasius, and seated him on the evangelical throne. And he wrote excellent treatises and many homilies; and he was called during his patriarchate the Apostolic, on account of the nobility of his deeds, which were like those of the Apostles. (*History of the Patriarchs of Alexandria*, PO 1:403)

Athanasius' death on 2 May 373 marked the passing of an era. Few men still lived who could remember the outbreak of the Great Persecution and the shock of Constantine's conversion, or who could recall the Council of Nicaea in its splendour. Athanasius had witnessed first hand the transformation of Christianity into the dominant religion of the Roman Empire, and through his long and often controversial career he had played a crucial part in shaping the new imperial Church. By the end of his life, his reputation was secure. A few opponents lingered, both inside and outside Egypt, but their voices were fading. Through his leadership and strength of character, his theological and ascetic convictions, and his pastoral dedication, Athanasius had become recognized as the great champion of his age. He had become a Father of the Church, a man whose name was known across the Christian world, and whose words and example would provide a source of inspiration for later men and women to follow.

The final years of Athanasius' episcopate had been relatively peaceful. Yet tensions remained. His chosen successor, Peter II, was exiled almost immediately and replaced by the 'Arian' Lucius, leaving the authority of the Alexandrian see once again under threat. The theological debates that exerted such an influence upon Athanasius continued unabated. The Cappadocian Fathers were refining the Trinitarian teachings that would be upheld at the Council of Constantinople in 381, and the seeds of the Christological divisions of the fifth century had already been sown. The ascetic movement had spread across the Mediterranean, not least through Athanasius' patronage and the impact of the *Life of Antony*. But asceticism took many forms, and its place within society and the organized Church still had to be resolved. Athanasius, like his contemporaries, had struggled with the need to define the very nature of Christianity in a changing world. For the subsequent generations who faced that same struggle in their own times, Athanasius became himself part of Christian tradition, a figure of authority to whom all might appeal. In this final chapter I wish to explore briefly the diverse legacy of Athanasius and the different interpretations of his memory that emerged in the Greek east and the Latin west, the Syriac and Armenian worlds, and the Coptic Egypt of his Alexandrian successors.

From the perspective of the modern student, it is all too easy to view Christian tradition as something fixed and static. Western university patristic courses trace the history and doctrinal development of the early Church through the Fathers, the men whose writings came to be regarded as authoritative, and through the creeds and canons of the ecumenical councils. Tradition, however, is neither fixed nor static. On the contrary, it is a living entity, constantly redefined as new controversies arise and contexts change. During his life Athanasius appealed repeatedly to the traditional faith of the Church, reinterpreting that faith according to his personal concerns. The vast majority of later Christians would come to share his views, just as they shared his definition of the canonical books of the New Testament and the meaning of the original Nicene Creed. Yet Athanasius' conception of tradition was by no means universal among his contemporaries, and nor was Athanasius alone in the fourth century in seeking to reinterpret earlier traditions. Athanasius' influence is a tribute to the power and clarity of his teachings and to his reputation as a heroic bishop and confessor. Nevertheless, his later influence should not lead us to exaggerate his status in his own time, while later generations would themselves interpret Athanasius' legacy in significantly different ways.

The various Christian traditions on Athanasius that I will examine share considerable common ground. All represent Athanasius as a leading bishop of the fourth-century Church, and all uphold Athanasius' conception of himself as a champion of orthodoxy and of the Council of Nicaea. There were dissident opinions, but in the fifth century they were being marginalized, and today they survive only in fragments. Even among those who revered his memory, however, Athanasius' legacy is not as monolithic as one might perhaps expect. Different linguistic and cultural traditions emphasized different elements of Athanasius' life and writings. Later authors reinterpreted and where necessary reshaped their material to suit their individual motives and contexts. The widely varying visions of Athanasius in modern scholarship are a continuation of this theme. Tracing Athanasius' legacy highlights the diverse ways in which a great Father of the Church could be remembered and reinvented to serve the changing needs of later centuries.[1]

ATHANASIUS IN THE GREEK EAST

Athanasius has remained a powerful figure within Greek Christian tradition down to the present day. His works were preserved, and the power of his name attracted further writings that were not his own. The polemical construction of the 'Arian Controversy' that he created would become enshrined in Greek ecclesiastical history, and his theological and ascetic teachings would be cited as authoritative in numerous later controversies. Athanasius' triumph came at a price: the loss of alternative interpretations of his career that were not preserved and in some instances deliberately destroyed. Here I am primarily interested in exploring how attitudes towards Athanasius in Greek Christian literature evolved over time, from his younger contemporary Gregory of Nazianzus to the divisions that emerged after the Council of Chalcedon in 451. As the historical Athanasius receded into the past, his image was continually reshaped and his life and teachings acquired new meanings, not all of which might have seemed familiar to the great bishop himself.

---

[1] '"Tradition" refers simultaneously to the process of communication and to its content. Thus tradition means the handing down of Christian teaching during the course of the history of the Church, but it also means that which was handed down' (Pelikan 1971: 7). For an overview of Christian tradition, see Pelikan (2003). On the reception of Athanasius in the diverse traditions discussed in this chapter, see also the contributions in Gemeinhardt (2011: 390–425).

Gregory of Nazianzus' *Oration* XXI in honour of Athanasius, composed
less than ten years after the latter's death, is an important landmark in the
development of the Alexandrian bishop's posthumous reputation.[2] There
is no indication that Gregory and Athanasius ever met, although as a youth
Gregory had studied in Alexandria in 348 during Athanasius' golden decade.
Like his friend Basil of Caesarea, Gregory admired Athanasius greatly,
although in his theology he moved beyond Athanasius' teachings, particularly on the importance of the Son's full humanity in the Incarnation.
Oration XXI, delivered in May 380, was a devout expression of that admiration for Athanasius as an ideal Christian leader and laid down a model for
subsequent episcopal panegyrics.[3]

Yet the speech was also rooted in Gregory's circumstances at the time
of composition. Leaving the small see of Sasima where Basil had ordained
him bishop in 372, Gregory had come to Constantinople to lead the Nicene
community there in 379. He faced considerable opposition, both from anti-
Nicenes within the city and from other Nicene groups. The church of the
Anastasia (from *anastasis*, 'resurrection'), which was the setting for the
oration, had been attacked at Easter 380 by hostile monks, and Gregory's
congregation had recently been increased by the arrival of a large body of
Egyptians who were not reconciled to his leadership. The feast of 2 May
380 to commemorate Athanasius was an ideal opportunity for Gregory to
associate himself with the great bishop and to construct an image of Athanasius that served his purposes.

'In praising Athanasius, I shall be praising virtue' (1). The opening line of
Gregory's oration immediately sets the tone. Athanasius is placed alongside
the patriarchs and prophets of the Old Testament and the disciples of
Christ and their successors. 'With some of these Athanasius vied, by some
he was slightly excelled, and others, if it is not bold to say so, he surpassed'
(4). Gregory knows little of Athanasius' early life and does not recount the
story of the child Athanasius on the beach that will appear in the ecclesiastical historians. He does assert, on no explicit evidence, that Athanasius
received a religious education and studied only sufficient literature and
philosophy to avoid ignorance (6). Athanasius then passed through the
orders of the clergy, and became bishop 'by the vote of the whole people'
(8). This is the sole allusion to Athanasius' contested election, for Gregory

---

[2] On Gregory, see Bernardi (1995), McGuckin (2001), and Daley (2006). For the *Oration's*
date and interpretation, see McGuckin (2001: 266–9).

[3] For the debates over the ideal 'model bishop' in Late Antiquity, see Rapp (2005).

wishes to concentrate upon his subject's episcopal virtues, as described in the quotation at the head of this chapter. Athanasius guided all alike, young and old, ascetics and laypeople, rich and poor (10). He led the congregation through peace and love, his pastoral dedication preceding the controversies into which he was drawn as a passive and innocent victim.

Gregory's narrative of the complex events of Athanasius' life is highly selective. Following Athanasius, he traces the divisions in the fourth-century Church back to Arius and regards Athanasius' later opponents as successors to the same 'Arian heresy'. These men denied the divinity of the Son and the Holy Spirit and so dishonoured the Trinity. But Athanasius resisted. 'He both happily preserved the Unity, which belongs to the Godhead, and religiously taught the Trinity, which refers to personality, neither confounding the Three persons in the Unity nor dividing the substance among the Three persons' (13). Gregory is the earliest extant source to make the fictional claim that Athanasius led the opposition to Arius at Nicaea, which would become a standard theme of Athanasian hagiography. 'Though not yet ranked among the bishops, he held the first rank among the members of the council, for preference was given to virtue just as much as to office' (14). His defence of orthodoxy made Athanasius a target for the 'Arians' when the Devil fanned the flames of conflict once more.

For Gregory and his Constantinopolitan audience, the story of Athanasius' original condemnation and exile was evidently well known and his innocence required no detailed defence. Gregory thus offers only a single passing allusion to the Council of Tyre, when he states that, 'if any of you have heard of the hand which was produced by the fraud against the saint and the corpse of the living man [Arsenius], and the unjust banishment, he knows what I mean' (15). Rather more of a concern in Gregory's eyes was the need to defend his own homeland, for, like himself, the two great rivals of Athanasius, Gregory of Alexandria and later George, hailed from Cappadocia. George in particular is condemned at length, with a comparison between the plight of Athanasius and the suffering of Job (16–19). In this context Gregory also praises Athanasius' devotion to the cause of asceticism. Athanasius 'arranged his exile most excellently, for he betook himself to the holy and divine homes of contemplation in Egypt where, secluding themselves from the world and welcoming the desert, men live to God more than all who exist in the body' (19). Through his teachings and example Athanasius brought together the solitary hermits, the communal monks, and the clergy, and the ascetics obeyed his decisions as the laws of Moses and protected him from those who hunted him (20).

The concluding sections of *Oration* XXI focus more strongly on theological concerns and Athanasius' efforts to achieve reconciliation. The Council of Seleucia in 359 rejected the term *homoousios* as unscriptural and so let in 'Arianism'. Persecution of the orthodox followed (23–5), but the death of Constantius led to George being lynched and the return of Athanasius, whose welcome in 362 rivalled the great procession of 346 (27–9). Despite the brief interruption caused by the reign of Julian, Athanasius laboured to reunite the Christian community by persuasion rather than violence (30–3). He maintained the equal divinity of the Holy Spirit with the Son and the Father and saw the need to rise above quarrels over words and seek doctrinal unity. Gregory proclaims as orthodox the teaching of one *ousia* and three *hypostases* in the Trinity. The Latins held the same teaching but, 'owing to the scantiness of their vocabulary and its poverty of terms' (35), they spoke of three *prosopa* and so were suspected of Sabellianism, while they in turn regarded three *hypostases* as 'Arian'. Athanasius 'conferred in his gentle and sympathetic way with both parties, and after he had carefully weighed the meaning of their expressions and found that they had the same sense and were in nowise different in doctrine, by permitting each party to use its own terms, he bound them together in unity of action' (35).

'His life and habits form an ideal of an episcopate and his teaching the law of orthodoxy' (37). Gregory's admiration for Athanasius was obvious and sincere. Nevertheless, his knowledge of his hero's career was by no means extensive, and he makes very little reference to Athanasius' actual writings. The pastoral and ascetic dimensions of Athanasius' episcopate are recognized, but ecclesiastical persecution and doctrine are Gregory's major themes. This was appropriate given the context in which the oration was delivered. In particular, the theological principles at stake were those of the greatest concern to Gregory and the other Cappadocian Fathers. The consubstantiality of the Holy Spirit with the Father and the Son was a teaching that Gregory developed in greater depth than Athanasius, and, while it is true that Athanasius accepted speaking of three *hypostases* in the *Tomus ad Antiochenos*, this was never his preferred formulation for the Trinity. These doctrines remained highly controversial in 380, and Gregory sought to convince his audience that his teachings were Athanasian and therefore orthodox. In this aim he failed. Although *Oration* XXI would exert considerable influence on the later memory of Athanasius, Gregory's efforts to associate himself with the great Alexandrian bishop were not enough to persuade his critics or avert his forced resignation from the Constantinopolitan see in 381.

The heroic vision of Athanasius presented by Gregory near the end of the fourth century had become firmly established by the time of the fifth-century ecclesiastical historians Socrates, Sozomen, and Theodoret. Yet dissenting views could still be heard. Our evidence is extremely limited, as later generations had little reason to preserve works that challenged the prevailing orthodox tradition. But we gain at least some idea of the anti-Athanasian arguments once in circulation from the fragmentary survival of the 'Neo-Arian' *Ecclesiastical History* of Philostorgius.[4] We know nothing of the author outside this text, which appeared in *c.*425–33. Philostorgius supported the 'Anomoion' teaching that the Father and Son were entirely unlike (*anomoios*) according to *ousia*, a doctrine condemned as heretical by the Nicene Church. His doctrinal allegiance is clearly stated, and so too is his bitter hostility towards the Nicene champion Athanasius.

It is Philostorgius who preserves the account of Athanasius' election in 328 as uncanonical and achieved only through compulsion:

Athanasius broke into the Church of Dionysius in the late afternoon, found two Egyptian bishops, shut the doors and barred them firmly with the help of his supporters, and in this way received ordination. Those ordaining resisted vigorously, but when the violence offered them proved too much for their will and their strength, Athanasius got what he wanted. (II.11)

When the emperor Constantine heard the truth of this forced ordination, he summoned Athanasius to explain himself at the Council of Tyre. Unlike our orthodox writers, Philostorgius has no doubts as to the justice of Athanasius' fate. In order to undermine his accuser, Eusebius of Nicomedia, Athanasius bribed a prostitute to claim that Eusebius had violated her. Unfortunately, the prostitute accused the wrong person, and Athanasius was then doubly condemned. A second council examined the case further and added accusations of violence, the hand of Arsenius, and the broken chalice. Athanasius was excommunicated, and the council appointed Gregory of Cappadocia in his place (II.11).

Philostorgius appears to have combined the Council of Tyre in 335, which led to Athanasius' first exile, with the Council of Antioch in 338/9, which preceded his second exile and appointed Gregory to his see. Later he similarly confuses Athanasius' return on Constantine's death in 337 with his return, after Gregory had died, in 346 (II.18). Such chronological errors

---

[4] Until recently, Philostorgius has received less scholarly attention than his orthodox counterparts. For an introduction, see Argov (2001), Leppin (2001), and the general works on the ecclesiastical historians cited below.

occur in many orthodox sources as well, notably Rufinus of Aquileia. So do stories like that of the prostitute, although elsewhere it is Eusebius who hired the woman and Athanasius who is accused of her violation.

Constantius subsequently drove Athanasius once more from Alexandria and installed 'George' in his place, while Athanasius departed for the west (III.3). 'George' here is another case of chronological confusion, for this passage seems to refer to Athanasius' second western exile in 339. While in the west Athanasius used persuasion and bribery at the court of Constantius' brother Constans to convince the latter to threaten war if the bishop was not restored.[5] Constantius complied, and recalled George. Athanasius returned and travelled through the east seeking supporters for the doctrine of *homoousios*. 'None of them agreed except Aetius, the bishop of Palestine, who had been denounced for fornication and, hoping to conceal his disgrace by yielding to Athanasius, defected to his doctrine. But he paid a very heavy penalty when his genitals putrefied and swarmed with worms, and thus he died' (III.12).

Such educational deaths are a feature of Philostorgius' *Ecclesiastical History*, and in a later passage the death of Constans is attributed to divine anger aroused by Constans' zeal for Athanasius (III.22). Of course, the fate of Arius is explained in equally providential terms in Athanasius' *De Morte Arii*. But it is ironic that Aetius of Palestinian Lydda, whose death is blamed by Philostorgius on his acceptance of *homoousios*, is a man whom Athanasius on the contrary regarded as 'Arian'. Philostorgius' conception of fourth-century Christianity is in fact exactly as polarized as that of Athanasius. Whereas Athanasius branded all those who opposed him as 'Arian', Philostorgius defines anyone who takes a view contrary to his own as a supporter of the Nicene Creed.

Elsewhere in the surviving fragments Philostorgius asserts that Athanasius was the true instigator behind the lynching of George during the reign of Julian 'the Apostate' (VII.2). He also, perhaps more surprisingly, compares Athanasius unfavourably to Apollinaris of Laodicea and the Cappadocians Basil and Gregory. 'These three men championed the *homoousion* doctrine at that time in opposition to that of "other in *ousia*" and were so far superior to all the other leaders of that sect before and after until my own time that Athanasius must be reckoned a child in comparison to them' (VIII.11a). It is a tribute to Athanasius that this 'Neo-Arian' writing half a

---

[5] Philostorgius' image of Athanasius may have been influenced by the contemporary activities of Cyril of Alexandria, whose careful organization of 'diplomatic gifts' to secure the aid of allies at court against Nestorius is preserved in Cyril, *Letter 96*.

century after the bishop's death still regarded him as a foe worthy of such condemnation. Philostorgius is without question a biased and frequently inaccurate historian, and we cannot take his arguments at face value merely because they preserve an alternative to our mainstream orthodox tradition. Nevertheless, it does need to be said that he shares much of the material he presents and the rhetorical devices he employs with those orthodox sources. It is certainly not self-evident that any of the assertions that Philostorgius makes against Athanasius are correct. It is not always self-evident that they are wrong.

Socrates, Sozomen, and Theodoret offer very different interpretations to that of their 'Neo-Arian' contemporary. In comparison to Philostorgius, they follow the orthodox tradition that glorified the Nicene Creed and Athanasius as its champion. We are therefore tempted to view them as representatives of a single monolithic vision of the fourth-century Church.[6] All three wrote their works as continuations of the original *Ecclesiastical History* of Eusebius of Caesarea (which ended in 324), and they are united not only in their conception of orthodoxy but in the framework of events and individuals through which they traced their histories. This may in part reflect the sources they read, although a number of fourth-century texts known to them have long since been lost.[7] Socrates used and corrected the Latin *Ecclesiastical History* of Rufinus of Aquileia, which is discussed further below. Sozomen and to a lesser extent Theodoret in turn used Socrates. It is hardly a surprise that their presentations of Athanasius' career are strikingly uniform. Yet that uniformity is far from complete. Socrates, Sozomen, and Theodoret each have their individual emphases, which shape the image of Athanasius that they choose to depict.

Athanasius' influence on the three historians is immediately apparent. All follow his polarized polemic in dividing the fourth-century Church between orthodoxy and heresy and represent Athanasius as an innocent victim persecuted by the 'Eusebians' for the sake of 'Arianism'. Their narratives of his initial trial and exile are markedly consistent (Socrates I.27–35; Sozomen II.22–3, 25, 28; Theodoret I.25–9). This is predictable, as those narratives were drawn from the *Apologia contra Arianos* and copy from the

---

[6] This was already true in the early sixth century, when Theodore Lector epitomized their writings together as the *Historia Tripartita*. For general introductions to the ecclesiastical historians, see Chesnut (1986), Urbainczyk (1997, 2002), Ferguson (2005), and the relevant articles in Rohrbacher (2002) and Marasco (2003).

[7] One such source may have been the *Ecclesiastical History* of Gelasius of Caesarea, whose influence on Rufinus and the fifth-century Greek historians has been much debated. There is a helpful survey of these debates in Van Deun (2003: 152–60).

documents that Athanasius collected in his defence.[8] Other Athanasian works quoted include those on the death of Arius (Socrates I.37–8; Sozomen II.29; Theodoret I.13–14) and the *Apologia de Fuga*, a work that Athanasius sought to circulate widely.[9] Theodoret further drew upon the *Epistula ad Afros* for Athanasius' account of Nicaea, although the status he assigns to Athanasius at that council owes more to Gregory of Nazianzus (Theodoret I.7; see likewise Socrates I.8; Sozomen I.17). Strikingly, none of the historians makes any use of the *Orationes contra Arianos*, the *De Decretis*, or the *Historia Arianorum*.

The independent value of these three ecclesiastical historians for our knowledge of Athanasius is limited. For eastern Christian tradition, their importance was immense. They preserved what became the standard narrative of the fourth-century controversies, drawn to a considerable degree from Athanasius' writings. Later authors turned to them for guidance, and their works were epitomized and translated. Socrates in particular became a foundational text for Syriac and Armenian Church historiography. He completed his *Ecclesiastical History* in Constantinople in *c*.440, covering from the reign of Constantine to 439. To modern eyes he is the most even-handed of the historians, and memorably described the doctrinal controversies as 'not unlike a contest in the dark; for neither party appeared to understand distinctly the grounds on which they calumniated one another' (I.23). His scepticism, however, did not extend to questioning Athanasius' interpretation of the 'Arian Controversy'. In his preface to book II, Socrates explains that he drew upon Rufinus while gathering material for his work:

Afterward we perused the writings of Athanasius, wherein he depicts his own sufferings and how through the calumnies of the Eusebians he was banished, and judged that more credit was due to him who had suffered, and to those who were witnesses of the things they describe, than to such as have been dependent on conjecture, and had therefore erred. (Socrates, II.1)

Socrates then revised the opening books of his work to correct Rufinus' errors. His *History* is more impartial than that of Rufinus and helps us to

---

[8] Every historian quotes the letter of Constantine II announcing Athanasius' restoration in 337 (*Apologia contra Arianos* 87 = Socrates, II.3; Sozomen, III.2; Theodoret, II.1). Other documents quoted include Constantine's letter to the bishops at Tyre (*Apologia contra Arianos* 86 = Sozomen, II.28) and the letters in favour of Athanasius' return from his second exile (*Apologia contra Arianos* 51–6 = Socrates, II.23). See further Barnes (1993: apps 5–7).

[9] See Socrates, II.28, III.8 (where Athanasius is said to have read out his defence at the Council of Alexandria in 362); Theodoret, I.7, II.4, II.10, II.11, II.12, II.18.

flesh out a more complete outline of the course of the fourth-century controversies (although his chronology is also occasionally at fault). But, given his dependence on the bishop's writings, he cannot provide external confirmation for Athanasius' presentation of his career.

Sozomen drew heavily on Socrates (without attribution), but had his own concerns. He too wrote in Constantinople, and his extant *Ecclesiastical History* covers the period from 323 to 425. The final book appears to be incomplete, and was probably still under preparation when Sozomen died in *c.*448/9. He was capable of original research, and went back to Athanasius' writings to correct at least one error that Socrates had made.[10] Sozomen professed greater sensitivity for the theological debates than Socrates, and, unlike his predecessor, refused to quote the Nicene Creed, which should not be read by non-believers (I.20). His greatest interest lay in asceticism. The teachings of the ascetics are hailed as 'the most useful thing that has been received by man from God' (I.12), and short biographies are provided for the leading fourth-century monks. Antony's career is summarized (I.13) and the bond between the hermit and Athanasius recognized (II.17, II.31). Unlike Socrates, however, even in those passages Sozomen never identifies Athanasius as the author of the *Life of Antony*.

Theodoret of Cyrrhus stands slightly apart from the laymen Socrates and Sozomen. A bishop and theologian, he had a greater commitment to and understanding of the issues at stake in the fourth-century controversies. His *Ecclesiastical History* covers from 324 to 429 and was probably completed in the late 440s, both from internal evidence and because Theodoret appears to have drawn upon Socrates but not Sozomen. He exhibits the same dependence on Athanasius' writings and offers the same panegyrical appraisal of Athanasius' career. But, while all the fifth-century historians wrote at a time when new doctrinal questions were dividing the eastern Church, only Theodoret was an active participant. The representation of Athanasius and 'Arianism' in his *Ecclesiastical History* was of direct relevance to those contemporary conflicts. Theodoret claimed to uphold the faith that Athanasius had defended. Yet he stood in opposition to Athanasius' greatest successor, Cyril of Alexandria (bishop 412–44), whom in his letters Theodoret repeatedly denounced as the heir of Arius, Eunomius, and Apollinaris.[11] Cyril likewise turned to the past to defend himself

---

[10] He corrected the name Apis to Alypius from *Apologia contra Arianos* 60: see Socrates, I.27, and Sozomen, II.22.

[11] Theodoret, *Letters* 151, 167, 168, 170. In the same letters he appeals to the authority of Athanasius and other orthodox Fathers in support of his own position.

and condemn his foes. Athanasius' theology and his reputation as a champion of orthodoxy made him an important figure of authority in the fifth-century controversies, and this had significant consequences for his legacy within eastern Christianity.

The theological debates of the fourth century had not ceased with Athanasius' death or with the Council of Constantinople in 381. In the fifth century discussion centred upon the humanity and divinity of Christ and the relationship of the two natures in the Incarnation. This is not the place for an in-depth assessment of the Christological controversies.[12] But even the briefest glimpse reveals striking similarities to the debates of the preceding century. The issues involved were once again fundamental to the Christian faith and focused around the promise of salvation for humanity through the Incarnate Christ. The different positions held were not as starkly separated as our polemical sources suggest, and all participants appealed to the support of Scripture and the traditional faith of the Church. This last argument played a more influential role in the fifth century.[13] Fourth-century writers did, of course, emphasize their agreement with past tradition, as Athanasius does most obviously in the *De Decretis* and *De Sententia Dionysii*. Basil of Caesarea in his work *On the Holy Spirit* was the first to prepare a detailed florilegium to reinforce his case, a compilation of extracts drawn both from the Fathers and from Scripture. In the fifth century, florilegia and appeals to the Fathers became ever more important. One of the greatest Fathers in the eyes of fifth-century Christians was Athanasius.

In 428/9 Cyril of Alexandria clashed with Nestorius of Constantinople over the latter's refusal to use the term *Theotokos* ('God-bearer') for the Virgin Mary. For Nestorius, such language threatened to blur the distinct humanity and divinity of Jesus Christ and to deny that Christ was fully man. For Cyril, to describe Mary as *Theotokos* was an essential statement of the unity of Christ's humanity and divinity, a unity that he believed was challenged by Nestorius' teachings. Both men appealed to Christian tradition to support their arguments and abuse their opponents. Nestorius was eventually condemned at the Council of Ephesus in 431, but this did not end the debates. Cyril died in 444, and at the Council of Chalcedon in 451 Christ was said to be 'in two natures', human and divine, united without confusion. Those who rejected this conclusion and maintained that Christ

---

[12] There are good recent assessments in McGuckin (2004) and Wessel (2004).

[13] For the role of tradition and the appeal to the Fathers in the formation of Christian identity in the fourth and early fifth centuries, see Graumann (2002).

had just one nature (*mia physis*), a formula used by Cyril, are known in modern scholarship as Monophysites or Miaphysites. Over the following centuries they came to form separate churches in Egypt, Syria, Armenia, and elsewhere.[14]

Athanasius featured prominently on every side of these debates. Unfortunately, as was also true of Scripture, appeal to Athanasius' authority could not resolve the questions under dispute. As we have seen, his theology placed great emphasis on the humanity and divinity of Christ and their role in salvation. But his Christological language was sufficiently imprecise by later standards that everyone could turn to him for support. Nestorius and his friend Theodoret quoted Athanasian works just as freely as Cyril of Alexandria.[15] The situation was further complicated by the existence of edited versions of Athanasius' writings and of pseudonymous works attributed to his name. Cyril was aware of corrupted texts of the *Letter to Epictetus* being circulated by his opponents in the early 430s.[16] It is therefore somewhat ironic that Cyril derived his famous expression 'one nature [*mia physis*] of the Word incarnate' from a work that he believed was written by Athanasius but was in fact a pseudonymous Apollinarian text, the *De Incarnatione Dei Verbi*.[17]

Nevertheless, Cyril's representation of himself as the natural successor of Athanasius was a major factor in his eventual triumph.[18] Against the rival claims of Nestorius, Cyril turned to Athanasius for proof that his own theology was the traditional orthodox faith. We see this argument in his *Letter to the Monks of Egypt*, written in 429 near the onset of the controversy. No one should doubt that the title *Theotokos* is appropriate to the Virgin, for 'the divine disciples handed on this faith to us even if they did not make mention of the term' (4). Cyril's defence of the unscriptural *Theotokos* recalls Athanasius' justification for *homoousios*. And he immediately invokes Athanasius to reinforce his argument:

[14] On the reinterpretation of Christian tradition that took place during the debates surrounding Chalcedon, see further Gwynn (2009) and other articles in the same volume. The classic overview of the emerging 'Monophysite' churches in the fifth and sixth centuries remains Frend (1972).

[15] Athanasius' works are cited repeatedly in the patristic florilegia of Nestorius' *Bazaar of Heracleides* and Theodoret's *Eranistes* (as well as in the latter's *Historia Ecclesiastica*).

[16] Cyril, *Letters* 39 (to John of Antioch) and 45 (First Letter to Succensus of Diocaesarea).

[17] On Apollinarian (or apparently Apollinarian) elements in Cyril, see still Galtier (1956). Cyril first used the formula 'one incarnate nature of God the Word' in the preface to his second book *Against Nestorius*.

[18] For discussion, see Wessel (2004: esp. 126–37).

We have been taught to think this way by the holy Fathers. Our Father Athanasius, of illustrious memory, was an ornament to the throne of the Church of Alexandria throughout forty-six years in all. He opposed an unconquered and apostolic wisdom to the sophistries of the evil heretics, and refreshed the whole world with his own writings as if they were some most fragrant balsam. His orthodoxy and godliness in teaching are confessed by all, and he composed a book for us concerning the holy and consubstantial Trinity where, throughout the third discourse, he calls the holy virgin the Mother of God. I will make use of his own sayings. (4)

Cyril quotes two passages from the third *Oratio contra Arianos* (III.29 and 33). He then continues:

This man is trustworthy and we ought to rely upon him as someone who would never say anything that was not in accordance with the sacred text. For how could such a brilliant and famous man, held in such reverence by everybody at the holy and great Council itself (I mean that which formerly gathered together in Nicaea) be mistaken as to the truth? At that time he did not occupy the episcopal throne, but was still only a cleric. Nonetheless because of his shrewdness, his purity of life, and his sharp and incomparably penetrating mind, he was taken along on that occasion by bishop Alexander of blessed memory, and he was to the old man like a son to a father, guiding him in everything useful and admirably showing him the way in all he did. (4)

Cyril's vision of Athanasius at Nicaea parallels the accounts in Gregory and the ecclesiastical historians, while his emphasis on Athanasius' relationship with Alexander is a recurring theme of the Coptic Egyptian tradition. Glorifying Athanasius glorified the see that Cyril now held, and was an appropriate theme for a letter addressed to the loyal Egyptian ascetics, who followed Cyril as they had followed Athanasius. Cyril similarly exploited Athanasius' reputation in the wider Church, particularly the ties he had forged between Alexandria and the west. Thus he secured the support of Celestine of Rome, just as Athanasius had won over Julius against the 'Eusebians', and led the bishops who condemned Nestorius at Ephesus in 431.

No less than his predecessor, Cyril is a historical figure of great complexity. His involvement in ecclesiastical politics and his use of the Egyptian monks as 'shock troops' for his cause have given him a negative reputation in some modern eyes. Yet, like Athanasius, Cyril was also a committed ascetic and theologian. The doctrine of the Incarnation that he taught moved beyond that of Athanasius in his conception of the relationship between Christ's humanity and divinity expressed through the communication of idioms.[19] In his focus upon the theology of salvation and his pastoral awareness, however, Cyril was Athanasius' worthy heir. For the bishops gathered at Chalcedon, and for subsequent Christian generations, he attained an equally exalted status. The two Alexandrians were recognized by Chalcedonians and Miaphysites alike as twin pillars of orthodoxy and Fathers of the Church.

ATHANASIUS IN THE LATIN WEST

From the time of his first involuntary visit to the western regions of the Roman Empire following his exile to Trier in 335, Athanasius found friendship and support in the Latin-speaking Church. His years in Italy and Gaul from 339 to 346 strengthened those bonds, and in the 350s defence of Athanasius and defence of the Nicene Creed became inseparable for many western bishops. Athanasius built a particularly close relationship between Alexandria and Rome, which Cyril exploited to his advantage, while the authority of his name elsewhere in the west in his later years is reflected in the *Epistula ad Afros*.

Later generations of Latin Christianity, like their counterparts in the Greek east, remembered Athanasius as the heroic champion of orthodoxy and as a propagator of asceticism. To a greater degree than in the east, however, the western memory of Athanasius became increasingly separated from the bishop's original writings and historical context. Relatively few of Athanasius' Greek works were widely read or translated into Latin.[20] His apologetic writings and doctrinal treatises held limited value in the west, even though so-called 'Germanic Arianism' endured there far longer than in the east. The key exception, as we would expect, was the *Life of Antony*, the one Athanasian text that did circulate across the western churches. Outside of ascetic contexts, Athanasius was only occasionally cited by the great Latin fathers of the late fourth and early fifth centuries. It is, therefore, perhaps unsurprising that throughout the Middle Ages Athanasius would be best known in the west for a creed that he did not write.

---

[19] In addition to McGuckin (2004) and Wessel (2004), on Cyril's theology see McKinion (2000), Russell (2000), and the articles in Weinandy and Keating (2003). For the argument that Cyril owes as much or more to the theology of Gregory of Nazianzus as to that of Athanasius, see Beeley (2009).

[20] Simon (1991); C. Müller (2010).

Hilary of Poitiers (*c.*300–*c.*368) was hailed in some later western circles as the 'Athanasius of the west'.[21] His career does bear a certain resemblance to that of the Alexandrian. After entering the episcopate in *c.*353, Hilary was exiled under controversial circumstances following the Council of Béziers in 356 (although he was not apparently condemned at that council). He came east to Phrygia and attended the Council of Seleucia in 359 before returning to his see in 360. Hilary's writings are an important albeit difficult source for the complex events of the mid-350s. In addition to defending his own legitimacy as bishop, Hilary sought to inform the western churches of the contemporary doctrinal controversies as he understood them. He wrote against the Balkan bishops Ursacius and Valens and against Constantius (after an initial appeal to the emperor had failed), an account of the recent church councils (*De Synodis*), and his major work, *De Trinitate*.

Athanasius and Hilary do have much in common. Hilary strongly opposed the campaigns to rally the western Church against Athanasius in the 350s, and Athanasius fully shared Hilary's hostility to Ursacius, Valens, and (eventually) Constantius. Although Hilary wrote that he had 'never heard the Nicene Creed until about to be exiled' (*De Synodis* 91), he provides one of the earliest explicit western statements of Athanasius' reputation as the innocent champion of Nicaea:

Athanasius, deacon at the Council of Nicaea and subsequently bishop of Alexandria, had stood forth, therefore, as the forceful instigator of this creed's publication to all. Holding fast to truth he had vanquished the Arian plague in the whole of Egypt and when witnesses conspired against him on that account, a false set of charges was prepared. (Hilary, *Against Valens and Ursacius* I.IX.6, in 356)[22]

In the light of their similarities, it is thus rather striking that Athanasius makes no reference to Hilary anywhere in his extant writings. Moreover, despite the respect that Hilary showed for Athanasius, there is little indication of Athanasian influence on his theology. During his time in the east, Hilary became an associate of Basil of Ancyra and the group known rather inaccurately as the 'Homoiousians'. Recent studies of Hilary's *De Trinitate* have emphasized the impact of Basil rather than Athanasius, and this led some extreme western Nicenes such as Lucifer of Cagliari to regard

---

[21] For his life, see Borchardt (1966) and Brennecke (1984). On Hilary's theology and his role in the doctrinal controversies, see now Weedman (2007) and Beckwith (2008).

[22] There is a translation of *Against Valens and Ursacius* with a detailed introduction in Wickham (1997).

Hilary as 'Arian'. This may help to explain Athanasius' silence, given his praise for other westerners who defended his cause, including Lucifer and Hilary's ally Eusebius of Vercellae. Whatever the cause, Hilary's writings set a pattern for Athanasius' legacy in the west, admiration for the Alexandrian's defence of Nicaea but little detailed knowledge of his thought and writings.

Shortly before his death, Hilary launched a failed attack on the leading Homoian bishop in the west, Auxentius of Milan. Athanasius too repeatedly denounced Auxentius as 'Arian' and continued to do so as late as the *Epistula ad Afros* and the *Letter to Epictetus*. Auxentius still held on to his see until his own death in 373/4. His successor, the governor of Aemilia-Liguria, who was hastily baptized and promoted through the clerical ranks, was Ambrose (bishop of Milan 373/4–97).[23] One of the leading figures in the history of Latin Christianity, Ambrose masterminded the condemnation of 'Arianism' at the Council of Aquileia in 381 and resisted pressure from the western imperial court in support of the Homoians. His theological and ascetic writings and sermons influenced Augustine of Hippo among many others and included *De Fide ad Gratianum*, *De Spiritu Sancto*, and *De Virginitate*.

Ambrose's accession to the episcopate followed very closely upon Athanasius' death, and the impact of Athanasius on Ambrose is difficult to assess. Unlike many of his western contemporaries, Ambrose read Greek fluently and had certainly studied a number of Athanasius' writings. However, he rarely acknowledges such debts. His treatise on virginity draws heavily on Athanasius' works on the same theme,[24] and the anti-'Arian' polemic of *De Fide* closely echoes Athanasian rhetoric.[25] Yet Athanasius is not mentioned by name in either work. Ambrose was fully aware of Athanasius' reputation, and cites Athanasius' appeal to the west as a precedent to justify western support for Maximus of Constantinople (the Egyptian who was an unsuccessful candidate for that see in 381).[26] But overall Athanasius is not a prominent figure in Ambrose's writings, a judgement that holds true for the other two members of the great triumvirate of late-antique Christianity in the west: Jerome and Augustine.

---

[23] On Ambrose, see McLynn (1994) and D. H. Williams (1995b).

[24] Particularly Athanasius' first *Letter to Virgins*: Duval (1974).

[25] On this Ambrosian work, and specifically the context and purpose of *De Fide* III–V, which were later additions to books I–II and have more Athanasian influence, see D. H. Williams (1995a: 524–31; 1995b: 128–53).

[26] For the context and translation of the letters, see Liebeschuetz (2005).

Before we turn to those two much-debated figures, we should consider one further contemporary writer who played a central part in the transmission of Athanasius' legacy to the western Church: Rufinus of Aquileia (c.345–410).[27] Born in Italy, Rufinus came to Egypt around 373 and was in Alexandria to witness the persecution after Athanasius' death and the election of Peter II.[28] He travelled widely among the Egyptian ascetic communities and then lived for many years in Jerusalem before returning to the west in 397. Having settled in Aquileia near where he was born, Rufinus translated Eusebius of Caesarea's *Ecclesiastical History* into Latin in 402 at the request of his bishop Chromatius, who sought moral support for the Christians of Aquileia under threat from Alaric and the Goths. He then wrote his own continuation of Eusebius covering from 324 to 395. We have seen that Rufinus was read by Socrates and Sozomen in the Greek east, and in the west he exerted a powerful influence, notably on the historical writings of Augustine and Augustine's disciple Orosius.

Athanasius is the hero of much of book X, the first of the two books of Rufinus' continuation of Eusebius. He is introduced as a deacon at Nicaea, aiding Alexander of Alexandria with his advice (X.5). His authorship of the *Life of Antony* is praised (X.8), as too is his ordination of Frumentius as the first bishop of Ethiopia (X.10). But Rufinus deliberately postpones a detailed account of Athanasius' career until after he has reported the death of Constantine (X.12) in order to separate Athanasius' sufferings from the reign of the first Christian emperor. Only then does Rufinus present the story of Athanasius' childhood discussed in my opening chapter, to lead into his narrative of Athanasius' endurance on behalf of the faith.

The whole world conspired to persecute him and the princes of the earth were moved, nations, kingdoms and armies gathered against him. But he guarded that divine utterance which runs: 'If camps are set up against me, my heart will not fear, if battle is waged against me, in him will I hope' [Psalm 27:3]. But because his deeds are so outstanding that their greatness does not allow me to omit any of them, yet their number compels me to pass over very many, and thus my mind is troubled by uncertainty, unable to decide which to keep and which to pass over. We shall therefore relate a few of the pertinent matters, leaving the rest to be told by his fame. (X.15)

---

[27] In addition to the general studies on the ecclesiastical historians cited earlier, see in particular Thelamon (1981).
[28] Rufinus describes the persecution in *Ecclesiastical History* XI.2–4: 'I speak of what I was there to see and I report the deeds of those whose sufferings I was granted to share' (XI.4).

This panegyrical tone is maintained throughout Rufinus' work, with significant implications. As the 'Arians' feared that Athanasius might draw the new emperor Constantius towards the true faith, they conspired against him and even showed the emperor the arm that they claimed Athanasius had cut from the body of Arsenius for magical purposes (X.16). Athanasius was summoned to trial at the Council of Tyre (X.17), but Arsenius came forward alive and unharmed, and the woman who was to accuse Athanasius of violating her accused his presbyter Timothy by mistake. Nevertheless, the council still condemned Athanasius (X.18). Now a fugitive pursued by the whole power of the empire, Athanasius hid for six years in a dry cistern without seeing the sun (X.19). Finally he withdrew from the realm of Constantius and came to the latter's brother Constans in the west. Constans threatened to restore Athanasius by force, and Constantius allowed the bishop to return until his brother's death. Athanasius was then driven again from Alexandria, and after Constantius had conquered the west he demanded that the western bishops condemn Athanasius and endorse 'Arianism' (X.20).

It is striking that so inaccurate a narrative could be composed less than a generation after Athanasius' death by a serious scholar who had lived in Alexandria. Rufinus has moved the Council of Tyre to the reign of Constantius to avoid blaming Constantine for Athanasius' original condemnation. He has likewise merged Athanasius' first and second periods of exile, while adding a legendary version of the six years of ascetic concealment from his third exile. The underlying interpretation of Athanasius' career is the bishop's own, with repeated 'Arian' conspiracies against the innocent champion of orthodoxy. But Rufinus' chronological and factual errors, which were already criticized by Socrates, mark an important stage in the separation of the hagiographical Athanasius from the historical bishop of Alexandria. Nor was Rufinus exceptional among educated Latin Christians of his time in his lack of in-depth knowledge of the earlier fourth century, at least on the evidence provided by the writings of Jerome and Augustine.

Jerome (*c.*347–420) was another highly controversial figure, both in his lifetime and in modern scholarship.[29] For his knowledge of Athanasius we can turn in the first instance to the entry that Jerome composed in 392/3 in his *De Viris Illustribus (On Illustrious Men)*:

Athanasius bishop of Alexandria, hard pressed by the wiles of the Arians, fled to Constans emperor of Gaul. Returning thence with letters and, after the death of

---

[29] Introductions to Jerome's life and writings can be found in Kelly (1975) and Rebenich (2002).

the emperor, again taking refuge in flight, he remained in hiding until the accession of Jovian, when he returned to the church and died in the reign of Valens. Various works by him are in circulation: two books Against the Nations, one Against Valens and Ursacius, On Virginity, very many On the Persecutions of the Arians, also On the Titles of the Psalms and the Life of Antony the monk, also Festal epistles and other works too numerous to mention. (*De Viris Illustribus* 87)

Elsewhere in the same work Jerome refers to Gregory of Nazianzus' oration in honour of Athanasius (117) and identifies his friend Evagrius of Antioch as the Latin translator of the *Life of Antony* (125). The entry on Athanasius does not reveal any deep knowledge, although it is necessarily brief, and we cannot assume that Jerome had actually read the writings he lists. He did have a grasp on the major events of Athanasius' career. This is confirmed by his continuation of Eusebius of Caesarea's *Chronicle* to cover the period 327–78, in which he praised the Alexandrian bishop as one of those who resisted heretical emperors in defence of orthodoxy. There is, likewise, some slight evidence for Athanasian influence on Jerome's theology and exegesis. He drew on Athanasius' polemical construction of 'Arianism' in his *Against the Luciferians*, the work that contains Jerome's notorious declaration that, after the Council of Constantinople in 360 had adopted the Dated Creed, then 'the whole world groaned, and was astonished to find itself Arian' (19). But, although aware of the *Tomus ad Antiochenos*, Jerome disliked the three *hypostases* formula, and was not prepared to follow Athanasius in admitting that those who held such a view could be orthodox (Jerome, *Letter* 15, to Damasus of Rome).

Neither Athanasius' ecclesiastical career nor his theology, however, lay at the heart of Jerome's admiration for him. Jerome was committed above all to asceticism, and played a crucial role in the promotion of ascetic ideals in the west. So too did Athanasius, and this Jerome fully recognized. Marcella, an older member of the circle of ascetic Roman women who gathered around Jerome in the early 380s before his departure for Bethlehem, is said to have become interested in the desert fathers through meeting Athanasius and later Peter of Alexandria during their periods of exile (Jerome, *Letter* 127.5). Given that Marcella would have been perhaps 10 or 12 when Athanasius was in Rome in 339–42, any close contact appears improbable. But Marcella, like many westerners of similar interests, must have read the *Life of Antony*, and possibly other Athanasian ascetic writings.[30] Jerome encouraged such reading, including in his treatise on the education of a

---

[30] See further Letsch-Brunner (1998).

young Christian virgin the recommendation that she study 'the letters of Athanasius' (*Letter* 107.12).[31]

Admiration for Athanasius' contribution to the ascetic movement not-withstanding, Jerome could not resist challenging the prestige of Antony and of Athanasius' *Life*. In the *Life of Paul the First Hermit*, Jerome maintained that Antony should not be held as the original model for the anchoretic lifestyle.[32] That place should, on the contrary, be awarded to the Egyptian hermit Paul, who died before Antony and from whom Antony received instruction. No external evidence supports the existence of Paul as a his-torical figure, and, whatever the truth, Jerome's *Life of Paul* is a further testimony to the influence of the *Life of Antony*. For Jerome as for later gen-erations of western ascetics, Athanasius provided inspiration and a model, although Jerome did modify some traits of the Athanasian Antony, notably when he insisted that Paul (unlike Antony, but like himself) received an excellent education.

Jerome's slightly younger contemporary Augustine of Hippo (354–430) was a very different man in career and personality.[33] He did not possess the linguistic attainments of Jerome or share the opportunity to live in the eastern Mediterranean, and to this extent his exposure to the writings of Athanasius may have been more limited. On the other hand, Augustine's experiences as a bishop gave him more in common with the Alexandrian than Jerome, while Augustine fully shared their abiding interest in asceti-cism. No analysis of Augustine's vast corpus can hope to be comprehensive. The rapid assessment offered here suggests that Augustine, like Jerome, had a basic knowledge of Athanasius' career and reputation, but was most familiar with the latter's ascetic contribution inevitably represented by the *Life of Antony*.

There are very few references to Athanasius in Augustine's numerous theological and exegetical works, and little indication of Athanasian influence. Athanasius is not mentioned in Augustine's *magnum opus*, the *City of God*, and perhaps more surprisingly not in the *De Trinitate* written during Augustine's anti-'Arian' campaign in the later years of his episco-pate.[34] Augustine recognized Athanasius' standing as the enemy of 'Arian-ism', and reports that some 'Arians' 'called catholics "Athanasians" ' (*Contra*

---

[31] For the possible influence of Athanasius' teachings on virginity upon Jerome's ascetic *Letter* 22, see Adkin (1992).

[32] On this work and its relationship to the *Life of Antony*, see Rebenich (2000).

[33] The classic study remains that of Brown (2000); see also Lancel (2002).

[34] On the *De Trinitate*, see Gioia (2008). There is a basic introduction to Augustine's anti-'Arian' campaigns in Sumruld (1994).

Julianum (Opus Imperfectum) 1.75.2). But he felt no real need to engage with Athanasius' arguments directly. One rare citation is given in Augustine's letter of instruction to Fortunatianus in 413/14, when he invokes 'the very blessed Athanasius, bishop of Alexandria' in support of the equal invisibility of Father, Son, and Holy Spirit against those who teach that only the Father is invisible (*Letter* 148.10). Later in the same letter Augustine includes Athanasius with Ambrose, Jerome, and Gregory of Nazianzus as the writers he has read (148.15). But the debt he owes to the two Latin fathers is by far the greater, and, to the extent that there is an eastern influence on his thought, the main source is Gregory not Athanasius.

We gain a similar impression from the few passing comments that Augustine makes concerning Athanasius' ecclesiastical career. He understood that Athanasius was the victim of 'Arian' persecution and endured periods of exile, but this is the limit of his knowledge, and it is extremely unlikely that he was familiar with Athanasius' apologetic writings at first hand. Late in his life, Augustine wrote a letter to his fellow bishop Honoratus on the question of whether a bishop should flee his city to avoid attack (*Letter* 228).[35] Honoratus had cited Scripture to justify the decision to flee: 'When they persecute you in one town, flee to the next' (Matthew 10:23). Augustine countered with new arguments from Scripture and insisted that flight was justified only when the bishop was the chief target of attack and his congregation could still be ministered by others. One example of this is the Apostle Paul escaping from Damascus. Another is Athanasius fleeing from Constantius (228.6). He left his people in good hands and rightly preserved himself. 'The whole catholic world knows how necessary it was to the Church that he should do so, and how useful was the prolonged life of the man who by his word and loving service defended her against the Arian heretics' (228.10). This appears to be all that Augustine knows of the context of Athanasius' flight, and he is unaware of Athanasius' arguments in the *Apologia de Fuga*. Nevertheless, the two great bishops were in essential agreement, and Athanasius would have approved of Augustine's own decision to remain within Hippo when his city came under Vandal attack just before his death.

This leaves the one Athanasian work that there is no doubt that Augustine knew very well indeed. Like Ambrose and Jerome, Augustine shared the ascetic enthusiasm of his age. A key moment in his conversion to asceticism was his discovery of the *Life of Antony*, and exceptionally we are even

---

[35] The letter is quoted by Possidius in his *Life of Augustine* 30.

informed how this revelation occurred. While Augustine and his friend Alypius were living in Milan in 386, before their final decision to commit their lives fully to Christianity, they were visited by a fellow North African named Ponticianus:

He began to tell us the story of Antony, the Egyptian monk, whose name was held in high honour by Your servants, although Alypius and I had never heard it until then. When Ponticianus realized this, he went into greater detail, wishing to instil some knowledge of this great man into our ignorant minds, for he was very surprised that we had not heard of him. For our part, we too were astonished to hear of the wonders You had worked so recently, almost in our own times, and witnessed by so many in the true faith and in the catholic Church. (*Confessions* VIII.6)

Ponticianus went on to recount how two associates of his dedicated themselves to serving God after reading the *Life of Antony* in Trier.[36] Augustine did not immediately make the same resolution, nor would he follow the anchoretic path of Antony. The inclusion of this episode in book VIII of the *Confessions*, however, reaffirms the impact that the story had on Augustine during his spiritual journey that culminated in the Garden of Milan.[37] In later years Augustine would continue to turn to Antony as a source of inspiration for himself and others.[38] It is no small tribute to the legacy of Athanasius that his work played such a role in the formation of one of the leading minds of Latin Christianity.

For Augustine, as for all the western churchmen discussed in the preceding pages, the memory of Athanasius of Alexandria inspired respect and admiration. His heroic commitment to the cause of orthodoxy made him a model for others to follow, and the rhetorical power of his anti-'Arian' polemic aided those who faced similar heretical challenges. But deep and genuine respect did not require close knowledge of Athanasius' ecclesiastical career or theology. The orthodoxy that he stood for was represented by the Nicene Creed. His doctrinal treatises, even the *Contra Gentes–De Incarnatione*, were less relevant to a Latin audience than in the east, and the specific nuances of his teachings did not need to be preserved. The

---

[36] For the romantic but very unlikely suggestion that one of these men was Jerome, see Courcelle (1950:181–5). Athanasius resided in Trier 335–7 and may have contributed to the city's rise as a monastic centre.

[37] See the thorough discussion in Stock (1996: 98–111).

[38] In his *De Doctrina Christiana* (Preface 4), Augustine urges his readers to study the Scriptures and cites the example of Antony, who was unlearned (as claimed in Athanasius' *Life*) but committed the Scriptures to memory and understood them through listening and meditation.

only Athanasian work that we can demonstrate maintained a widespread circulation was the *Life of Antony*, which after its early translation into Latin remained essential reading in western monasticism.

There was one other 'Athanasian' text that circulated as widely as the *Life of Antony* in the early medieval west. It has been known for centuries that the so-called Athanasian Creed (or Quicunque from its opening word) has no connection whatsoever to the Alexandrian bishop.[39] Understandably, the creed has therefore played little or no part in modern Athanasian studies. Yet for over a thousand years this was the work that the majority of Latin Christianity associated most strongly with Athanasius' name. It is a document of fundamental importance to the western legacy of Athanasius, and deserves to be quoted in full.

Whoever desires to be saved must above all things hold the catholic faith. Unless a man keeps it in its entirety inviolate, he will assuredly perish eternally.

Now this is the catholic faith, that we worship one God in Trinity and Trinity in unity, without either confusing the persons or dividing the substance. For the Father's person is one, the Son's another, the Holy Spirit's another; but the Godhead of the Father, the Son and the Holy Spirit is one, their glory is equal, their majesty coeternal.

Such as the Father is, such is the Son, such also the Holy Spirit. The Father is increate, the Son increate, the Holy Spirit increate. The Father is infinite, the Son infinite, the Holy Spirit infinite. The Father is eternal, the Son eternal, the Holy Spirit eternal. Yet there are not three eternals, but one eternal; just as there are not three increates or three infinites, but one increate and one infinite. In the same way the Father is almighty, the Son almighty, the Holy Spirit almighty; yet there are not three almighties, but one almighty.

Thus the Father is God, the Son God, the Holy Spirit God; and yet there are not three Gods, but there is one God. Thus the Father is Lord, the Son Lord, the Holy Spirit Lord; and yet there are not three Lords, but there is one Lord. Because just as we are obliged by Christian truth to acknowledge each person separately both God and Lord, so we are forbidden by the catholic religion to speak of three Gods or Lords.

The Father is from none, not made nor created nor begotten. The Son is from the Father alone, not made nor created but begotten. The Holy Spirit is from the Father and the Son, not made nor created nor begotten but proceeding. So there is one Father, not three Fathers; one Son, not three Sons; one Holy Spirit, not three Holy Spirits. And in this Trinity there is nothing before or after, nothing greater or less, but all three persons are coeternal with each other and coequal. Thus in all

---

[39] The standard English work remains Kelly (1964), which traces the scholarly history of the creed and provides the translation quoted here. See also Drecoll (2007).

things, as has been stated above, both Trinity in unity and unity in Trinity must be worshipped. So he who desires to be saved should think thus of the Trinity.

It is necessary, however, to eternal salvation that he should also faithfully believe in the Incarnation of our Lord Jesus Christ. Now the right faith is that we should believe and confess that our Lord Jesus Christ, the Son of God, is equally both God and man.

He is God from the Father's substance, begotten before time; and he is man from his mother's substance, born in time. Perfect God, perfect man composed of a rational soul and human flesh, equal to the Father in respect of his divinity, less than the Father in respect of his humanity.

Who, although he is God and man, is nevertheless not two but one Christ. He is one, however, not by the transformation of his divinity into flesh, but by the taking up of his humanity into God; one certainly not by confusion of substance, but by oneness of person. For just as rational soul and flesh are a single man, so God and man are a single Christ.

Who suffered for our salvation, descended to hell, rose from the dead, ascended to heaven, sat down at the Father's right hand, whence he will come to judge living and dead; at whose coming all men will rise again with their bodies, and will render an account of their deeds; and those who have behaved well will go to eternal life, those who have behaved badly to eternal fire.

This is the catholic faith. Unless a man believes it faithfully and steadfastly, he will not be able to be saved.

The original author of the Quicunque creed remains a subject for debate. The language of composition was Latin, and the theology is post-Athanasian (particularly in Christology) and western in the double procession of the Spirit. Our earliest definite witness appears to be Caesarius of Arles (bishop 502–42), and the creed was probably composed in southern Gaul in the late fifth or early sixth century. Caesarius promoted the Quicunque as an aid for the instruction of catechumens and clergy alike. Canon 1 of the Second Council of Autun in Burgundy in c.670 required that all clergy should be able to recite 'the Faith of the holy primate Athanasius' without error. The creed featured prominently in the Carolingian period, and was in widespread educational and liturgical use until its identification with Athanasius came under attack in the mid-sixteenth century. Even then the Quicunque still found champions until the twentieth century, when uncertainty over the authorship and distaste for the dogmatic fundamentalism of the opening and closing lines saw the creed fall into neglect.

In the memory of western Christianity, the prominence of Athanasius owed much to the false attribution of the Athanasian Creed, perhaps almost as much as to the *Life of Antony*. It is perhaps ironic that a work that he did not write helped to preserve Athanasius' legacy and indeed to promote many of the theological values that he had fought to defend. The fundamental doctrines of the Quicunque are teachings that Athanasius upheld. The equality and unity of the persons of the Trinity are strongly maintained, but so too are their individual identities. The Incarnate Christ is fully God and fully man, and therein lies our salvation. However erroneous its attribution to him may be, the fact that this enormously influential and popular creed acquired his name is too important to ignore. For the Latin west no less than for the Greek east, Athanasius remained a symbol of orthodoxy for future generations and an integral figure in the concept of Christian tradition that bound the later Church to the patristic age.

ATHANASIUS IN SYRIAC TRADITION

Syriac Christianity has preserved an enormous volume of literary material, both translations from Greek and original Syriac language compositions, and I cannot attempt to do justice to this great tradition here. In addition to the works of Athanasius preserved in Syriac manuscripts, the Alexandrian bishop features prominently in Syriac histories of the early Church. His prominence opens a rare window of opportunity. The Syriac tradition is extremely diverse, for Syriac Christianity came to be divided between Chalcedonian and Miaphysite churches and the Church of the East (often inaccurately described as the 'Nestorian Church'). Did this diversity impact upon the Syriac memory of Athanasius?

In terms of Syriac historiography, the answer would seem to be no. This is significant. Despite the theological differences that split the Syriac churches, the image of Athanasius preserved in Syriac historical texts is remarkably uniform. To cite two examples from many, take the East Syrian Barhadbesabba of 'Arbaya's *Ecclesiastical History: Stories of the Holy Fathers who were Persecuted on Behalf of the Truth*[40] and the West Syrian *Chronicle* of Pseudo-Dionysius of Tel-Mahre.[41] These works differ dramatically in form and ideology. Barhadbesabba, who wrote in the late sixth century, was a representative of the Church of the East, and his *Ecclesiastical History*, like the Coptic *History of the Patriarchs*, is a collection of biographies rather than a historical narrative. Pseudo-Dionysius, whose identity remains uncertain but who is dated to the eighth century, compiled his *Chronicle* in

---

[40]　Nau (1913, 1932).
[41]　Chabot (1949), with discussion in Witakowski (1987).

a more annalistic style and represented a Miaphysite view of the Christian past. Yet, for the fourth century, the two authors share the same pool of knowledge, and their interpretations follow very similar lines. They derived their information from the Greek ecclesiastical historians, particularly Socrates,[42] and are content to endorse Athanasius as the champion of orthodoxy, even if they each understand 'orthodoxy' in their own way.

Where the diversity of Syriac Christianity does impact upon Athanasius, however, lies in the complex manuscript transmission of the Syriac Athanasian corpus. This corpus has proved of the utmost value to modern editors of Athanasius' writings, for the surviving Syriac corpus is the oldest Athanasian collection now extant.[43] But, unlike the Greek corpora of Athanasius' writings, the Syriac collection omits his major polemical and doctrinal works.[44] The works that later Syriac generations found most valuable were, on the contrary, Athanasius' letters and ascetica. Moreover, a number of Athanasius' writings in Syriac reveal editing, particularly in the light of the Christological debates following the Council of Chalcedon. The eighth-century Syriac Athanasian corpus is Chalcedonian, with a number of passages inserted in favour of a two-nature doctrine of Christ. Unfortunately, the corpus' editor was apparently unaware that several of the texts he included (three of which are Apollinarian rather than Athanasian) had already been edited by an earlier Syriac scribe with Miaphysite tendencies.[45]

ATHANASIUS IN ARMENIAN TRADITION

The literary tradition of Armenian Christianity is perhaps less diverse than the Syriac tradition but no less worthy of study. In the centuries after the Council of Chalcedon, the Armenian Church became predominantly Miaphysite. This influenced both the Armenian preservation of Athanasius' writings and his place in Armenian historiography. Even more than

[42] No Syriac translation of Socrates survives intact, but, on the Syriac witnesses to Socrates' text, see further Hansen (1995: pp. xxxi–iii). There is little indication that either Barhadbesabba or Pseudo-Dionysius knew Athanasius' apologetic-historical writings at first hand.

[43] The single Syriac Athanasian corpus dates to the eighth century, whereas the oldest extant Greek corpus belongs to the tenth century; see further Thomson (1963, 1965–77).

[44] The Syriac 'Short Recension' of Athanasius' *De Incarnatione* survives in a separate manuscript dated to 564 (Vatican Syr. 104). On the significance of this text, see Thomson (1964; 1971: pp. xxiv–ix).

[45] Thomson (1963).

in Syriac, the Armenian Athanasius was reworked to serve a context far removed from fourth-century Egypt.

Athanasius plays no role at all in the greatest formative work of the early Armenian historical tradition, the eighth-century *History of the Armenians* of Moses Khorenats'i.[46] Moses' *History* is focused almost exclusively on the region of Armenia, and the Alexandrian bishop does not appear. When Moses does refer to the wider fourth-century Christian context, he, like Barhadbesabba or Pseudo-Dionysius in Syriac, derives his knowledge from the *Ecclesiastical History* of Socrates translated into Armenian in the sixth century.[47]

Whereas the Syriac authors were content to summarize Socrates' account of Athanasius, however, the Armenian tradition went further. Shortly before the time of Moses Khorenats'i, in the late seventh century, the so-called 'Shorter Socrates' was compiled. This was an Armenian adaptation of Socrates' *Ecclesiastical History*, which abridged sections of the text but also added material not found in the original.[48] A number of those additions concern Athanasius, and reflect the image of the saint that the Armenian author wished to construct. Athanasius is repeatedly emphasized as a moral and orthodox champion, who 'with his peace-loving teaching advised and taught a life of virtue' (III.10, 234). He is also credited with the composition of a creed (not the western Athanasian Creed), in which he proclaimed the Incarnation of the Son, who is 'without seed from the Virgin, and mingles the unmingled in the womb ineffably and incomprehensibly' (III.10, 238). This is the language not of Athanasius, but of the Christological controversies of the seventh century, during which the 'Shorter Socrates' was compiled.

The same process of adaptation is reflected in the Armenian manuscript transmission of Athanasiana. Like the older Syriac corpus, the Armenian corpora of Athanasius' writings omit his major polemical and doctrinal works.[49] And, like the Syriac corpus, the Armenian material has been edited in the light of the later Christological debates. The Armenian text of Athanasius' *Letter to Epictetus* provides a glimpse of how such editorial

---

[46] Thomson (1978).

[47] Thomson (1978: 36–8). The Armenian translation of Socrates contributed significantly to the modern critical edition of Socrates' text: see Hansen (1995: pp. xxv–xxxi).

[48] Thomson (2001), from which the translations here derive.

[49] There are three extant Armenian corpora of Athanasian writings, dating from approximately the ninth to the fourteenth centuries; see Casey (1931). They do not derive from any known Greek corpus or from the extant Syriac corpus.

intervention could occur.[50] The original *Letter* included the reading that 'the body that the Word indwelt was not co-essential with the Godhead but truly born of Mary, and the Word himself was not converted into flesh and bones' (*Letter to Epictetus* 8). In one Armenian version, Athanasius' teachings were converted into an explicit affirmation of the later Cyrillian doctrine of the *Theotokos* and the indissoluble union of the natures of Christ.[51]

For the body was united to the Word, and the divinity of the Word and the body were not one nature, but it was truly born from the holy Mother of God, Mary; and it was not that the Word of God was altered and changed into a body, but the Word was indissolubly united to his body which He took from the Virgin; and the uniting shows the indissolubility and unity of the natures.[52]

ATHANASIUS IN COPTIC TRADITION

Athanasius was held in high regard by all the diverse traditions of eastern and western Christianity in the centuries after his death. For the Coptic Church of Egypt, however, the great bishop of Alexandria possessed a special importance. Alongside his eventual successor Cyril, Athanasius was venerated as the founding father of late-antique Egyptian Christianity. Our knowledge of early Coptic literature is fragmentary, and much of our evidence survives in later translations from lost Coptic language writings.[53] But what does survive provides an essential insight into Athanasius' achievement and his legacy.

The earliest Coptic historical text of which traces still exist is the *Histories of the Church*.[54] This anonymous work probably reached its final form in the episcopate of Timothy Aelurus (bishop of Alexandria 457–77), while drawing upon earlier sources.[55] Today, the fragments of the Coptic *Histories*

---

[50] See Casey (1933) and Thomson (1965).

[51] In the words of Thomson (1965: 47): 'The Athanasius known to the Armenians was different from the Athanasius familiar to modern Patristic students. He was known as one who had spent his life fighting the dyophysites, dedicated to the cause: "one nature of the incarnate Word".'

[52] Quotation from Thomson (1965: 52).

[53] For an introduction to the evidence and the issues involved in the study of Coptic literature, see Orlandi (1986) and Emmel (2007).

[54] See Orlandi (1968a), Johnson (1973, 1977), and most recently Orlandi (2007).

[55] One of those sources may have been the *History of the Episcopate of Alexandria* recently identified by Camplani from a new Ethiopian manuscript. Camplani (2006) has proposed that this text may have been compiled in the late fourth century, shortly after the death of Athanasius, although the extant fragments cut off in the early fourth century and do not cover Athanasius' episcopate.

are largely preserved in Arabic translation in the most important extant
witness to the Coptic historiographical tradition: the *History of the Patriarchs of Alexandria*.[56] The *History of the Patriarchs* was compiled by a series
of scribes across almost a millennium. In contrast to the Greek ecclesiastical historians, the Coptic scribes composed a collection of biographies
focused upon Egypt and Alexandria not a universal Christian narrative.[57]
The section that includes the life of Athanasius depends heavily on the
earlier *Histories* but attained its present form in the late eleventh century.
Our other leading representative of Coptic historiography is the seventh-
century *Chronicle* of John of Nikiu.[58] John almost certainly wrote in Coptic,
but his *Chronicle* survives only in a late Ethiopic translation of an Arabic
translation of the original. He draws upon a number of shared traditions
with the *History of the Patriarchs*, although he had access to other now lost
sources and his factual knowledge of Athanasius' career is superior.

We saw in my opening chapter that the *History of the Patriarchs* describes
the young Athanasius holding doggedly to his ascetic principles against
the pleas of his pagan mother. Eventually she brought the youth before
Alexander, who baptized him and oversaw his upbringing. The Coptic
tradition places particular emphasis on the relationships between different bishops of Alexandria, and later stories associated Athanasius with his
future successor Theophilus as well as Theophilus more naturally with his
nephew Cyril.[59] Even so, the bond between Athanasius and Alexander is presented as being especially close. Once Athanasius' education was complete,
Alexander 'made him his scribe, and he became as though he were the
interpreter of the aforesaid father, and a minister of the word which he
wished to utter' (*HPA* PO 1:408). Immediately after this statement, the *History of the Patriarchs* offers a dramatic account of the conflict between Alexander, Athanasius, and Arius that led to the heresiarch's death.

When the emperor Constantine died, his son Constantius was corrupted
by Arius. Constantius therefore summoned Alexander from Alexandria to
Constantinople and asked him to restore Arius. Athanasius accompanied

---

[56] Text and translation by Evetts (1907–15). On the complex history and chronology of this
work, see den Heijer (1989).

[57] There is no indication that any of the fifth-century Greek ecclesiastical histories were
ever translated into Coptic, unlike in the Syriac and Armenian traditions.

[58] Translation by Charles (1916).

[59] In the *History of the Patriarchs*, Theophilus is Athanasius' secretary and companion
(*HPA* PO 1:425). John of Nikiu (*Chronicle* 79) recounts another probably legendary story of
how Athanasius met Theophilus and his sister (the mother of Cyril) and supervised their
upbringing.

Alexander to the imperial court as 'his interpreter and scribe and mouth-piece' (*HPA* PO 1:409), and refuted Arius in debate until Arius withdrew. The next day, Arius bribed the royal attendants not to allow Athanasius to enter the debating room, but Alexander refused to speak, for 'how shall I speak without a tongue?' (*HPA* PO 1:410). Athanasius was now allowed to enter, and Arius fled and remained condemned. After Alexander of Alexandria had died, Arius then appealed again to Constantius for aid and demanded that he be received by bishop Alexander of Constantinople. When this Alexander tried to resist, Arius presented a creed that falsely concealed his heresy, and Alexander agreed that he would receive Arius into the priest-hood the following Sunday. Arius came to the church, dressed in his finest garments, but during the reading he had to leave to relieve himself: 'all his bowels gushed out from his body' and he died (*HPA* PO 1:411–13).

This account of the famous death of Arius bears careful analysis. The reported debate in which Athanasius represented Alexander of Alexandria against Arius in the presence of Constantius is entirely absent from the Greek historical tradition. It is also chronologically impossible. Alexander died in 328 and Constantius succeeded his father in 337. The episode rein-forces the *History of the Patriarch*'s depiction of Athanasius as the 'tongue' of Alexander, an image known elsewhere from Egyptian writings.[60] In addition, by placing the recall of Arius in the reign of Constantius, the *History of the Patriarchs* protected the reputation of Constantine, who is praised repeatedly as the defender of Nicaea but who was in fact respon-sible for Arius' return from banishment after 325. John of Nikiu followed the same principle, alleging that Arius is said to have appeared in the days of Constantius, who attached himself to the heresy (*Chronicle* 78.5). The Coptic tradition is not alone in protecting Constantine in this manner, for, as we have seen, the recall of Arius is similarly falsely attributed to Constan-tius by Rufinus, an error (almost certainly deliberate) that was corrected by Socrates.

Arius' clash with Alexander of Constantinople in the *History of the Patri-archs* is closer to the version found in the Greek ecclesiastical historians, although here too there are differences. Most notably, the *History of the Patriarchs* describes Arius actually attending the church on the day of his death, scented and perfumed and dressed in all his finery, and only then

---

[60] In the *c*.sixth-century Coptic text of Pseudo-Dioscorus, *Panegryic on Macarius of Tkôw*, Dioscorus prays to Athanasius 'let your spirit be doubled upon me, for this is the crucial time when I have need of the tongue of the elder, Alexander' (13.2–3) (translation from Johnson 1980).

having to leave to relieve himself. In the Greek versions, Arius died in a procession before he could enter the church, and according to Socrates (I.39) the place of his death was commemorated at the rear of the Forum of Constantine. These differences may be minor, but they are significant. All the narratives originally drew their material from the same common source: Athanasius' description of Arius' death in the *De Morte Arii* and the *Encyclical Letter to the Bishops of Egypt and Libya*. The later Greek and Coptic writers took from Athanasius the essential elements—the resistance of Alexander of Constantinople, Arius' deceptive creed, and the description of his actual death—but felt free to embellish the story and add their own details.

In the *History of the Patriarchs*, the death of Arius is followed by a short narrative of Athanasius' episcopate under Constantius. To support the friends of Arius, the emperor sent George of Cappadocia with five hundred horsemen to seize the bishopric of Alexandria. They killed the followers of Athanasius in his church, and Athanasius went into hiding. After six years, 'Athanasius showed himself, and went to the prince, thinking that he would kill him, and that he would receive the crown of martyrdom'. Constantius set Athanasius adrift alone in a small boat, but the waves carried him to Alexandria, where the clergy and people received him with joy, and he expelled George. Seven years later, a new rival named Gregory came, bringing with him two thousand soldiers. Athanasius was arrested and almost killed, but he escaped with Liberius, bishop of Rome, and Dionysius, bishop of Antioch. He remained with Liberius until Constantius' death, and Constantius' orthodox son Constans then restored Athanasius to his see (*HPA* PO 1:413–15).

The chronological and historical problems raised by this narrative are almost too numerous to mention. The arrival of George as bishop of Alexandria occurred in February 357, a full year after Athanasius had fled into hiding following the attack on the Church of Theonas on the night of 8/9 February 356. His return six years later was made possible by the death of Constantius and the accession of Julian, and George was lynched by the pagans of Alexandria not expelled by Athanasius. The claim that Athanasius surrendered himself to Constantius for execution directly contradicts Athanasius' own denial of voluntary martyrdom in his *Apologia de Fuga*,[61]

---

[61] For the importance of persecution and martyrdom to the self-identity of the later Coptic Church, which styled itself as the 'Church of the Martyrs', see Papaconstantinou (2006).

while the story that Constantius set Athanasius adrift appears to be a conventional hagiographic legend.[62] The joyful response of the Alexandrians may recall the welcome that Athanasius received on his return from his second exile in 346. That exile had seen Athanasius replaced by Gregory, whose episcopate is wrongly placed in the *History of the Patriarchs* after that of George rather than before. Liberius was indeed an ally of Athanasius in the 350s under Constantius, together with Dionysius (who was bishop of Milan not of Antioch). But the reference to Constans, who was Constantius' brother and died in 350, is again confused. The only instance in which the son of an emperor restored Athanasius upon his father's death was Constantine II in 337.

I have catalogued these errors at some length, for they shed valuable light on the nature of Coptic historiography. The account of Athanasius' life in the *History of the Patriarchs* has little or no narrative or chronological cohesion.[63] To a degree, this is equally true of the relevant section of the *Chronicle* of John of Nikiu, although John is able to identify Constans as Constantius' brother rather than his son and correctly places both the attack on Athanasius in his church and the exile of Liberius of Rome after Constans' death (*Chronicle* 78.11–22). Neither the *History of the Patriarchs* nor John of Nikiu ever refers to Athanasius' original condemnation and exile under Constantine after the Council of Tyre in 335, which forms the essential background to Athanasius' experiences under Constantius. Nor is either apparently aware of how the relationship between Athanasius and Constantius fluctuated throughout the 340s and 350s, from imperial favour to open hostility. The wider context of Athanasius' life, described in detail by the Greek ecclesiastical historians, played only a marginal role in the Coptic tradition of their great fourth-century bishop.[64]

---

[62] The same combination of hagiography and history occurs in the Coptic *Life of Athanasius* and *Encomium of Athanasius* edited by Orlandi (1968b), again drawing on material from the Coptic *Histories of the Church*.

[63] According to the *History*, Athanasius was bishop for forty-seven years, of which he passed the first twenty-two in exile and conflict and the final twenty-five in tranquillity and peace (*HPA* PO 1:416). The forty-seven years date Athanasius' episcopate incorrectly from 326 rather than 328, while the division of those years into conflict and peace is at best rhetorical. The earlier statement in the *History* that Athanasius was exiled three times and that his third exile lasted eleven years (*HPA* PO 1:404) must likewise be rejected.

[64] The minimal attention paid in these works to Athanasius' long theological struggle with those he condemned as 'Arian' contrasts markedly with the life of Cyril presented in the *History of the Patriarchs*, which is dominated by his ongoing debate with Nestorius and quotations from his polemical writings (*HPA* PO 1:432–43).

To modern eyes, this may seem surprising. It is certainly notable that the Greek ecclesiastical historians display a far more extensive knowledge of Athanasius' apologetic writings, from which they drew their material, than do their Coptic counterparts. Yet the historical inaccuracy of the presentation of Athanasius' career in these Coptic texts must not cause us to overlook the true value of this Athanasian tradition. The Coptic Church showed very limited interest in Athanasius' polemic, and did not even collect translations of his apologetic or theological works into corpora.[65] Instead, the Athanasian writings that dominate our Coptic evidence are precisely those writings that either do not survive in Greek or were ignored by the Greek ecclesiastical historians. Near the end of Athanasius' biography in the *History of the Patriarchs*, the bishop is said to have written 'many homilies and treatises' (*HPA* PO 1:422). The works then named are not Athanasius' apologetic or theological writings. They are the *Life of Antony*, the *Festal Letters*, and an otherwise unknown work on virginity.[66] Other Athanasian or pseudo-Athanasian writings known in Coptic reflect the same ascetic and pastoral concerns, including the moral homilies preserved (rightly or wrongly) in his name and the undoubtedly pseudonymous *Life of Syncletica* and the 107 Canons of Athanasius.[67]

For our knowledge of the events and controversies of Athanasius' lifetime, his own writings and to a lesser degree the Greek ecclesiastical historians remain our primary resource. But the evidence that the Greek tradition provides can never fully explain Athanasius' ultimate triumph. Across the long and often difficult years of his episcopate, Athanasius united the diverse communities of Christian Egypt under his leadership and redefined the authority of the Alexandrian see. It is the memory of this achievement that the Coptic tradition above all preserves. The Athanasius who dominates Coptic historiography, and whose works that tradition valued, was not a controversialist but an ascetic and pastoral leader. It is an image encapsulated in the final vision of Athanasius recalled by John of Nikiu, the spiritual bishop guiding and protecting his flock:

---

[65] This is not to deny the importance of Athanasius in Coptic theological tradition, on which see further Davis (2008).

[66] The content of this work, the only Athanasian text quoted at any length in the *History* (*HPA* PO 1:405), closely parallels Athanasius' first *Letter to Virgins*, which likewise survives only in Coptic. See Brakke (1994a: 37–8).

[67] For the homilies, see Orlandi (1981). For the *Life of Syncletica* and the Canons, see respectively Bongie (1998) and Riedel and Crum (1904).

In those days [the reign of Emperor Valens] there appeared a miracle through the intervention of the apostolic Saint Athanasius, the father of the faith, patriarch of Alexandria. When the sea rose against the city of Alexandria and, threatening an inundation, had already advanced to a place called Heptastadion, the venerable father accompanied by all the priests went forth to the borders of the sea, and holding in his hand the book of the holy Law he raised his hand to heaven and said 'O Lord, Thou God who liest not, it is Thou that didst promise to Noah after the flood and say: "I will not again bring a flood of waters upon the earth." ' And after these words of the saint the sea returned to its place and the wrath of God was appeased. Thus the city was saved through the intercession of the apostolic Saint Athanasius, the great star. (John of Nikiu, *Chronicle* 82.21–3)

Conclusion

Amidst the storms of persecution, the archbishop of Alexandria was patient of labour, jealous of fame, careless of safety; and, although his mind was tainted by the contagion of fanaticism, Athanasius displayed a superiority of character and abilities which would have qualified him, far better than the degenerate sons of Constantine, for the government of a great monarchy.

(Edward Gibbon, *The History of the Decline and Fall of the Roman Empire* (1776–88), ch. 21)

Athanasius was a truly lovable man. That he was not flawless—that his words could be somewhat too sharp in controversy, or somewhat unreal in addressing a despot, that he was not always charitable in his interpretation of his adversaries' conduct... this may be, and has been, admitted; but after all, and looking at the whole man, we shall not be extravagant if we pronounce his name to be the greatest in the Church's post-apostolic history.

(William Bright, *Dictionary of Christian Biography* (1877), 202)

If the violence of Athanasius leaves fewer traces in the surviving sources than similar behaviour by later bishops of Alexandria like Theophilus, Cyril, and Dioscorus, the reason is not that he exercised power in a different way, but that he exercised it more efficiently and that he was successful in presenting himself to posterity as an innocent in power, as an honest, sincere and straightforward 'man of God'.

(Timothy Barnes, *Athanasius and Constantius* (1993), 33)

Harnack's assessment is probably the most balanced: that judged 'by the standard of his time, we can discover nothing ignoble or mean about him'.

(John Behr, *The Nicene Faith* (2004), 167, quoting Adolf von Harnack (1898))

Athanasius of Alexandria has divided modern opinions just as surely as he divided those of his contemporaries. The story of his life has been a source of inspiration for some, a cautionary tale for others. In later Christian tradition Athanasius' reputation stood secure. He was the champion of orthodoxy, the defender of the Nicene faith against the 'Arian heresy'. Even Edward Gibbon, a man rarely moved to praise a Christian saint, acknowledged Athanasius' gifts while deploring his fanaticism. Today, in the early years of the twenty-first century, Athanasius' legacy still shines brightly. But darker interpretations have gathered in strength. Ecclesiastical politics and polemic have seemed more relevant to many modern eyes than theology and asceticism, and older praises now read uncomfortably like hagiographical hero worship. The evidence presented in the preceding chapters can support a variety of different verdicts, and whatever judgement one makes will shed light on Athanasius but also on the judge.

This book is not a traditional biography. My hope is that readers will decide for themselves what manner of man they believe Athanasius was and what lessons they will learn from his example. As an embattled bishop, he possessed the courage and strength to endure years of persecution and exile. His methods may at times have been violent, and his misrepresentation of his foes resembles rather too closely the partisan rhetoric of a modern politician. Yet the convictions that drove Athanasius rose far above personal ambition and desire for power or fame. Despite the trials he faced, we never hear Athanasius question his faith or doubt his duty to God and to those who looked to him for leadership. It was that duty to which he dedicated his life.

No student of Athanasius would question the sincerity or depth of his religious beliefs. But, for those of us who live in an increasingly secular world, Athanasius' devotion to Christian doctrine and his admiration for ascetic renunciation can appear alien and even dangerous. The complex questions that split the fourth-century Church no longer strike a chord with modern audiences. It is all too easy to dismiss such concerns as incomprehensible and irrelevant, the domain of a theological and monastic elite. An integral part of Athanasius' genius, however, lay in his capacity to bridge the gulf that threatened to separate just such an elite from the wider Christian population. The orthodox faith that he fought to defend was not an arcane formula but confirmation of the salvation promised to humanity through the Incarnation. The virtues of asceticism were not the exclusive preserve of a holy man such as Antony but could be emulated by every believer in his or her own measure. Athanasius' pastoral concern thus drew together the ecclesiastical, theological, and ascetic challenges that he faced and laid the foundation for his eventual triumph.

Athanasius was a bishop and a theologian, an ascetic and a pastoral father. Each of these roles merits careful attention, and each offers a different vision of Athanasius from which the modern viewer can learn. But, as we have seen throughout this volume, these roles were never mutually exclusive. On the contrary, they were inseparable from each other. Whatever judgements we may draw from his life and writings, all these elements are equally essential to our understanding of Athanasius as an individual. He was a product of his times, and his career offers a valuable insight into the great formative period of Late Antiquity. Like other great men and women of history, he also transcended his times, and continues to teach lessons from which later generations may benefit.

Bibliography

EDITIONS, TEXTUAL *CRITICA*, AND TRANSLATIONS

The Writings of Athanasius

Barnard, L. W. (1994). *The Monastic Letters of Saint Athanasius the Great*. Oxford.

Bartelink, G. M. J. (1994). *Athanase d'Alexandrie: Vie d'Antoine*. Sources Chrétiennes, 400. Paris.

Brakke, D. (1994a). 'The Authenticity of the Ascetic Athanasiana', *Orientalia*, NS 63: 17–56.

Brennecke, H. C. (2006). 'Zwei Apologien des Athanasius an Kaiser Constantius II', *ZAC* 10: 67–85.

——Heil, U., and Stockhausen, A. von (2006). *Athanasius Werke 2. Die 'Apologien'.* Volume 8. *Apologia ad Constantium, Epistula ad Joannem et Antiochum, Epistula ad Palladium, Epistula ad Dracontium, Epistula ad Afros, Tomus ad Antiochenos, Epistula ad Jovianum, Epistula Joviani ad Athanasium, Petitiones Arianorum*. Berlin and New York.

Bright, W. (1881). *The Historical Writings of Athanasius*. Oxford.

Burgess, H. (1854). *The Festal Letters of Saint Athanasius*. Oxford.

Camplani, A. (1989). *Le Lettere Festali di Atanasio di Alexandria*. Rome.

——(2003). *Atanasio di Alessandria. Lettere festali. Anonimo. Indice delle Lettere festali.* Milan.

Casey, R. P. (1931). 'Armenian Manuscripts of St Athanasius of Alexandria', *HThR* 24: 43–59.

——(1933). 'An Armenian Version of Athanasius's *Letter to Epictetus*', *HThR* 26: 127–50.

Cureton, W. (1848). *The Festal Letters of Athanasius*. London.

Gregg, R. (1980). *Athanasius: The Life of Antony and the Letter to Marcellinus*. Mahwah, NJ.

Heil, U. (1999). *Athanasius von Alexandrien: De Sententia Dionysii. Einleitung, Übersetzung und Kommentar*. Berlin and New York.

Lefort, L. T. (1955). *Saint Athanase: Lettres festales et pastorales en Copte*. Scriptores Coptici 19: 1–72, and 20: 1–55.

Lorenz, R. (1986). *Der zehnte Osterfestbrief des Athanasius von Alexandrien*. Berlin and New York.

Meijering, E. P. (1996–8). *Athanasius, die dritte Rede gegen die Arianer: Einleitung, Übersetzung, Kommentar*. 3 vols. Amsterdam.

Metzler, K., and Simon, F. (1991) (eds). *Ariana et Athanasiana: Studien zur Überlieferung und zu philologischen Problemen der Werke des Athanasius von Alexandrien*. Opladen.

Müller, G. (1952). *Lexicon Athanasianum.* Berlin.

Opitz, H.-G. (1935). *Athanasius Werke II.1.* Volume 3. *Die Apologien: 1. De Decretis Nicaenae Synodi.* Berlin and Leipzig.

——(1936). *Athanasius Werke II.1.* Volume 4. *Die Apologien: 2. De Sententia Dionysii, 3. Apologia De Fuga Sua (1–18).* Berlin and Leipzig.

——(1938a). *Athanasius Werke II.1.* Volume 5. *Die Apologien: 3. Apologia De Fuga Sua (19–27), 4. Apologia Secunda (1–43).* Berlin.

——(1938b). *Athanasius Werke II.1.* Volume 6. *Die Apologien: 4. Apologia Secunda (43–80).* Berlin.

——(1940a). *Athanasius Werke II.1.* Volume 7. *Die Apologien: 4. Apologia Secunda (80-schluß), 5. Epistula Encyclica, 6. De Morte Arii, 7. Ep. Ad Monachos, 8. Historia Arianorum (1–32).* Berlin.

——(1940b). *Athanasius Werke II.1.* Volume 8. *Die Apologien: 8. Historia Arianorum (32-schluß), 9. De Synodis (1–13).* Berlin.

——(1941). *Athanasius Werke II.1.* Volume 9. *Die Apologien: 9. De Synodis (13–55), 10. Apologia ad Constantium (1–3).* Berlin.

Robertson, A. (1892). *Select Writings and Letters of Athanasius, Bishop of Alexandria. Nicene and Post-Nicene Fathers.* Second Series 4. London.

Seiler, R. (1932). *Athanasius, Apologia contra Arianos (Ihre Entstehung und Datierung).* Diss. Tübingen.

Simon, F. (1991). 'Athanasius latinus', in Metzler and Simon (1991), 87–130.

Stockhausen, A. von (2002). *Athanasius von Alexandrien, Epistula Ad Afros: Einleitung, Kommentar und Übersetzung.* Berlin and New York.

——and Brennecke, H. C. (2010) (eds). *Von Arius zum Athanasianum: Studien zur Edition der 'Athanasius Werke'.* Berlin and New York.

Szymusiak, J. M. (1987). *Athanase d'Alexandrie. Deux Apologies: A L'Empereur Constance, Pour sa Fuite.* Sources Chrétiennes, 56. Rev. edn. Paris.

Tetz, M. (1988). 'Ein enzyklishes Schreiben der Synode von Alexandrien (362)', *ZNW* 79: 262–81; repr. in Tetz (1995), 207–25.

——(1996). *Athanasius Werke 1.1. Die Dogmatischen Schriften.* Volume 1. *Epistula ad Episcopos Aegypti et Libyae.* Berlin and New York.

——(1998). *Athanasius Werke 1.1. Die Dogmatischen Schriften.* Volume 2. *Orationes I et II Contra Arianos.* Berlin and New York.

——and Wyrwa, D. (2000). *Athanasius Werke 1.1. Die Dogmatischen Schriften.* Volume 3. *Oratio III Contra Arianos.* Berlin and New York.

Thomson, R. W. (1963). 'The Text of the Syriac Athanasian Corpus', in J. N. Birdsall and R. W. Thomson (eds), *Biblical and Patristic Studies in Memory of Robert Pierce Casey,* Freiburg, 250–64.

——(1964). 'Some Remarks on the Syriac Version of Athanasius' *De Incarnatione*', *Le Muséon,* 77: 17–28.

——(1965). 'The Transformation of Athanasius in Armenian Theology (a Tendentious Version of the *Epistula ad Epictetum*)', *Le Muséon,* 78: 47–69; repr. in Thomson, *Studies in Armenian Literature and Christianity* (Aldershot, 1994), XIII.

——(1965–77). *Athanasiana Syriaca* I (CSCO 257), II (CSCO 272), III (CSCO 324), IV (CSCO 386). Louvain.

——(1971). *Athanasius, Contra Gentes and De Incarnatione*. Oxford.

Other Primary Sources

Bidez, J. (3rd edn by F. Winkelmann) (1981). *Philostorgius Kirchengeschichte mit dem Leben des Lucian von Antiochien und den Fragmenten eines arianischen Historiographen*. Berlin.

Bongie, E. B. (1998). *The Life and Regimen of the Blessed and Holy Syncletica*. Toronto.

Brakke, D. (2002). *Pseudo-Athanasius On Virginity*. CSCO 592. Louvain.

Brennecke, H. C., Heil, U., Stockhausen, A. von, and Wintjes, A. (2007). *Athanasius Werke III.1. Urkunden zur Geschichte des arianischen Streites 318–328*, Volume 3, *Bis zur Ekthesis Makrostichos*. Berlin.

Cameron, Averil, and Hall, S. G. (1999). *Eusebius: Life of Constantine. Introduction, Translation and Commentary*. Oxford.

Chabot, J.-B. (1949). *Incerti auctoris chronicon Pseudo-Dionysianum vulgo dictum I.* CSCO 121. Louvain.

Charles, R. H. (1916). *The Chronicle of John, Bishop of Nikiu*. London.

Den Heijer, J. (1989). *Mawhūb ibn Manṣūr ibn Mufarriǧ et l'historiographie copte-arabe: etude sur la composition de l'Histoire des Patriarches d'Alexandrie*. Louvain.

Draguet, R. (1980). *La Vie primitive de saint Antoine conservée en syriaque*. CSCO 417–18. Louvain.

Evetts, B. (1907–15). *History of the Patriarchs of the Coptic Church of Alexandria*. PO 1(2 and 4), 5(1), 10(5). Paris.

Fitschen, K. (1992). *Serapion von Thmuis: Echte und unechte Schriften sowie die Zeugnisse des Athanasius und Anderer*. Berlin and New York.

Goehring, J. E. (1985). *The Letter of Ammon and Pachomian Monasticism*. Berlin and New York.

Hansen, G. C. (1995). *Sokrates Kirchengeschichte*. Berlin.

——(2004). *Sozomenos Historia Ecclesiastica Kirchengeschichte: Übersetzt und Eingeleitet*. Turnhout.

Johnson, D. W. (1973). 'Coptic Sources of the History of the Patriarchs of Alexandria'. Upublished Ph.D. thesis, The Catholic University of America, Washington.

——(1977). 'Further Remarks on the Arabic History of the Patriarchs of Alexandria', *Oriens Christianus*, 61: 7–17.

——(1980). *A Panegyric on Macarius, Bishop of Tkôw, Attributed to Dioscorus of Alexandria*. Louvain.

Klostermann, E. (2nd edn by G. C. Hansen) (1972). *Eusebius Werke*. Volume 4. *Gegen Marcell, Über Die Kirchliche Theologie, Die Fragmente Marcells*. Berlin.

Liebeschuetz, J. H. W. G. (2005). *Ambrose of Milan: Political Letters and Speeches*. Liverpool.

Martin, A. (1985) (ed.). *Histoire 'Acéphale' et Index Syriaque des Lettres festales d'Athanase d'Alexandrie*. Sources Chrétiennes, 317. Paris.

Nau, F. (1913). *La Seconde Partie de l'Histoire de Barhadbesabba 'Arbaia*. PO 9(5). Paris.

——(1932). *La Première Partie de l'Histoire de Barhadbesabba 'Arbaia*. PO 23(2). Paris.

Opitz, H.-G. (1934–5). *Athanasius Werke II.1*. Volumes 1–2. *Urkunden zur Geschichte des arianischen Streites 318–328*. Berlin and Leipzig.

Orlandi, T. (1968a). *Storia della Chiesa di Alessandria. Testo copto, traduzione e commento, I. Da Pietro ad Atanasio*. Milan and Varese.

——(1968b). *Testi Copti: 1) Encomio di Atanasio; 2) Vita di Atanasio*. Milan.

——(1981). *Omelie copte: Scelte e tradotte, con una introduzione sulla letteratura copta*. Turin.

——(2007). 'The Coptic Ecclesiastical History', in J. E. Goehring and J. A. Timbie (eds), *The World of Early Egyptian Christianity: Language, Literature, and Social Context. Essays in Honor of David W. Johnson*, Washington, 3–24.

Parmentier, L. (3rd edn. by G. C. Hansen) (1998). *Theodoret Kirchengeschichte*. Berlin.

Riedel, W., and Crum, W. E. (1904). *The Canons of Athanasius of Alexandria*. London and Oxford.

Robinson, J. M. (1996) (ed.). *The Nag Hammadi Library in English*. 4th rev. edn. Leiden.

Thomson, R. W. (1978). *Moses Khorenats'i, History of the Armenians (translation and commentary)*. Cambridge, MA, and London.

——(2001). *The Armenian Adaptation of the Ecclesiastical History of Socrates (translation and commentary)*. Leuven, Paris, and Sterling, VA .

Vinzent, M. (1993). *Asterius von Kappadokien: De Theologischen Fragmente. Einleitung, Kritischer Text, Übersetzung und Kommentar*. Leiden, New York, and Cologne.

——(1996). *Pseudo-Athanasius* Contra Arianos IV: *Eine Schrift gegen Asterius von Kappadokien, Eusebius von Cäsarea, Markell von Ankyra und Photin von Sirmium*. Leiden, New York, and Cologne.

Wickham, L. R. (1997). *Hilary of Poitiers: Conflicts of Conscience and Law in the Fourth-Century Church*. Liverpool.

Witakowski, W. (1987). *The Syriac Chronicle of Pseudo-Dionysius of Tel-Mahre: A Study in the History of Historiography*. Uppsala.

Modern Authors

Abramowski, L. (1982). 'Dionysius of Rome (d. 268) and Dionysius of Alexandria (d. 264/5) in the Arian Controversies of the Fourth Century' (German original, *ZKG* 93: 240–72), trans. in L. Abramowski, *Formula and Context: Studies in Early Christian Thought* (London, 1992), XI, 1–35.

Adkin, N. (1992). 'Athanasius' *Letter to Virgins* and Jerome's *Libellus de virginitate servanda*', *Rivista di Filologia e di Istruzione Classica*, 120: 185–203.

Anatolios, K. (1998). *Athanasius: The Coherence of his Thought*. London and New York.

——(2004). *Athanasius*. London and New York.

Argov, E. (2001). 'Giving the Heretic a Voice: Philostorgius of Borissus and Greek Ecclesiastical Historiography', *Athenaeum*, 89: 497–524.

Arnold, D. W. H. (1989). 'Sir Harold Idris Bell and Athanasius: A Reconsideration of *London Papyrus* 1914', *StP* 21: 377–83.

——(1991). *The Early Episcopal Career of Athanasius of Alexandria*. Notre Dame, IN.

Aubineau, M. (1966). 'Les 318 serviteurs d'Abraham (Gen., XIV, 14) et le nombre des pères au concile de Nicée (325)', *Revue d'histoire ecclésiastique*, 61: 5–43.

Ayres, L. (2004a). 'Athanasius' Initial Defence of the Term *homooúsios*: Rereading the *De Decretis*', *JECS* 12: 337–59.

——(2004b). *Nicaea and its Legacy: An Approach to Fourth-Century Trinitarian Theology*. Oxford.

Bagnall, R. S. (1993). *Egypt in Late Antiquity*. Princeton.

——(2007) (ed.). *Egypt in the Byzantine World 300–700*. Cambridge.

Baldovin, J. (1987). *The Urban Character of Christian Worship: The Origins, Development, and Meaning of Stational Liturgy*. Rome.

Bardy, G. (1936). *Recherches sur Lucien d'Antioche et son école*. Paris.

Barnard, L. W. (1973). 'Athanasius and the Meletian Schism in Egypt', *JEA* 59: 181–9.

——(1974). 'Athanase et les empereurs Constantin et Constance', in Kannengiesser (1974), 127–43; repr. in revised English translation in Barnard (1978), 312–28.

——(1975). 'Two Notes on Athanasius', *Orientalia Christiana Periodica* 41/2: 344–56; repr. in Barnard (1978), 329–40.

——(1978). *Studies in Church History and Patristics*. Thessaloniki.

——(1983). *The Council of Serdica 343 AD*. Sofia.

——(1989). 'Athanasius and the Emperor Jovian', *StP* 21: 384–9.

——(1993). 'Did Athanasius know Antony?', *Ancient Society*, 23: 139–49.

Barnes, M. R., and Williams, D. H. (1993) (eds). *Arianism after Arius: Essays in the Development of the Fourth Century Trinitarian Conflicts*. Edinburgh.

Barnes, T. D. (1981). *Constantine and Eusebius*. Cambridge, MA, and London.

——(1986). 'Angel of Light or Mystic Initiate? The Problem of the *Life of Antony*', *JThS*, NS 37: 353–68.

——(1989). 'The Career of Athanasius', *StP* 21: 390–401.

——(1993). *Athanasius and Constantius: Theology and Politics in the Constantinian Empire*. Cambridge, MA, and London.

Bauer, F. A. (1996). *Stadt, Platz und Denkmal in der Spätantike: Untersuchungen zur Ausstattung des öffentlichen Raumes in den spätantiken Städten Rom, Konstantinopel und Ephesos*. Mainz.

Bauer, W. (1971). *Orthodoxy and Heresy in Earliest Christianity* (German original 1934, English translation from the 2nd German edn (ed. G. Strecker, 1963) and ed. R. A. Kraft and G. Krodel). Philadelphia.

Baynes, N. H. (1925). 'Athanasiana', *JEA* 11: 58–69; partially reprinted in Baynes (1960).

——(1926). 'Alexandria and Constantinople: A Study in Ecclesiastical Diplomacy', *JEA* 12: 145–56; reprinted in Baynes (1960), 97–115.

——(1960). *Byzantine Studies and Other Essays*. London.

Beckwith, C. L. (2008). *Hilary of Poitiers on the Trinity: From De Fide to De Trinitate.* Oxford.

Beeley, C. A. (2009). 'Cyril of Alexandria and Gregory Nazianzen: Tradition and Complexity in Patristic Christology', *JECS* 17: 381–419.

Behr, J. (2001). *The Way to Nicaea.* The Formation of Christian Theology, 1. New York.

——(2004). *The Nicene Faith.* The Formation of Christian Theology, 2. New York.

Bell, H. I. (1924). *Jews and Christians in Egypt.* London.

Bernardi, J. (1995). *Saint Grégoire de Nazianze: Le Théologien et son temps (330–390).* Paris.

Bertonière, G. (1972). *The Historical Development of the Easter Vigil and Related Services in the Greek Church.* Rome.

Bienert, W., and Kühneweg, U. (1999) (eds). *Origeniana Septima: Origenes in den Auseinandersetzungen des 4. Jahrhunderts.* Leuven.

Böhm, T. (1991). *Die Christologie des Arius. Dogmengeschichtliche Überlegungen unter besonderer Berücksichtigung der Hellenisierungsfrage.* Ottilien.

Bolman, E. S. (2002) (ed.). *Monastic Visions: Wall Paintings in the Monastery of St Antony at the Red Sea.* New Haven and London.

Borchardt, C. F. A. (1966). *Hilary of Poitier's Role in the Arian Struggle.* The Hague.

Bradshaw, P. F. (1996). *Early Christian Worship: A Basic Introduction to Ideas and Practice.* London.

——and Hoffman, L. A. (1999) (eds). *Passover and Easter: Origin and History to Modern Times.* Notre Dame, IN.

Brakke, D. (1994b). 'Canon Formation and Social Conflict in Fourth-Century Egypt: Athanasius of Alexandria's Thirty-Ninth *Festal Letter*', *HThR* 87: 395–419.

——(1994c). 'The Greek and Syriac Versions of the *Life of Antony*', *Le Muséon* 107: 29–53.

——(1995). *Athanasius and the Politics of Asceticism.* Oxford.

——(1998). ' "Outside the Places, Within the Truth": Athanasius of Alexandria and the Localization of the Holy', in D. Frankfurter (ed.), *Pilgrimage and Holy Space in Late Antique Egypt*, Leiden, Boston, and Cologne, 445–81.

——(2001). 'Jewish Flesh and Christian Spirit in Athanasius of Alexandria', *JECS* 9: 453–81.

——(2006). *Demons and the Making of the Monk: Spiritual Combat in Early Christianity.* Cambridge, MA, and London.

——(2010). 'A New Fragment of Athanasius's Thirty-Ninth *Festal Letter*: Heresy, Apocrypha and the Canon', *HThR* 103: 47–66.

Brennan, B. R. (1985). 'Athanasius' *Vita Antonii*: A Sociological Interpretation', *VC* 39: 209–27.

Brennecke, H. C. (1984). *Hilarius von Poitiers und die Bischofsopposition gegen Konstantius II: Untersuchungen zur dritten Phase des arianischen Streites (337–361).* Berlin and New York.

——(1988). *Studien zur Geschichte der Homöer: Der Osten bis zum Ende der homöischen Reichskirche.* Tübingen.

Bright, P. (1997). 'Singing the Psalms: Augustine and Athanasius on the Integration of the Self', in D. E. Aune and J. McCarthy (eds), *The Whole and Divided Self*, New York, 115–29.

Bright, W. (1877). 'Athanasius', in W. Smith and H. Wace (eds), *A Dictionary of Christian Biography*, London, i. 178–203.

Brown, P. (1970). 'Sorcery, Demons and the Rise of Christianity: From Late Antiquity into the Middle Ages', in M. Douglas (ed.), *Witchcraft Confessions and Accusations*, London, 17–45; repr. in P. Brown, *Religion and Society in the Age of Saint Augustine* (London, 1972), 119–46.

——(1971). 'The Rise and Function of the Holy Man in Late Antiquity', *JRS* 61: 80–101, repr. and rev. in P. Brown, *Society and the Holy in Late Antiquity* (London, 1982), 103–52.

——(1988). *The Body and Society: Men, Women and Sexual Renunciation in Early Christianity*. New York.

——(1992). *Power and Persuasion in Late Antiquity: Towards a Christian Empire*. Madison.

——(1995). *Authority and the Sacred: Aspects of the Christianisation of the Roman World*. Cambridge.

——(1998). 'The Rise and Function of the Holy Man in Late Antiquity, 1971–1997', *JECS* 6: 353–76.

——(2000). *Augustine of Hippo: A Biography*. Rev. edn. London.

——(2002). *Poverty and Leadership in the Later Roman Empire*. Hanover, NH, and London.

Bumazhnov, D. F. (2007). 'The Evil Angels in the *Vita* and the *Letters* of St Antony the Great: Some Observations concerning the Problem of the Authenticity of the *Letters*', ZAC 11: 500–16.

Burrus, V. (1991). 'The Heretical Woman as Symbol in Alexander, Athanasius, Epiphanius and Jerome', *HThR* 84: 229–48.

Butterweck, C. (1995) (ed.). *Athanasius von Alexandrien: Bibliographie*. Opladen.

Cameron, Averil (1991). *Christianity and the Rhetoric of Empire: The Development of Christian Discourse*. Berkeley and Los Angeles.

Camplani, A. (2006). 'L'Identità del patriarcato di Alessandria tra storia e rappresentazione storiografica', *Adamantius* 12: 8–42.

——and Filoramo, G. (2007) (eds). *Foundations of Power and Conflicts of Authority in Late-Antique Monasticism*. Leuven.

Caner, D. (2002). *Wandering, Begging Monks: Spiritual Authority and the Promotion of Monasticism*. Berkeley and Los Angeles, and London.

Chadwick, H. (1960). 'Faith and Order at the Council of Nicaea: A Note on the Background of the Sixth Canon', *HThR* 53: 171–95; repr. in H. Chadwick, *History and Thought of the Early Church* (London, 1982), XII.

——(1967). *The Early Church*. London.

——(1980). *The Role of the Christian Bishop in Ancient Society*. Berkeley.

Chadwick, H. (1993). 'Bishops and Monks', *StP* 24: 45–61.

——(2003). *East and West: The Making of a Rift in the Church*. Oxford.

Chesnut, G. F. (1986). *The First Christian Histories: Eusebius, Socrates, Sozomen, Theodoret, and Evagrius*. 2nd edn. Macon.

Chitty, D. J. (1966). *The Desert a City: An Introduction to the Study of Egyptian and Palestinian Monasticism under the Christian Empire*. Oxford.

Christensen, M. J., and Wittung, J. A. (2007) (eds). *Partakers of the Divine Nature: The History and Development of Deification in the Christian Traditions*. Madison.

Clark, E. A. (1999). *Reading Renunciation: Asceticism and Scripture in Early Christianity*. Princeton.

Cloke, G. (1995). *This Female Man of God: Women and Spiritual Power in the Patristic Age, AD 350–450*. London.

Cooper, K. (1996). *The Virgin and the Bride: Idealized Womanhood in Late Antiquity*. Cambridge.

Courcelle, P. (1950). *Recherches sur les Confessions de saint Augustin*. Paris.

Cox Miller, P. (1983). *Biography in Late Antiquity: A Quest for the Holy Man*. Berkeley.

Cross, F. L. (1945). *The Study of Saint Athanasius*. Oxford.

Cunningham, M. B., and Allen, P. (1998) (eds). *Preacher and Audience: Studies in Early Christian and Byzantine Homiletics*. Leiden, Boston, and Cologne.

Daley, B. E. (2006). *Gregory of Nazianzus*. London and New York.

Davis, S. J. (2004). *The Early Coptic Papacy: The Egyptian Church and its Leadership in Late Antiquity*. Cairo and New York.

——(2008). *Coptic Christology in Practice: Incarnation and Divine Participation in Late Antique and Medieval Egypt*. Oxford.

De Clercq, V. C. (1954). *Ossius of Cordova: A Contribution to the History of the Constantinian Period*. Washington.

Demacopoulos, G. E. (2007). *Five Models of Spiritual Direction in the Early Church*. Notre Dame, IN.

Diamond, E. (2004). *Holy Men and Hunger Artists: Fasting and Asceticism in Rabbinic Culture*. Oxford.

Di Berardino, A., and Studer, B. (1996) (eds). *History of Theology*, i: *The Patristic Period*. Collegeville, MN.

DiMaio, M. (1996). '*Imago veritatis aut verba in speculo*: Athanasius, the Meletian Schism, and Linguistic Frontiers in Fourth-Century Egypt', in R. W. Mathisen and H. S. Sivan (eds), *Shifting Frontiers in Late Antiquity*, Aldershot, 277–84.

Dix, G. (1945). *The Shape of the Liturgy*. London.

Dörries, H. (1949). 'Die *Vita Antonii* als Geschichtsquelle', *Nachrichten von der Akademie der Wissenschaften in Göttingen, Philologisch-Historische Klasse* 14: 359–410.

Dragas, G. D. (2005). *Saint Athanasius of Alexandria: Original Research and New Perspectives*. Rollinsford, NH.

Drake, H. A. (1986). 'Athanasius' First Exile', *GRBS* 27: 193–204.

——(2000). *Constantine and the Bishops: The Politics of Intolerance*. Baltimore and London.

Drecoll, V. H. (2007). 'Das Symbolum Quicumque als Kompilation augustinischer Tradition', *ZAC* 11: 30–65.

Drijvers, J. W. (2004). *Cyril of Jerusalem: Bishop and City.* Leiden.

Dunn, M. (2000). *The Emergence of Monasticism: From the Desert Fathers to the Early Middle Ages.* Oxford.

Dunn-Wilson, D. (2005). *A Mirror for the Church: Preaching in the First Five Centuries.* Grand Rapids, MI, and Cambridge.

Duval, Y.-M. (1974). 'L'Originalité du "De virginibus" dans le mouvement ascetique occidental: Ambroise, Cyprien, Athanase', in Y.-M. Duval (ed.), *Ambroise de Milan: Dix études*, Paris, 9–66.

Ehrhardt, C. T. H. R. (1980). 'Constantinian Documents in Gelasius of Cyzicus, *Ecclesiastical History*', *JAC* 23: 48–57.

Elliott, T. G. (1992). 'Constantine and "The Arian Reaction after Nicaea"', *JEH* 43: 169–94.

——(2007). 'Was the *Tomus ad Antiochenos* a Pacific Document?', *JEH* 58: 1–8.

Elm, S. (1994). *Virgins of God: The Making of Asceticism in Late Antiquity.* Oxford and New York.

——Rebillard, E., and Romano, A. (2000) (eds). *Orthodoxie, christianisme, histoire = Orthodoxy, Christianity, History.* Rome.

Eltester, W. (1937). 'Die Kirchen Antiochias im IV. Jahrhundert', *ZNW* 36: 251–86.

Emmel, S. (2007). 'Coptic Literature in the Byzantine and Early Islamic World', in Bagnall (2007), 83–102.

Ernest, J. D. (2004). *The Bible in Athanasius of Alexandria.* Leiden and Boston.

Evans, G. R. (2004) (ed.). *The First Christian Theologians: An Introduction to Theology in the Early Church.* Oxford.

Ferguson, T. C. (2005). *The Past is Prologue: The Revolution of Nicene Historiography.* Leiden and Boston.

Finlan, S., and Kharlamov, V. (2006) (eds). *Theosis: Deification in Christian Theology.* Eugene, OR.

Francis, J. A. (1995). *Subversive Virtue: Ascetics and Authority in the Second-Century Pagan World.* University Park, PA.

Frank, G. (2000). *The Memory of the Eyes: Pilgrims to Living Saints in Christian Late Antiquity.* Berkeley and Los Angeles, and London.

Frankfurter, D. (1998). *Religion in Roman Egypt: Assimilation and Resistance.* Princeton.

Frend, W. H. C. (1972). *The Rise of the Monophysite Movement: Chapters in the History of the Church in the Fifth and Sixth Centuries.* Cambridge.

——(1974). 'Athanasius as an Egyptian Christian Leader in the Fourth Century', *New College Bulletin* 8: 20–37; repr. in W. H. C. Frend, *Religion Popular and Unpopular in the Early Christian Centuries* (London, 1976), XVI.

Gaddis, M. (2005). *There is No Crime for Those who have Christ: Religious Violence in the Christian Roman Empire.* Berkeley and Los Angeles, and London.

Galtier, P. (1956). 'Saint Cyrille et Apollinaire', *Gregorianum* 37: 584–609.

Gavrilyuk, P. (2004). *The Suffering of the Impassible God*. Oxford.

Gemeinhardt, P. (2006). 'Der Tomus ad Antiochenos (362) und die Vielfalt ortho-
doxer Theologien im 4. Jahrhundert', *ZKG* 117: 169–96.

——(2011) (ed.), *Athanasius Handbuch*. Tübingen.

Gioia, L. (2008). *The Theological Epistemology of Augustine's De Trinitate*. Oxford.

Girardet, K. M. (1975). *Kaisergericht und Bischofsgericht: Studien zu den Anfängen
des Donatistenstreites (313–315) und zum Prozeß des Athanasius von Alexandrien
(328–346)*. Bonn.

Goehring, J. E. (1986). 'New Frontiers in Pachomian Studies', in Pearson and Goehring (1986), 236–57, repr. in Goehring (1999a), 162–86.

——(1996). 'Withdrawing from the Desert: Pachomius and the Development
of Village Monasticism in Upper Egypt', *HThR* 89: 267–85; repr. in Goehring
(1999a), 89–109.

——(1999a). *Ascetics, Society, and the Desert: Studies in Early Egyptian Monasticism*.
Harrisburg, PA.

——(1999b). 'Hieracas of Leontopolis: The Making of a Desert Ascetic', in Goehring (1999a), 110–33.

——(2007). 'Monasticism in Byzantine Egypt: Continuity and Memory', in Bagnall
(2007), 390–407.

Graumann, T. (2002). *Die Kirche der Väter: Vätertheologie und Väterbeweis in den Kirchen
des Ostens bis zum Konzil von Ephesus (431)*. Tübingen.

Gregg, R. C. (1985) (ed.). *Arianism: Historical and Theological Reassessments*. Philadelphia.

——and Groh, D. E. (1981). *Early Arianism: A View of Salvation*. Philadelphia.

Griggs, C. W. (1990). *Early Egyptian Christianity: From its Origins to 451 CE*. Leiden.

Grillmeier, A. (1975). *Christ in Christian Tradition*, i. *From the Apostolic Age to Chalcedon (451)*. 2nd rev. edn, trans. J. Bowden. Oxford.

Grossman, P. (2002). *Christliche Architektur in Ägypten*. Leiden.

Gwatkin, H. M. (1882). *Studies of Arianism*. Cambridge.

Gwynn, D. M. (2007). *The Eusebians: The Polemic of Athanasius of Alexandria and the
Construction of the 'Arian Controversy'*. Oxford.

——(2009). 'The Council of Chalcedon and the Definition of Christian Tradition',
in R. Price and M. Whitby (eds), *Chalcedon in Context: Church Councils 400–700*,
Liverpool, 7–26.

——(2010). 'Archaeology and the "Arian Controversy" in the Fourth Century', in
D. M. Gwynn and S. Bangert (eds), *Late Antique Archaeology 6: Religious Diversity
in Late Antiquity*, Leiden, 229–63.

Haas, C. (1997). *Alexandria in Late Antiquity: Topography and Conflict*. Baltimore and
London.

Hahn, J. (2004). *Gewalt und religiöser Konflikt: Studien zu den Auseinandersetzungen
zwischen Christen, Heiden und Juden im Osten des Römischen Reiches (von Konstantin
bis Theodosius II.)*. Berlin.

Hall, S. G. (1991). *Doctrine and Practice in the Early Church*. London.

Hanson, R. P. C. (1985). 'The Arian Doctrine of the Incarnation', in Gregg (1985),
181–212.

——(1987). 'The Influence of Origen on the Arian Controversy', in L. Lies (ed.), *Origeniana Quarta*, Innsbruck, 410–23.

——(1988). *The Search for the Christian Doctrine of God: The Arian Controversy 318–381.* Edinburgh.

Harmless, W. (2004). *Desert Christians: An Introduction to the Literature of Early Monasticism.* New York and Oxford.

Harnack, A. von (1898). *History of Dogma*, vol. 4 (trans. N. Buchanan from 3rd German edn). London and Edinburgh.

Hauben, H. (1998). 'The Melitian "Church of the Martyrs": Christian Dissenters in Ancient Egypt', in T. W. Hillard, R. A. Kearsley, C. E. V. Nixon, and A. M. Nobbs (eds), *Ancient History in a Modern University*, ii. *Early Christianity, Late Antiquity and Beyond*, Macquarie, 329–49.

——(2001). 'Le Papyrus London VI (P.Jews) 1914 dans son contexte historique (mai 335)', in *Proceedings of the Twenty-Second International Congress of Papyrology*, Florence, 605–18.

Hauschild, W.-D. (1967). *Die Pneumatomachen: Eine Untersuchung zur Dogmengeschichte des vierten Jahrhunderts.* Hamburg.

Haykin, M. A. G. (1994). *The Spirit of God: The Exegesis of 1 and 2 Corinthians in the Pneumatomachian Controversy of the Fourth Century.* Leiden.

Heil, U. (2006). 'Athanasius und Basilius', *ZAC* 10: 103–20.

——(2007). 'Athanasius als Apologet des Christentums. Einleitungsfragen zum Doppelwerk *Contra gentes/De incarnatione*', in A. C. Jacobsen and J. Ulrich (eds), *Drei griechische Apologeten: Origenes, Eusebius und Athanasius*, Frankfurt am Main, 159–87.

Heinen, H. (2002). 'Überfüllte Kirchen: Bischof Athanasius über den Kirchenbau in Alexandrien, Trier und Aquileia', *Trierer Theologische Zeitschrift* 111: 194–211.

Heron, A. (1974). 'Zur Theologie der "Tropici" in den Serapionbriefen des Athanasius', *Kyrios: Vierteljahresschrift für Kirchen- und Geistesgeschichte Europas*, NF 14: 3–24.

Hess, H. (2002). *The Early Development of Canon Law and the Council of Serdica.* Oxford.

Honigmann, E. (1939). 'La Liste Originale des Pères de Nicée', *Byz* 14: 17–76.

Hunter, D. G. (1989) (ed.). *Preaching in the Patristic Age.* New York and Mahwah, NJ.

Jakab, A. (2001). *Ecclesia Alexandrina: Evolution sociale et institutionnelle du christianisme alexandrin (IIe et IIIe siècles).* Bern and Oxford.

Jones, C., Wainwright, G., Yarnold, E., and Bradshaw, P. F. (1992) (eds). *The Study of Liturgy.* Rev. edn. London.

Jungmann, J. (1959). *The Early Liturgy to the Time of Gregory the Great.* English trans. F. A. Brunner. Notre Dame, IN.

Kannengiesser, C. (1964). 'Le temoignage des Lettres Festales de saint Athanase sur la date de l'Apologie *Contre les Paiens, Sur l'Incarnation du Verbe*', *RSR* 52: 91–100; repr. in Kannengiesser (1991), V.

——(1970). 'La Date de l'Apologie d'Athanase *Contre les Paiens* et *Sur l'incarnation du Verbe*', *RSR* 58: 383–428; repr. in Kannengiesser (1991), VI.

Kannengiesser, C. (1974) (ed.). *Politique et Théologie chez Athanase d'Alexandrie*. Paris.

—— (1981). 'Holy Scripture and Hellenistic Hermeneutics in Alexandrian Christology: The Arian Crisis', *Colloquy* 41 of the Centre for Hermeneutical Studies, Berkeley (pp. 1–40); repr. in Kannengiesser (1991), I.

—— (1982). 'Athanasius of Alexandria: *Three Orations against the Arians*: A Reappraisal', *StP* 17/3: 981–95; repr. in Kannengiesser (1991), IX.

—— (1983). *Athanase d'Alexandrie eveque et ecrivain*. Paris.

—— (1985a). 'The Blasphemies of Arius: Athanasius of Alexandria *De Synodis* 15', in Gregg (1985), 59–78; repr. in Kannengiesser (1991), III.

—— (1985b). 'The Athanasian Decade 1974–1984: A Bibliographical Report', *ThS* 46: 524–41; repr. in Kannengiesser (1991), XI.

—— (1986). 'Athanasius of Alexandria vs. Arius: the Alexandrian Crisis', in Pearson and Goehring (1986), 204–15; repr. in Kannengiesser (1991), XII.

—— (1989). 'The Homiletic Festal Letters of Athanasius', in Hunter (1989), 73–100; repr. in Kannengiesser (1991), XV.

—— (1991). *Arius and Athanasius: Two Alexandrian Theologians*. London.

—— (1993a). 'Athanasius' so-called *Third Oration against the Arians*', *StP* 26: 375–88.

—— (1993b). '(Ps.-)Athanasius, *Ad Afros* Examined', in H. C. Brennecke, E. L. Grasmück, and C. Markschies (eds), *Logos: Festschrift für Luise Abramowski zum 8. Juli 1993*, Berlin and New York, 264–80.

—— (1998). 'Athanasius of Alexandria and the Ascetic Movement of his Time', in Wimbush and Valantasis (1998), 479–92.

—— (2001). 'Prolegomena to the Biography of Athanasius', *Adamantius* 7: 25–43.

—— (2006). 'The Dating of Athanasius' Double Apology and Three Treatises against the Arians', *ZAC* 10: 19–33.

Karmann, T. R. (2009). *Meletius von Antiochien. Studien zur Geschichte des trinitätstheologischen Streits in den Jahren 360–364 n.Chr.* Frankfurt am Main.

Kelly, J. N. D. (1964). *The Athanasian Creed*. London.

—— (1972). *Early Christian Creeds*. 3rd edn. London.

—— (1975). *Jerome: His Life, Writings, and Controversies*. London.

—— (1977). *Early Christian Doctrines*. 5th edn. London.

Klein, R. (1977). *Constantius II und die christliche Kirche*. Darmstadt.

Kolbet, P. R. (2006). 'Athanasius, the Psalms, and the Reformation of the Self', *HThR* 9: 85–101.

Kopecek, T. A. (1979). *A History of Neo-Arianism*, vols I–II. Cambridge, MA.

Krause, M. (1998) (ed.). *Ägypten in spätantik-christlicher Zeit: Einführung in die koptische Kultur*. Wiesbaden.

Lancel, S. (2002). *St Augustine*, trans. A. Nevill. London.

Layton, R. A. (2004). *Didymus the Blind and his Circle in Late-Antique Alexandria: Virtue and Narrative in Biblical Scholarship*. Urbana, IL.

Le Boulluec, A. (1985). *La Notion d'heresie dans la literature greque II–III siècles*. Paris.

Leemans, J. (2000). 'Thirteen Years of Athanasius Research (1985–1998): A Survey and Bibliography', *Sacris Erudiri* 39: 105–217.

—— (2003). 'The Idea of "Flight from Persecution" in the Alexandrian Tradition from Clement to Athanasius', in L. Perrone (ed.), *Origeniana Octava: Origen and the Alexandrian Tradition = Origene e la tradizione alessandrina*, Leuven, ii. 901–10.

Lefort, L. T. (1933). 'St Athanase, écrivain copte', *Le Muséon* 46: 1–33.

Leppin, H. (2001). 'Heretical Historiography: Philostorgius', *StP* 34: 111–24.

Letsch-Brunner, S. (1998). *Marcella—discipula et magistra. Auf den Spuren einer römischen Christin des 4. Jahrhunderts*. Berlin and New York.

Leyser, C. (2000). *Authority and Asceticism from Augustine to Gregory the Great*. Oxford.

Liebeschuetz, J. H. W. G. (1972). *Antioch: City and Imperial Administration in the Later Roman Empire*. Oxford.

—— (1997). 'The Rise of the Bishop in the Christian Roman Empire and the Successor Kingdoms', *Electrum* 1: 113–25.

Lienhard, J. T. (1985). 'The Epistle of the Synod of Ancyra, 358: A Reconsideration', in Gregg (1985), 313–19.

—— (1987). 'The "Arian" Controversy: Some Categories Reconsidered', *ThS* 48: 415–37.

—— (1993). 'Did Athanasius reject Marcellus?', in Barnes and Williams (1993), 65–80.

—— (1999). *Contra Marcellum: Marcellus of Ancyra and Fourth-Century Theology*. Washington.

—— (2006). 'Two Friends of Athanasius: Marcellus of Ancyra and Apollinaris of Laodicea', *ZAC* 10: 56–66.

Lieu, S. N. C. (1992). *Manichaeism in the Later Roman Empire and Medieval China: A Historical Survey*. 2nd edn. Tübingen.

Lizzi Testa, R. (2009). 'The Late Antique Bishop: Image and Reality', in P. Rousseau (ed.), *A Companion to Late Antiquity*, Chichester, 525–38.

Logan, A. H. B. (1987). 'Origen and the Development of Trinitarian Theology', in L. Lies (ed.), *Origeniana Quarta*, Innsbruck, 424–9.

Löhr, W. (1986). *Die Entstehung der homöischen und homöusianischen Kirchenparteien—Studien zur Synodalgeschichte des 4. Jahrhunderts*. Bonn.

—— (1993). 'A Sense of Tradition: The Homoiousian Church Party', in Barnes and Williams (1993), 81–100.

—— (2005). 'Arius Reconsidered (Part 1)', *ZAC* 9: 524–60.

—— (2006). 'Arius Reconsidered (Part 2)', *ZAC* 10: 121–57.

Lorenz, R. (1979). *Arius Judaizans? Untersuchungen zur dogmengeschichtlichen Einordnung des Arius*. Göttingen.

Louth, A. (1985). 'Athanasius' Understanding of the Humanity of Christ', *StP* 16: 309–18.

Luibheid, C. (1976). 'The Arianism of Eusebius of Nicomedia', *IThQ* 43: 3–23.

—— (1982). *The Council of Nicaea*. Galway.

Lyman, J. R. (1993). *Christology and Cosmology: Models of Divine Activity in Origen, Eusebius and Athanasius*. Oxford.

McDonald, L. M. (1995). *The Formation of the Christian Biblical Canon*. Rev. edn. Peabody, MA.

McGrath, A. E. (1994). *Christian Theology: An Introduction*. Oxford and Cambridge, MA.

McGuckin, J. (2001). *Saint Gregory of Nazianzus: An Intellectual Biography*. Crestwood, NY.

——(2004). *Saint Cyril of Alexandria and the Christological Controversy*. Crestwood, NY.

McKenzie, J. (2007). *The Architecture of Alexandria and Egypt, c.300 BC to AD 700*. New Haven and London.

McKinion, S. A. (2000). *Words, Imagery, and the Mystery of Christ: A Reconstruction of Cyril of Alexandria's Christology*. Leiden.

McLynn, N. B. (1994). *Ambrose of Milan: Church and Court in a Christian Capital*. Berkeley and London.

Marasco, G. (2003) (ed.). *Greek and Roman Historiography in Late Antiquity Fourth to Sixth Century A.D*. Leiden and Boston.

Martin, A. (1974). 'Athanase et les Mélitiens (325–335)', in Kannengiesser (1974), 31–61.

——(1996). *Athanase d'Alexandrie et L'Église d'Égypte au IVe siècle (328–373)*. Rome.

——(1998). 'Alexandrie à l'époque romaine tradive: L'Impact du christianisme sur la topographie et les institutions', in C. Décobert and J.-Y. Empereur (eds), *Alexandrie médievale*, Cairo, i. 9–21.

——(2007). 'Les relations entre le monachisme égyptien et l'institution ecclésiastique au IVème siècle', in Camplani and Filoramo (2007), 13–46.

Maxwell, J. L. (2007). *Christianization and Communication in Late Antiquity: John Chrysostom and his Congregation in Antioch*. Cambridge.

May, G. (1994). *Creatio ex Nihilo: The Doctrine of Creation out of Nothing in Early Christian Thought* (German original 1978, trans. A. S. Worrall). Edinburgh.

Meijering, E. P. (1968). *Orthodoxy and Platonism in Athanasius: Synthesis or Antithesis?* Leiden.

Merendino, P. (1965). *Paschale Sacramentum. Eine Untersuchung über die Osterkatechese des Hl. Athanasius von Alexandrien in ihrer Beziehung zu den frühchristlichen exegetisch-theologischen Überlieferungen*. Münster.

Metzler, K. (1997). *Welchen Bibeltext benutzte Athanasius im Exil? Zur Herkunft der Bibelzitate in den Arianerreden im Vergleich zur ep. ad epp. Aeg*. Opladen.

Morales, X. (2006). *La Théologie Trinitaire d'Athanase d'Alexandrie*. Paris.

Mosshammer, A. A. (2008). *The Easter computus and the Origins of the Christian Era*. Oxford.

Müller, C. (2010). 'Das Phänomen des "lateinischen Athanasius"', in Stockhausen and Brennecke (2010), 3–42.

Müller, C. D. G. (1974). 'Athanasios I. von Alexandrien als koptischer Schriftsteller', *Kyrios: Vierteljahresschrift für Kirchen- und Geistesgeschichte Europas*, NF 14: 195–204.

Munro-Hay, S. (1997). *Ethiopia and Alexandria: The Metropolitan Episcopacy of Ethiopia*. Warsaw and Wiesbaden.

Newman, J. H. (1833). *The Arians of the Fourth Century* (1968 edn). Westminster.

Ng, N. K.-K. (2001). *The Spirituality of Athanasius: A Key for Proper Understanding of this Important Church Father.* Bern.

Nispel, M. D. (1999). 'Christian Deification and the Early *Testimonia*', *VC* 53: 289–304.

Nordberg, H. (1964). *Athanasius and the Emperor.* Helsinki.

Norton, P. (2007). *Episcopal Elections 250–600: Hierarchy and Popular Will in Late Antiquity.* Oxford.

Opitz, H.-G. (1934). 'Die Zeitfolge des arianischen Streites von den Anfangen bis zum Jahr 328', *ZNW* 33: 131–59.

Orlandi, T. (1986). 'Coptic Literature', in Pearson and Goehring (1986), 51–81.

Papaconstantinou, A. (2006). 'Historiography, Hagiography, and the Making of the Coptic "Church of the Martyrs" in Early Islamic Egypt', *DOP* 60: 65–86.

Parvis, S. (2006). *Marcellus of Ancyra and the Lost Years of the Arian Controversy 325–345.* Oxford.

Patlagean, E. (1977). *Pauvreté économique et pauvreté sociale à Byzance, 4e–7e siècles.* Paris.

Patterson, L. G. (1982). 'Methodius, Origen, and the Arian Dispute', *StP* 17/2: 912–23.

Pearson, B. A., and Goehring, J. E. (1986) (eds). *The Roots of Egyptian Christianity.* Philadelphia.

Peeters, P. (1945). 'L'Épilogue du Synode de Tyr en 335', *Analecta Bollandiana* 63: 131–44.

Pelikan, J. (1971). *The Christian Tradition: A History of the Development of Doctrine*, i. *The Emergence of the Catholic Tradition (100–600).* Chicago and London.

——(2003). *Credo: A Historical and Theological Guide to Creeds and Confessions of Faith in the Christian Tradition.* New Haven and London.

Pettersen, A. (1984). ' "To Flee or Not to Flee": An Assessment of Athanasius' *De Fuga Sua*', in W. J. Shiels (ed.), *Persecution and Toleration*, Oxford, 29–42.

——(1990). 'The Arian Context of Athanasius of Alexandria's *Tomus ad Antiochenos* VII', *JEH* 41: 183–98.

——(1995). *Athanasius.* London.

Rapp, C. (2005). *Holy Bishops in Late Antiquity: The Nature of Christian Leadership in an Age of Transition.* Berkeley and Los Angeles, and London.

Rebenich, S. (2000). 'Der Kirchenvater Hieronymus als Hagiograph: Die *Vita s. Pauli primi eremitae*', in K. Elm (ed.), *Beiträge zur Geschichte des Paulinerordens*, Berlin, 23–40.

——(2002). *Jerome.* London and New York.

Roberts, C. H. (1979). *Manuscript, Society and Belief in Early Christian Egypt.* London.

Robertson, J. M. (2007). *Christ as Mediator: A Study of the Theologies of Eusebius of Caesarea, Marcellus of Ancyra, and Athanasius of Alexandria.* Oxford.

Rohrbacher, D. (2002). *The Historians of Late Antiquity.* London and New York.

Roldanus, J. R. (1977). *Le Christ et l'homme dans la théologie d'Athanase d'Alexandrie.* Leiden.

Rondeau, M. J. (1968). 'L'Épître à Marcellinus sur les Psaumes', *VC* 22: 176–97.

Rousseau, P. (1978). *Ascetics, Authority, and the Church in the Age of Jerome and Cassian.* Oxford.

——(1994). *Basil of Caesarea.* Oxford.

——(1999). *Pachomius: The Making of a Community in Fourth-Century Egypt.* Rev. edn. Berkeley.

Rubenson, S. (1995). *The Letters of St Antony: Monasticism and the Making of a Saint.* 2nd edn. Minneapolis.

Russell, N. (2000). *Cyril of Alexandria.* London and New York.

——(2004). *The Doctrine of Deification in the Greek Patristic Tradition.* Oxford.

Schneemelcher, W. (1950). 'Athanasius von Alexandrien als Theologe und als Kirchenpolitiker', *ZNW* 43: 242–55; repr. in Schneemelcher (1974*b*), 274–89.

——(1974*a*). 'Die Epistula Encyclica des Athanasius', in Schneemelcher (1974*b*), 290–337.

——(1974*b*). *Gesammelte Aufsätze zum Neuen Testament und zur Patristik.* Thessaloniki.

——(1977). 'Die Kirchweihsynode von Antiochen 341', in *Bonner Festgabe Johannes Straub zum 65. Geburtstag am 18.October 1977,* Bonn, 319–46.

Schwartz, E. (1935). 'Zur Kirchengeschichte des vierten Jahrhunderts', *ZNW* 34: 129–213.

——(1959). *Gesammelte Schriften,* iii. *Zur Geschichte des Athanasius* (first published in *Nachrichten der königlichen Gesellschaft der Wissenschaften zu Göttingen,* 1904–11). Berlin.

Seeck, O. (1911). *Geschichte des Untergangs der antiken Welt,* iv. Berlin.

Seibt, K. (1994). *Die Theologie des Markell von Ankyra.* Berlin and New York.

Shaw, T. (1998). *The Burden of the Flesh: Fasting and Sexuality in Early Christianity.* Minneapolis.

Simonetti, M. (1965). *Studi sull'Arianesimo.* Rome.

——(1975). *La Crisi Ariana nel Quarto Secolo.* Rome.

Sizgorich, T. (2009). *Violence and Belief in Late Antiquity.* Philadelphia.

Slusser, M. (1993). 'Traditional Views of Late Arianism', in Barnes and Williams (1993), 3–30.

Spoerl, K. M. (1993). 'The Schism at Antioch since Cavallera', in Barnes and Williams (1993), 101–26.

——(2006). 'Athanasius and the Anti-Marcellan Controversy', *ZAC* 10: 34–55.

Stark, R. (1996). *The Rise of Christianity: A Sociologist Reconsiders History.* Princeton.

Stead, G. C. (1976). 'Rhetorical Method in Athanasius', *VC* 30: 121–37; repr. in Stead (1985), VIII.

——(1978). 'The *Thalia* of Arius and the Testimony of Athanasius', *JThS,* NS 29: 20–52; repr. in Stead (1985), X.

——(1985). *Substance and Illusion in the Christian Fathers.* London.

——(1988). 'Athanasius' Earliest Written Work', *JThS*, ns 39: 76–91; repr. in Stead (2000), X.

——(1994). 'Arius in Modern Research', *JThS*, ns 45: 24–36; repr. in Stead (2000), IV.

——(2000). *Doctrine and Philosophy in Early Christianity.* Aldershot.

Steenson, J. N. (1985). 'Basil of Ancyra on the Meaning of *Homoousios*', in Gregg (1985), 267–79.

Sterk, A. (2004). *Renouncing the World yet Leading the Church: The Monk-Bishop in Late Antiquity.* Cambridge, MA.

Stock, B. (1996). *Augustine the Reader: Meditation, Self-Knowledge, and the Ethics of Interpretation.* Cambridge, MA, and London.

Stockhausen, A. von (2006). 'Athanasius in Antiochien', *ZAC* 10: 86–102.

Sumruld, W. A. (1994). *Augustine and the Arians: The Bishop of Hippo's Encounters with Ulfilan Arianism.* Selinsgrove and London.

Talley, T. J. (1982). 'The Origin of Lent at Alexandria', *StP* 17/2: 594–612.

Tetz, M. (1975). 'Über nikäische Orthodoxie. Der sog. *Tomus ad Antiochenos* des Athanasios von Alexandrien', *ZNW* 66: 194–222; repr. in Tetz (1995), 107–34.

——(1979a). 'Athanasius von Alexandrien', *Theologische Realenzyklopädie* 4: 333–49; repr. in Tetz (1995), 1–22.

——(1979b). 'Zur Biographie des Athanasius von Alexandrien', *ZKG* 90: 304–38; repr. in Tetz (1995), 23–60.

——(1989). 'Die Kirchweihsynode von Antiochien (341) und Marcellus von Ancyra', in D. Papandreou, W. A. Bienert, and K. Schäferdiek (eds), *Oecumenica et Patristica. Festschrift für Wilhelm Schneemelcher zum 75. Geburtstag,* Stuttgart, Berlin, and Cologne, 199–217; repr. in Tetz (1995), 227–48.

——(1995). *Athanasiana: Zu Leben und Lehre des Athanasius.* Berlin and New York.

Thelamon, F. (1981). *Païens et chrétiens au IVe siècle: L'Apport de l''Histoire ecclésiastique' de Rufin d'Aquilée.* Paris.

Torrance, T. F. (1995). *Divine Meaning: Studies in Patristic Hermeneutics.* Edinburgh.

Twomey, V. (1982). Apostolikos Thronos: *The Primacy of Rome as Reflected in the Church History of Eusebius and the Historico-Apologetical Writings of Saint Athanasius the Great.* Münster.

Urbainczyk, T. (1997). *Socrates of Constantinople: Historian of Church and State.* Ann Arbor.

——(2002). *Theodoret of Cyrrhus: The Bishop and the Holy Man.* Ann Arbor.

Vaggione, R. (2000). *Eunomius of Cyzicus and the Nicene Revolution.* Oxford.

Van Deun, P. (2003). 'The Church Historians after Eusebius', in Marasco (2003), 151–76.

Vivian, T. (1988). *St. Peter of Alexandria: Bishop and Martyr.* Philadelphia.

Wahba, M. F. (1998). 'The Spirituality of St Athanasius according to his Paschal Letters', in P. Allen, R. Canning and L. Cross with B. J. Caiger (eds), *Prayer and Spirituality in the Early Church,* Everton Park, Queensland, i. 113–24.

Wallace-Hadrill, D. S. (1982). *Christian Antioch: A Study of Early Christian Thought in the East.* Cambridge.

Watts, E. J. (2006). *City and School in Late Antique Athens and Alexandria*. Berkeley and Los Angeles, and London.

Weber, M. (1978). *Economy and Society: An Outline of Interpretative Sociology*, ed. G. Roth and C. Wittich. 2 vols. Berkeley and Los Angeles, and London.

Weedman, M. (2007). *The Trinitarian Theology of Hilary of Poitiers*. Leiden and Boston.

Weinandy, T. G. (2007). *Athanasius: A Theological Introduction*. Aldershot.

——and Keating, D. A. (2003) (eds). *The Theology of St Cyril of Alexandria: A Critical Appreciation*. London and New York.

Wessel, S. (2004). *Cyril of Alexandria and the Nestorian Controversy: The Making of a Saint and of a Heretic*. Oxford.

Widdicombe, P. (1994). *The Fatherhood of God from Origen to Athanasius*. Oxford.

Wiles, M. (1962). 'In Defence of Arius', *JThS*, ns 13: 339–47.

——(1965). 'The Nature of the Early Debate about Christ's Human Soul', *JEH* 16: 139–51.

——(1993). 'A Textual Variant in the Creed of the Council of Nicaea', *StP* 26: 428–33.

——(1996). *Archetypal Heresy: Arianism through the Centuries*. Oxford.

Williams, D. H. (1995a). 'Polemics and Politics in Ambrose of Milan's *De Fide*', *JThS*, ns 46: 519–31.

——(1995b). *Ambrose of Milan and the End of the Nicene-Arian Conflicts*. Oxford.

——(1997). 'Necessary Alliance or Polemical Portrayal? Tracing the Historical Alignment of Arians and Pagans in the Later Fourth Century', *StP* 29: 178–94.

Williams, R. D. (1985). 'The Quest for the Historical *Thalia*', in Gregg (1985), 1–35.

——(1986). 'Arius and the Melitian Schism', *JThS*, ns 37: 35–52.

——(1987). *Arius: Heresy and Tradition*. London.

——(1989) (ed.). *The Making of Orthodoxy: Essays in Honour of Henry Chadwick*. Cambridge.

——(2001a). *Arius: Heresy and Tradition*. 2nd edn. London.

——(2001b). 'Defining Heresy', in A. Kreider (ed.), *The Origins of Christendom in the West*, Edinburgh and New York, 313–35.

Wimbush, V. L. (1990) (ed.). *Ascetic Behaviour in Greco-Roman Antiquity*. Minneapolis.

——and Valantasis, R. (1998) (eds). *Asceticism*. Oxford.

Wipszycka, E. (1996). *Études sur le christianisme dans l'Égypte de l'antiquité tardive*. Rome.

——(2004). 'La *Vita Antonii* confrontée avec la réalité géographique', in U. Zanetti and E. Lucchesi (eds), *Ægyptus christiana: Mélanges d'hagiographie égyptienne et orientale dédiés à la mémoire du p. Paul Devos bollandiste*, Geneva, 135–48.

——(2007). 'The Institutional Church', in Bagnall (2007), 331–49.

Worp, K. A. (1994). 'A Checklist of Bishops in Byzantine Egypt (A.D. 325–c.750)', *ZPE* 100: 283–318.

Young, F. (1983). *From Nicaea to Chalcedon: A Guide to the Literature and its Background*. Philadelphia.

——(1991). *The Making of the Creeds*. London and Philadelphia.

Index of Athanasian Texts

Index of Biblical Citations

General Index

Palestine 5, 21, 24, 27, 31, 63, 166

Papyrus London 1914 28–9, 122

Paul (apostle) 38, 73, 115, 133, 147–8,
  153–4, 180

Paulinus of Antioch (bishop) 50–1, 53

persecution and religious violence 2,
  6, 14, 16, 21, 23, 47, 49, 54, 79,
  107, 109, 121, 151, 153, 159,
  164, 166, 176, 190

  against Athanasius 13, 16, 17, 19,
    31–4, 35, 43–5, 46, 51, 52, 93, 103,
    125.n.47, 136, 144, 147, 151, 153,
    164, 167, 176, 180, 190–1, 195–6

  against Athanasius' followers 13,
    32–4, 35, 43–5, 46, 54, 93, 122–3,
    125.n.47, 126, 127–8, 130, 137–8,
    144, 147, 163, 164, 176, 190–1

  attributed to Athanasius 8, 28–9, 31,
    36, 122, 195–6

Peter I of Alexandria (bishop) 1,
  23, 121

Peter II of Alexandria (bishop) 53–4,
  160, 176, 178

Philagrius (prefect) 32

Philostorgius (historian) 3, 165, 167
  on Athanasius 3, 165–7

Philumenus (official) 27

Photinus of Sirmium (bishop) 42, 94

physis (nature) 56, 57, 60–3, 66–70,
  71–2, 72–4, 78, 80–2, 84,
  87–9, 90–2, 97, 101–3, 119, 153,
  170–1, 185, 187

Pistus (bishop of Alexandria?) 30.n.26

poiēma (made) 60.n.11, 62, 73, 78, 81,
  84, 88–9, 95

prayer 12, 25, 43, 108, 109, 124.n.46,
  139, 140, 189.n.60

  Athanasius' promotion of 43,
    112–13, 115–16, 117–18, 139,
    142, 146–7, 150

preaching 19, 40, 72, 79, 126, 135, 138

  Athanasius' lost sermons 6–7, 40,
    132, 138

Rome 20, 22, 34.n.35, 54

  Athanasius and 8, 33, 34, 54,
    173, 178

Rufinus (historian) 3, 21.n.5, 41.n.47,
  166, 167, 168, 176–7, 189
  on Athanasius 2–3, 51, 176–7

Sabellianism / Modalism 58, 60–2, 65,
  71, 79, 85, 91–2, 97, 164

Scripture 10, 33, 56–7, 62, 64, 75–6, 81,
  87–9, 94, 126, 149–52, 152–6,
  164, 170–1, 180

  Athanasius' approach towards 3, 10,
    47, 68, 72–3, 75–6, 82, 87–9, 91,
    97, 152–6

  canon of 2, 16, 52, 56–7, 75, 132,
    148.n.23, 152–6, 160

  contemplation by ascetics 112–13,
    117–18, 150, 181.n.38

  pastoral use of 38, 126, 132–4,
    137, 141, 142.n.17, 144, 147–8,
    149–52, 152–6

  Psalter 43, 147, 149–52, 178

  see also Index of Scriptural Citations

Secundus of Ptolemais
  (bishop) 45.n.51

Serapion of Thmuis (bishop) 9, 14,
  33, 39, 42, 90, 124, 125, 126,
  130, 141

sexuality 105, 111–18, 133–4, 146–9

Socrates (historian) 3, 165, 167–9,
  176–7, 185, 186, 189, 190

  on Athanasius 3, 13.n.24, 165,
    167–9, 186

  'Shorter Socrates' (Armenian) 186

Son 4, 15, 55–6, 57–9, 60–5, 66–76,
  78–82, 83–5, 87–9, 90–2, 93–5,
  96–8, 100, 101–3, 114, 118–19,
  123, 129, 135, 142–6, 153, 155,
  162–4, 170–3, 180, 182–4, 196

  created 60–4, 66–70, 72–3, 75–6,
    78–82, 84, 87–9, 90–1, 95, 97,
    100, 123, 129, 145, 153, 182